EACL Hackashop on News Media Content Analysis and Automated Report Generation 2021

Online
19 April 2021

Editors:

Hannu Toivonen
Michele Boggia

ISBN: 978-1-7138-2960-7

Printed from e-media with permission by:

Curran Associates, Inc.
57 Morehouse Lane
Red Hook, NY 12571

CURRAN ASSOCIATES INC. proceedings .com

Some format issues inherent in the e-media version may also appear in this print version.

Association for Computational Linguistics
209 N. Eighth Street
Stroudsburg, Pennsylvania 18360

Phone: 1-570-476-8006
Fax: 1-570-476-0860

acl@aclweb.org

Additional copies of this publication are available from:

Curran Associates, Inc.
57 Morehouse Lane
Red Hook, NY 12571 USA
Phone: 845-758-0400
Fax: 845-758-2633
Email: curran@proceedings.com
Web: www.proceedings.com

EACL 2021
The 16th conference of the European Chapter
of the Association for Computational Linguistics

EACL Hackashop on News Media Content Analysis and Automated Report Generation

Proceedings

Hannu Toivonen and Michele Boggia, Editors

April 19, 2021

The hackashop has been organized by the EMBEDDIA project (Cross-Lingual Embeddings for Less-Represented Languages in European News Media) with support from the European Union's Horizon 2020 research and innovation program under grant 825153.

Preface

Automated content analysis of news media, including both news articles and users' comments on them, can provide unparalleled insight into current events, interests and opinions, as well as trends and changes in them. The needs are varied, from the readers who consume news of their personal interest to journalists who keep track of what is going on in the world, try to understand what their readers think of various topics, or want to automate routine reporting.

The aim of Hackashop 2021 is to foster discussion and research on the combination of language technology and news media content. The hackashop provides a forum for both discussing scientific advances in analysis of news stories and their reader comments and in automated generation of reports, as well as for experimental work on identifying interesting phenomena in reader comments and reporting on them.

Accordingly, the hackashop was implemented in a dual format. A traditional track consisted of submission of scientific papers, their reviews and finally paper presentations. It was complemented by an active, experimentation-based track consisting of an online hackathon preceding the workshop, with presentation of the results in the joint workshop event. Both tracks shared the same topic, news media analysis and generation, and participants to the two tracks had a good amount of overlap.

In the workshop track, we encouraged submissions of long and short papers. Based on three experts reviews for each submission, weighing the contributions of the submission against its length, 13 papers were selected for presentation in the workshop event.

The online hackathon was organized during a three-week period in February 2021, with six participating teams. The challenges they addressed covered a broad range, as each team had the freedom to define their own aims. In the spirit of providing a joint forum for discussing both scientific advances and experimental work, five hackathon teams submitted short reports to be included in this proceedings.

We also include in this proceedings an overview paper on all the tools, models, datasets and challenges collected and provided for the hackathon, as a resource for future scientific and empirical work in the area of news media content analysis and automated report generation.

We were very happy to see several cross-disciplinary and cross-sector collaborations involving, e.g., computer scientists, social scientists and media industry, both in workshop papers and hackathon contributions. We were also happy to have numerous contributions that address multilingual settings and low-resource languages.

The workshop event on 19 April 2021 brings both tracks together, with presentations of both scientific workshop papers and empirical hackathon reports.

We would like to thank all workshop paper authors and hackathon participants for their contributions to the hackashop! We are thankful to the programme committee members for their insightful reviews of the workshop papers. We are equally thankful to the large number of experts who made tools, models, data and challenges available for the hackathon and provided support for the participants.

We are grateful to EACL for giving the opportunity to organize the hackashop with them and to experiment with a novel format. The organization was supported by the European Union's Horizon 2020 research and innovation program under grant 825153 (EMBEDDIA).

Organizing committee

Organizing Committee

- Hannu Toivonen (University of Helsinki, Finland), Chair
- Matthew Purver (Queen Mary University of London, UK)
- Senja Pollak (Jozef Stefan Institute, Slovenia)
- Nada Lavrač (Jozef Stefan Institute, Slovenia)
- Marko Robnik-Šikonja (University of Ljubljana, Slovenia)
- Michele Boggia (University of Helsinki, Finland)
- Carl-Gustav Linden (University of Bergen, Norway)

Workshop Programme Committee

- Emanuela Boros (University of La Rochelle, France)
- Zoran Bosnić (University of Ljubljana, Slovenia)
- Hilde van den Bulck (Drexel University, USA)
- Nicholas Diakopoulos (Northwestern University, USA)
- Antoine Doucet (University of La Rochelle, France)
- Mark Granroth-Wilding (University of Helsinki, Finland)
- Adam Jatowt (Kyoto University, Japan)
- Maria Liakata (Queen Mary University of London, UK)
- Saturnino Luz (University of Edinburgh, UK)
- Matej Martinc (Jozef Stefan Institute, Slovenia)
- Marko Milosavljević (University of Ljubljana, Slovenia)
- Jose Moreno (IRIT, France)
- Kiem Hieu Nguyen (Hanoi university of science and technology, Vietnam)
- Lidia Pivovarova (University of Helsinki, Finland)
- Matej Ulčar (University of Ljubljana, Slovenia)
- Renata Vieira (University of Evora, Portugal)
- Carl Vogel (Trinity College Dublin, Ireland)
- Ivan Vulić (University of Cambridge, UK)
- Slavko Žitnik (University of Ljubljana, Slovenia)

Hackathon Experts

- Emanuela Boros (University of La Rochelle)
- Luis Adrián Cabrera-Diego (University of La Rochelle)
- Linda Freienthal (TEXTA OÜ)
- Boshko Koloski (Jožef Stefan Institute)
- Janez Kranjc (Jožef Stefan Institute)
- Ivar Krustok (Ekspress Meedia)
- Leo Leppänen (University of Helsinki)
- Matej Martinc (Jožef Stefan Institute)
- Jose G. Moreno (University of Toulouse)
- Tarmo Paju (Ekspress Meedia)
- Andraž Pelicon (Jožef Stefan Institute)
- Vid Podpečan (Jožef Stefan Institute)
- Marko Pranjić (Trikoder d.o.o.)
- Salla Salmela (Suomen Tietotoimisto STT)
- Shane Sheehan (University of Edinburgh)
- Ravi Shekhar (Queen Mary University of London)
- Blaž Škrlj (Jožef Stefan Institute)
- Silver Traat (TEXTA OÜ)
- Matej Ulčar (University of Ljubljana)
- Martin Žnidaršič (Jožef Stefan Institute)
- Elaine Zosa (University of Helsinki)

Table of Contents

Peer-reviewed Workshop Papers

Adversarial Training for News Stance Detection: Leveraging Signals from a Multi-Genre Corpus.
Costanza Conforti, Jakob Berndt, Marco Basaldella, Mohammad Taher Pilehvar, Chryssi Giannitsarou, Flavio Toxvaerd and Nigel Collier 1

Related Named Entities Classification in the Economic-Financial Context
Daniel De Los Reyes, Allan Barcelos, Renata Vieira and Isabel Manssour 8

BERT meets Shapley: Extending SHAP Explanations to Transformer-based Classifiers
Enja Kokalj, Blaž Škrlj, Nada Lavrač, Senja Pollak and Marko Robnik-Šikonja 16

Extending Neural Keyword Extraction with TF-IDF tagset matching
Boshko Koloski, Senja Pollak, Blaž Škrlj and Matej Martinc 22

Zero-shot Cross-lingual Content Filtering: Offensive Language and Hate Speech Detection
Andraž Pelicon, Ravi Shekhar, Matej Martinc, Blaž Škrlj, Matthew Purver and Senja Pollak 30

Exploring Linguistically-Lightweight Keyword Extraction Techniques for Indexing News Articles in a Multilingual Set-up
Jakub Piskorski, Nicolas Stefanovitch, Guillaume Jacquet and Aldo Podavini 35

No NLP Task Should be an Island: Multi-disciplinarity for Diversity in News Recommender Systems
Myrthe Reuver, Antske Fokkens and Suzan Verberne 45

TeMoTopic: Temporal Mosaic Visualisation of Topic Distribution, Keywords, and Context
Shane Sheehan, Saturnino Luz and Masood Masoodian 56

Using contextual and cross-lingual word embeddings to improve variety in template-based NLG for automated journalism
Miia Rämö and Leo Leppänen 62

Aligning Estonian and Russian news industry keywords with the help of subtitle translations and an environmental thesaurus
Andraž Repar and Andrej Shumakov 71

Exploring Neural Language Models via Analysis of Local and Global Self-Attention Spaces
Blaž Škrlj, Shane Sheehan, Nika Eržen, Marko Robnik-Šikonja, Saturnino Luz and Senja Pollak 76

Comment Section Personalization: Algorithmic, Interface, and Interaction Design
Yixue Wang 84

Unsupervised Approach to Multilingual User Comments Summarization
Aleš Žagar and Marko Robnik-Šikonja 89

News Media Resources

EMBEDDIA Tools, Datasets and Challenges: Resources and Hackathon Contributions
Senja Pollak, Marko Robnik-Šikonja, Matthew Purver, Michele Boggia, Ravi Shekhar, Marko Pranjić, Salla Salmela, Ivar Krustok, Tarmo Paju, Carl-Gustav Linden, Leo Leppänen, Elaine Zosa, Matej Ulčar, Linda Freienthal, Silver Traat, Luis Adrián Cabrera-Diego, Matej Martinc, Nada Lavrač, Blaž Škrlj, Martin Žnidaršič, Andraž Pelicon, Boshko Koloski, Vid Podpečan, Janez Kranjc, Shane Sheehan, Emanuela Boros, Jose G. Moreno, Antoine Doucet and Hannu Toivonen 99

Hackathon Reports

A COVID-19 news coverage mood map of Europe
Frankie Robertson, Jarkko Lagus and Kaisla Kajava 110

Interesting cross-border news discovery using cross-lingual article linking and document similarity
Boshko Koloski, Elaine Zosa, Timen Stepišnik-Perdih, Blaž Škrlj, Tarmo Paju and Senja Pollak 116

EMBEDDIA hackathon report: Automatic sentiment and viewpoint analysis of Slovenian news corpus on the topic of LGBTIQ+
Matej Martinc, Nina Perger, Andraž Pelicon, Matej Ulčar, Andreja Vezovnik and Senja Pollak 121

To Block or not to Block: Experiments with Machine Learning for News Comment Moderation
Damir Korencic, Ipek Baris, Eugenia Fernandez, Katarina Leuschel and Eva Salido 127

Implementing Evaluation Metrics Based on Theories of Democracy in News Comment Recommendation
Myrthe Reuver and Nicolas Mattis 134

Adversarial Training for News Stance Detection: Leveraging Signals from a Multi-Genre Corpus.

Costanza Conforti[1], **Jakob Berndt**[2], **Mohammad Taher Pilehvar**[1,3],
Marco Basaldella[1], **Chryssi Giannitsarou**[2], **Flavio Toxvaerd**[2], **Nigel Collier**[1]

[1] Language Technology Lab, University of Cambridge
[2] Faculty of Economics, University of Cambridge
[3] Tehran Institute for Advanced Studies, Iran
{cc918,jb2088}@cam.ac.uk

Abstract

Cross-target generalization constitutes an important issue for news Stance Detection (SD). In this short paper, we investigate *adversarial cross-genre SD*, where knowledge from annotated user-generated data is leveraged to improve news SD on targets unseen during training. We implement a BERT-based adversarial network and show experimental performance improvements over a set of strong baselines. Given the abundance of user-generated data, which are considerably less expensive to retrieve and annotate than news articles, this constitutes a promising research direction.

1 Introduction

Stance Detection (SD) is an important NLP task (Mohammad et al., 2017) with widespread applications, ranging from rumor verification (Derczynski et al., 2017) and fact checking (Hanselowski et al., 2019). Traditionally, research in SD focused on user-generated data, such as Twitter or Reddit (Gorrell et al., 2019): this is mainly due to the abundance of such data, which are usually freely available online; moreover, user-generated data tend to be relatively short and compact, and thus more affordable to annotate and process. Starting from popular shared tasks such as Pomerleau and Rao (2017), SD on complex and articulated input, such as news articles, has gained increasing popularity. Notably, effective news SD would constitute an invaluable tool to enhance the performance of human journalists in rumor and fake news debunking (Thorne and Vlachos, 2018).

In line with the general trend in NLP, deep learning-based models have long since established state-of-the-art results in news SD (Hanselowski et al., 2018). Notably, training neural networks relies heavily on the availability of large labeled datasets, which are especially expensive to obtain for items such as news articles. As a consequence, following research on other text classification tasks such as sentiment analysis (Du et al., 2020), research in SD investigated effective methods for *cross-domain SD*, where the scarcity of data for a specific dataset is supplemented with stance-annotated data from other domains. In this context, preliminary research in adversarial domain adaptation obtained promising results for both Twitter (Wang et al., 2020) and news (Xu et al., 2019) SD.

In this paper, we focus on the new task of *cross-genre SD*: we consider adversarial knowledge transfer from two datasets, WT–WT and STANDER, which collect samples in the *same domain* (i.e. the financial domain), but which belong to *different genres* (i.e. Twitter and news). We show experimentally that improvements in news SD performance can be achieved through cross-genre SD, which constitutes a promising direction for future research.

2 An Aligned Multi-Genre Stance Detection Corpus

In this work, we rely on two recently released datasets for news and Twitter SD: the STANDER corpus for the news genre (Conforti et al., 2020a), and the WT–WT corpus for Twitter (Conforti et al., 2020b). Both corpora collect samples discussing four mergers and acquisition (M&A) operations in the healthcare industry (Table 2): an M&A operation, or *merger*, is the process in which a company (the *buyer*) attempts to acquire the ownership of another company (the *target*). A merger succeeds if ownership of the target is transferred, but can fail at any stage of discussions or can be blocked by authorities due to, e.g., antitrust concerns (Bruner and Perella, 2004).

Proceedings of the EACL Hackashop on News Media Content Analysis and Automated Report Generation, pages 1–7
April 19, 2021 © Association for Computational Linguistics

	AET_HUM		ANTM_CI		CI_ESRX		CVS_AET	
Label	tweets	articles	tweets	articles	tweets	articles	tweets	articles
support	1,013	463	959	367	763	207	2,438	372
refute	1,110	537	1,966	313	265	64	530	104
comment	2,776	197	3,101	248	935	70	5,491	294
unrelated	2,930	5	4,995	14	548	5	3,058	31
total	7,829	1,009	11,021	1,199	2,511	376	11,517	831

Table 1: Label distribution in the STANDER News SD corpus and in the WT–WT Twitter SD corpus.

Samples in both STANDER and WT–WT are manually stance-labeled by domain experts using a four-classes annotation schema distinguishing between *support, refute, comment* and *unrelated*, which expresses the sample's orientation about the outcome of the M&A (succeeded or rejected).

As observed in Conforti et al. (2020a), the two corpora present comparable signals, but display different characteristics which reflect the diverse genres they belong to. The Twitter samples are abundant and noisy, as indicated by the high percentage of *unrelated* and *commenting* samples (Figure 1 and Table 1). On the other hand, STANDER collects considerably fewer samples, which are substantially longer and articulated; moreover, news articles in STANDER have been published in high-reputation outlets after careful editorial review, and thus contain a more formal and orthographically correct language with respect to user-generated tweets.

3 Adversarial Training for News Stance Detection

3.1 Motivation

Given the scarcity of news articles in STANDER, which are around one order of magnitude less abundant than tweets in WT–WT, and considering that both corpora collect the same targets in the same domain, *cross-genre* SD from WT–WT to STANDER seems to constitute an interesting research direction. However, due to the consistent genre differences, transferring knowledge from WT–WT to STANDER is non-trivial. To allow the model to capture the stance-specific features from the WT–WT samples which are useful to perform news SD, while ignoring the Twitter-specific features, we propose to treat the task adversarially.

Merger	Buyer	Target	Outcome
AET_HUM	Aetna	Humana	rejected
ANTM_CI	Anthem	Cigna	rejected
CI_ESRX	Cigna	Express Scripts	succeeded
CSV_AET	CVS	Aetna	succeeded

Table 2: Mergers considered in this work. Note that two companies appear both as *Buyer* and as *Target*.

3.2 Models

We propose to consider two classification problems – SD and genre identification (GI) – with a shared BERT-based feature extractor, as shown in Figure 2. To derive genre-invariant features, the GI component is trained adversarially.

The model receives an input sample as:

`[CLS] Target [SEP] Text [SEP],`

where `Target` is the SD target, expressed as the sentence "*A (a) will merge with B (b)*" (where upper- and lowercase *a* and *b* refers resp. to the buyer's and the target's company names and acronyms); for tweets, `Text` is the entire sample's text, while for news, we concatenate the article's title and its first four sentences into a single string. In this way, the target input is always the same over both genres, and it changes over targets only in the company names.

Feature Extractor. As shared feature extractor, we adopt the pretrained $\text{BERT}_{\text{base}}$ uncased model (Devlin et al., 2019).

Stance Classifier. The stance label is predicted

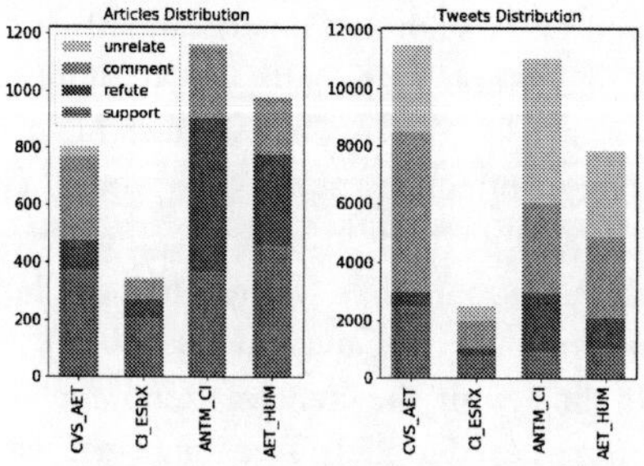

Figure 1: Distribution and number of samples in the STANDER news SD and the WT–WT Twitter SD corpus (Figure taken from Conforti et al. (2020a)).

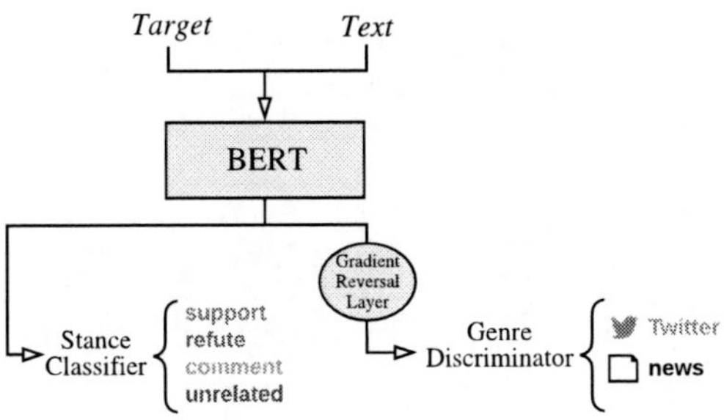

Figure 2: Architecture of our model for news SD.

with a dense layer followed by a softmax operation operating on the hidden state $h_{[CLS]}$ of the special classification embedding `[CLS]`:

$$y_s = \text{softmax}(W_s h_{[CLS]} + b_s) \quad (1)$$

The stance classifier is trained with categorical cross-entropy.

Genre Discriminator. The genre discriminator aims to predict gender labels of samples (Twitter or news). The feature extractor parameters are optimized to maximize the loss of the genre discriminator, thus encouraging BERT to generate genre-invariant features. In practice, the hidden state $h_{[CLS]}$ is first fed to a Gradient Reversal Layer (GRL, Ganin and Lempitsky (2014)). During the forward propagation, the GRL acts as an identity transformation:

$$GRL_\lambda(x) = x \quad (2)$$

but, during the backpropagation, it multiplies the gradient by a negative factor λ:

$$\frac{\delta GRL_\lambda(x))}{\delta x} = -\lambda I \quad (3)$$

The genre label y_g is finally obtained with a dense layer followed by a sigmoid operation:

$$y_g = \text{sigmoid}(W_g GRL(h_{[CLS]}) + b_g) \quad (4)$$

The genre discriminator is trained with binary cross-entropy.

Joint Learning. The two components are jointly trained, resulting in the total loss:

$$L_{total} = L_{stance} + L_{genre} \quad (5)$$

The GI component is adversarial because it is trained to maximise the loss, while the SD component attempts to minimise it. In this way, the more the GI component is unable to correctly classify the samples, the more the system has learned to extract genre-invariant features.

4 Experimental Setting

Baselines. We report results with the three baseline models proposed in Conforti et al. (2020a): a dummy *random* and *majority vote* baseline, abd *BertEmb*, an MLP leveraging sentence-BERT embeddings (Reimers and Gurevych, 2019); moreover, we also consider two further baselines:

- $BERT_{news}$: A vanilla BERT finetuned on news samples only;
- $BERT_{CoTrain}$: A vanilla BERT finetuned on Tweet and news samples, but without the adversarial component (Blum and Mitchell, 1998; Chen et al., 2011).

Training Setting and Preprocessing. We train in a cross-target setting (train on three mergers, test on the fourth) with the Adam optimizer. For each configuration, we randomly select 20% of the training samples as heldout data. For experiments with adversarial cross-genre SD, we randomly select a number of Twitter samples equal to the news training samples (i.e. we double the size of the training set). This ratio was found to perform best in preliminary experiments (refer to the Appendix for further details). The test set contains news samples only. We lowercase both tweets and news samples.

Hyperparameters. We set 128 as maximum sample length (including special tokens). We initialize our architecture with BERT large uncased[1]. BERT's weights are updated during training. We train using Adam (Kingma and Ba, 2015) on baatches of 23 samples, for a maximum of 70 epochs, with early stopping monitoring the SD loss on the development set.

Evaluation. As in Conforti et al. (2020a,b), and in line with other works on news SD (Hanselowski et al., 2018, 2019), we report on macro-averaged F_1 and consider both per-target operation scores, and average scores weighted by target operation size. For the adversarial cross-genre experiments, we compute accuracy for the binary GI task. For computing the evaluation metrics, we use the sklearn's implementations[2].

Computing Infrastructure. We run experiments on an NVIDIA GeForce GTX 1080 GPU.

[1]https://tfhub.dev/tensorflow/bert_en_uncased_L-12_H-768_A-12/3

[2]https://scikit-learn.org/stable/modules/classes.html#module-sklearn.metrics

Model	per-target F_1				$avgF_1$
	CVS AET	CI ESRX	ANTM CI	AET HUM	
Baselines from Conforti et al. (2020a)					
Majority	12.0	12.0	12.0	12.0	12.0
Random	17.5	17.4	17.1	16.5	17.1
BertEmb	42.5	33.2	46.4	43.9	45.7
BERT_{news}	45.5	60.6	47.7	48.8	48.9
$\text{BERT}_{CoTrain}$	47.1	64.8	48.4	51.5	50.8
BERT_{adv}					
$\lambda = 0.2$	**48.0**	64.5	**52.4**	**52.0**	**52.5**
$\lambda = 0.5$	46.9	**66.6**	51.5	50.8	51.8
$\lambda = 0.7$	45.9	64.8	48.9	50.1	50.2
$\lambda = 1.0$	42.6	60.2	47.2	46.1	47.2

Table 3: Results on the STANDER target operations. Macro F_1 scores are obtained by testing on the target operation while training on the other three. Average scores are weighted by the target operation size.

Model	GI $avgAcc$	SD $avgF_1$	Avg. per-class F_1			
			sup	*ref*	*com*	*unr*
BERT_{news}		48.9	70.4	65.8	43.6	18.2
$\text{BERT}_{CoTrain}$		50.8	70.5	67.6	45.4	18.5
BERT_{adv}						
$\lambda = 0.2$	65.8	**52.5**	**72.5**	70.4	**48.0**	19.2
$\lambda = 0.5$	65.3	51.8	69.3	**71.0**	46.5	**20.4**
$\lambda = 0.7$	43.6	50.2	68.9	68.5	44.0	16.4
$\lambda = 1.0$	13.7	47.2	69.3	68.2	34.5	12.0

Table 4: Per-target averaged accuracy for Gender Identification (GI) and per-target averaged F_1 score for Stance Detection (SD), along with single-label per-target averaged F_1 scores.

5 Experiments and Discussion

In this Section, we report on our cross-genre SD experiments. The discussion is organized around three research questions.

RQ1 *What is the effect on news SD of including annotated data from a different genre?*
As shown in Table 3, $\text{BERT}_{CoTrain}$ performs better than all baselines, including the BERT_{news} model, which was trained on in-genre data only. This seems to suggest that exposing the model to in-domain stance-annotated data, even if from a completely different genre, improves the generalizability over unseen targets.

RQ2 *Is adversarial training effective to improve cross-genre SD?*
Adding an adversarial component to the $\text{BERT}_{CoTrain}$ model leads to gains in performance over all considered targets, with improvements ranging from +0.5 (AET_HUM) and +4.0 (ANTM_CI) in macro-averaged F_1 score. (Table 3). Such performance gains are driven by improved performance over all stance labels(Table 4), with *refute* samples benefiting most from the adversarial component.

Such results suggest that a model which is punished for identifying the input's genre can still perform SD.

RQ3 *How does a decrease in GI through adversarial training correlate with SD performance?*
To understand to which extent genre-invariant representations are useful for SD, we experiment with different values of λ, the GRL hyperparameter in Equation 3. As expected, GI performance lowers with increasing λ (Table 4), reaching 13.7 GI accuracy for the model with $\lambda = 1$; this proves the GRL efficacy in forcing the model to learn genre-independent features. However, this also correlates with a steady decrease in SD performance, which holds true all target operations (Table 3), with the only exception of the relatively small CI_ESRX target, which also exhibit very strong label unbalancy (Table 1).

Moving to single-label classification, higher losses in performance are observed for *comment* and *unrelated* samples (resp. −13.5 and −8.3 in weighted accuracy), while *support* and *refute* label seem to be more robust to changes in the values of λ. A possible explanation for this might be in the stylistic differences between the two corpora: *unrelated* and *comment* samples in the Twitter WT–WT corpus were often retrieved because of keywords homonymy[3], and, as such, they tend to discuss completely different topics; on the contrary, such samples in the news STANDER corpus are actually covering the target companies. For this reason, completely genre-unaware knowledge transfer might not be optimal for those stance labels.

This is in line with previous work by McHardy et al. (2019) on satire detection, and seems to indicate that, while learning partially genre-invariant features is beneficial for cross-target performance, features which are completely opaque with respect to the genre component are not ideal for SD.

[3]For example, 'cvs' not referring to the company 'CVS Health', but used as as plural of 'resume'.

6 Conclusions

In this paper, we discussed the new task of *cross-genre SD*: our experiments with a range of BERT-based architectures show that partially obfuscating the genre component through adversarial training leads to better generalization, especially considering low-frequency labels. Cross-genre SD thus constitutes a promising future research direction. Future work might include experiments using different underlying feature extractors, such as RoBERTa, or with adapters, to study the robustness of cross-genre SD over modeling choices. The integration of cross-genre and cross-domain adaptation, possibly in a multi-task setting as in Conforti et al. (2020a), also offers interesting ideas for future investigation.

Acknowledgements

We thank the anonymous reviewers of this paper for their efforts and for the constructive comments and suggestions. We gratefully acknowledge funding from the Keynes Fund, University of Cambridge (grant no. JHOQ). CC is grateful to NERC DREAM CDT (grant no. 1945246) for partially funding this work. CG and FT are thankful to the Cambridge Endowment for Research in Finance (CERF).

References

Avrim Blum and Tom M. Mitchell. 1998. Combining labeled and unlabeled data with co-training. In *Proceedings of the Eleventh Annual Conference on Computational Learning Theory, COLT 1998, Madison, Wisconsin, USA, July 24-26, 1998.*, pages 92–100.

Robert F Bruner and Joseph R Perella. 2004. *Applied mergers and acquisitions*, volume 173. John Wiley & Sons.

Minmin Chen, Kilian Q. Weinberger, and John Blitzer. 2011. Co-training for domain adaptation. In *Advances in Neural Information Processing Systems 24: 25th Annual Conference on Neural Information Processing Systems 2011. Proceedings of a meeting held 12-14 December 2011, Granada, Spain*, pages 2456–2464.

Costanza Conforti, Jakob Berndt, Mohammad Taher Pilehvar, Chryssi Giannitsarou, Flavio Toxvaerd, and Nigel Collier. 2020a. STANDER: an expert-annotated dataset for news stance detection and evidence retrieval. In *Proceedings of the 2020 Conference on Empirical Methods in Natural Language Processing: Findings, EMNLP 2020, Online Event, 16-20 November 2020*, pages 4086–4101. Association for Computational Linguistics.

Costanza Conforti, Jakob Berndt, Mohammad Taher Pilehvar, Chryssi Giannitsarou, Flavio Toxvaerd, and Nigel Collier. 2020b. Will-they-won't-they: A very large dataset for stance detection on twitter. In *Proceedings of the 58th Annual Meeting of the Association for Computational Linguistics, ACL 2020, Online, July 5-10, 2020*, pages 1715–1724. Association for Computational Linguistics.

Leon Derczynski, Kalina Bontcheva, Maria Liakata, Rob Procter, Geraldine Wong Sak Hoi, and Arkaitz Zubiaga. 2017. Semeval-2017 task 8: Rumoureval: Determining rumour veracity and support for rumours. In *Proceedings of the 11th International Workshop on Semantic Evaluation, SemEval@ACL 2017, Vancouver, Canada, August 3-4, 2017*, pages 69–76.

Jacob Devlin, Ming-Wei Chang, Kenton Lee, and Kristina Toutanova. 2019. BERT: pre-training of deep bidirectional transformers for language understanding. In *Proceedings of the 2019 Conference of the North American Chapter of the Association for Computational Linguistics: Human Language Technologies, NAACL-HLT 2019, Minneapolis, MN, USA, June 2-7, 2019, Volume 1 (Long and Short Papers)*, pages 4171–4186. Association for Computational Linguistics.

Chunning Du, Haifeng Sun, Jingyu Wang, Qi Qi, and Jianxin Liao. 2020. Adversarial and domain-aware BERT for cross-domain sentiment analysis. In *Proceedings of the 58th Annual Meeting of the Association for Computational Linguistics*, pages 4019–4028, Online. Association for Computational Linguistics.

Yaroslav Ganin and Victor Lempitsky. 2014. Unsupervised domain adaptation by backpropagation. *arXiv preprint arXiv:1409.7495.*

Genevieve Gorrell, Elena Kochkina, Maria Liakata, Ahmet Aker, Arkaitz Zubiaga, Kalina Bontcheva, and Leon Derczynski. 2019. SemEval-2019 task 7: RumourEval, determining rumour veracity and support for rumours. In *Proceedings of SemEval 2019.*

Andreas Hanselowski, Avinesh P. V. S., Benjamin Schiller, Felix Caspelherr, Debanjan Chaudhuri, Christian M. Meyer, and Iryna Gurevych. 2018. A retrospective analysis of the fake news challenge stance-detection task. In *Proceedings of the 27th International Conference on Computational Linguistics, COLING 2018, Santa Fe, New Mexico, USA, August 20-26, 2018*, pages 1859–1874. Association for Computational Linguistics.

Andreas Hanselowski, Christian Stab, Claudia Schulz, Zile Li, and Iryna Gurevych. 2019. A richly annotated corpus for different tasks in automated fact-checking. In *Proceedings of the 23rd Conference on Computational Natural Language Learning*

(CoNLL), pages 493–503, Hong Kong, China. Association for Computational Linguistics.

Diederik P. Kingma and Jimmy Ba. 2015. Adam: A method for stochastic optimization. In *3rd International Conference on Learning Representations, ICLR 2015, San Diego, CA, USA, May 7-9, 2015, Conference Track Proceedings*.

Robert McHardy, Heike Adel, and Roman Klinger. 2019. Adversarial training for satire detection: Controlling for confounding variables. In *Proceedings of the 2019 Conference of the North American Chapter of the Association for Computational Linguistics: Human Language Technologies, NAACL-HLT 2019, Minneapolis, MN, USA, June 2-7, 2019, Volume 1 (Long and Short Papers)*, pages 660–665. Association for Computational Linguistics.

Saif M. Mohammad, Parinaz Sobhani, and Svetlana Kiritchenko. 2017. Stance and sentiment in tweets. *ACM Trans. Internet Techn.*, 17(3):26:1–26:23.

Dean Pomerleau and Delip Rao. 2017. Fake news challenge.

Nils Reimers and Iryna Gurevych. 2019. Sentence-bert: Sentence embeddings using siamese bert-networks. In *Proceedings of the 2019 Conference on Empirical Methods in Natural Language Processing*. Association for Computational Linguistics.

James Thorne and Andreas Vlachos. 2018. Automated fact checking: Task formulations, methods and future directions. In *Proceedings of the 27th International Conference on Computational Linguistics, COLING 2018, Santa Fe, New Mexico, USA, August 20-26, 2018*, pages 3346–3359. Association for Computational Linguistics.

Zhen Wang, Qiansheng Wang, Chengguo Lv, Xue Cao, and Guohong Fu. 2020. Unseen target stance detection with adversarial domain generalization. *2020 International Joint Conference on Neural Networks (IJCNN)*.

Brian Xu, Mitra Mohtarami, and James Glass. 2019. Adversarial domain adaptation for stance detection. *CoRR*, abs/1902.02401.

A Appendix

In this Appendix, we report on the results of preliminary experiments which were run in order to find the best proportion between news and Twitter samples. We consider six settings, with increasing proportion of Twitter to news samples: 50%, 100%, 150%, 200%, 250% and a last setting in which all Twitter samples were included. For each setting, experiments were run in a cross-validation setting (training on data on three operations, and testing on the fourth).

% of Twitter data	per-target F_1 CVS AET	CI ESRX	ANTM CI	AET HUM	$avgF_1$
BERT$_{news}$	43.3	62.2	48.5	50.9	49.4
= 50	42.5	63.5	49.5	51.2	49.8
= 100	48.0	64.5	52.4	52.0	52.5
= 150	48.9	65.5	47.3	52.5	51.2
= 200	56.1	63.6	47.3	51.7	52.3
= 250	51.4	61.1	51.6	51.8	52.5
all	54.6	62.1	48.3	47.7	51.2

Table 5: Stance Detection performance with the genre-adversarial model ($\lambda = 0.2$), by adding different proportion of Twitter data from the WT–WT corpus to the STANDER news samples. A % of 100 corresponds to the proportion used in the experiments reported in the paper. *all* corresponds to all the samples in the WT–WT corpus (33,668).

Interestingly, we observe gains in overall performance w.r.t. the BERT$_{news}$ baseline, which is trained on news data only (Table 5), with all adversarial models. This holds true even in the case of the model trained on the union of STANDER (2945) with *all* tweets from the WT–WT corpus (30711): the model's considerable performance gain with respect to the BERT$_{news}$ model testifies the ability of the adversarial model to learn partially genre-invariant features even when exposed to extremely unbalanced training data. Single-label results (Table 6) show that increasing the ratio of Twitter samples included in the training data tends to correlate with performance gains in recall, at the expense of losses in performance. The best news-to-tweets ratio lies between 100 and 250, with small differences between target operations and stance labels. Thus, our adversarial cross-genre models seem to be relatively robust over the exact amount of out-of-genre samples which are included during training.

% of Twitter data	SD			Avg. per-class performance											
				sup			*ref*			*com*			*unr*		
	avgP	avgR	$avgF_1$	P	R	F_1	P	R	F_1	P	R	F_1	P	R	F_1
50	52.2	49.9	49.8	69.5	73.5	70.4	69.1	70.3	69.5	47.5	42.6	44.9	15.3	20.8	15.4
100	54.6	55.2	**52.5**	**75.3**	70.9	**72.2**	67.8	73.6	70.5	49.8	51.6	49.0	25.9	24.1	**18.8**
150	**56.4**	52.4	51.2	68.7	74.1	69.8	**73.4**	67.3	69.9	48.8	48.8	46.7	**34.6**	19.4	18.1
200	54.9	54.1	52.3	73.7	70.8	71.8	72.6	67.9	70.0	49.0	**57.7**	**52.0**	24.2	20.1	16.5
250	55.2	**55.3**	**52.5**	71.3	**73.6**	71.8	68.9	**75.3**	**71.9**	**54.0**	46.0	48.9	26.1	**27.2**	18.6
all	52.1	53.5	51.1	72.0	70.5	70.1	70.5	71.8	71.1	49.6	45.4	46.7	16.2	25.7	17.0

Table 6: Per-label detailed performance when adding different percentage of tweets to the STANDER news samples. A % of 100 corresponds to the proportion used in the experiments reported in the paper. All results are obtained with the genre-adversarial model ($\lambda = 0.2$). Considering macro-averaged Precision, Recall and F_1 measures, weighted according to the target operation's size.

Related Named Entities Classification in the Economic-Financial Context

Daniel De Los Reyes[1], Allan Barcelos[1], Renata Vieira[2], Isabel H. Manssour[1]
[1]Pontifical Catholic University of Rio Grande do Sul, PUCRS.
School of Technology. Porto Alegre, Brazil.
[2]CIDEHUS, University of Évora, Portugal.
{daniel.reyes, allan.silva}@edu.pucrs.br, renatav@uevora.pt, isabel.manssour@pucrs.br

Abstract

The present work uses the Bidirectional Encoder Representations from Transformers (BERT) to process a sentence and its entities and indicate whether two named entities present in a sentence are related or not, constituting a binary classification problem. It was developed for the Portuguese language, considering the financial domain and exploring deep linguistic representations to identify a relation between entities without using other lexical-semantic resources. The results of the experiments show an accuracy of 86% of the predictions.

1 Introduction

In the context of the financial market, the news bring information regarding sectors economy, industrial policies, acquisitions and partnerships of companies, among others. The analysis of this data, in the form of financial reports, headlines and corporate announcements, can support personal and corporate economic decision making (Zhou and Zhang, 2018). However, thousands of news items are published every day and this number continues to increase, which makes the task of using and interpreting this huge amount of data impossible through manual means.

Information Extraction (IE) can contribute with tools that allow the monitoring of these news items in a faster way and with less effort, through automation of the extraction and structuring of information. IE is the technology based on natural language, that receives text as input and generates results in a predefined format (Cvitaš, 2011). Among the tasks of the IE area, it is possible to highlight both Named Entity Recognition (NER) and Relation Extraction (RE). For example, it is possible to extract that a given organization (first entity) was purchased (relation) by another organization (second entity) (Sarawagi, 2008).

A model based on the BERT language model (Devlin et al., 2018) is proposed to classify whether a sentence containing a tuple entity 1 and entity 2 (e1,e2), expresses a relation among them. Leveraging the power of BERT networks, the semantics of the sentence can be obtained without using enhanced feature selection or other external resources.

The contribution of this work is in building an approach for extracting entity relations for the Portuguese language on the financial context.

The remainder of this work is organized as follows. Section 2 presents news processing for the Competitive Intelligence (CI) area. Section 3 presents the related work. Section 4 provides a detailed description of the proposed solution. Section 5 explains the experimental process in detail, followed by section 6, which shows the relevant experimental results. Finally, section 7 presents our conclusions, as well as future work.

2 Competitive Intelligence and News Processing

Some of the largest companies in the financial segment have a Competitive Intelligence (CI) sector where information from different sources is strategically analyzed, allowing to anticipate market trends, enabling the evolution of the business compared to its competitors. This sector is usually formed by one or more professionals dedicated specifically to monitor the movements of the competition.

In a time of competitiveness that is based on knowledge and innovation, CI allows companies to exercise pro-activity. The conclusions obtained through this process allow the company to know if it really remains competitive and if there is sustainability for its business model. CI can provide some advantages to companies that use it, such as: minimizing surprises from competitors, identify-

Proceedings of the EACL Hackashop on News Media Content Analysis and Automated Report Generation, pages 8–15
April 19, 2021

ing opportunities and threats, obtaining relevant knowledge to formulate strategic planning, understanding the repercussions of their actions in the market, among others.

The process of capturing information through news still requires a lot of manual effort, as it often depends on a professional responsible for carefully reading numerous news about organizations to highlight possible market movements that also retain this knowledge. It is then estimated that a system, that automatically filters the relations between financial market entities, can reduce the effort and the time spent on these tasks. Another benefit is that this same system can feed the Business Intelligence (BI) systems and, thus, establish a historical database with market events. Thus, knowledge about market movements can be stored and organized more efficiently.

3 Related Work

ER is a task that has been the subject of many studies, especially now when information and communication technologies allow the storage of and processing of massive data.

Zhang (Zhang et al., 2017) proposes to incorporate the position of words and entities into an approach employing combinations of N-grams for extracting relations. Presenting a different methodology to extract the relations, Wu (Wu and He, 2019) proposed to use a pre-trained BERT language model and the entity types for RE on the English language. In order to circumvent the problem of lack of memory for very large sequences in convolutional networks, some authors (Li et al., 2018; Florez et al., 2019; Pandey et al., 2017) have adopted an approach using memory cells for neural networks, Long short-term memory (LSTM). In this sense, Qingqing's Li work (Li et al., 2018) uses a Bidirectional Long Short-Term Memory (Bi-LSTM) network, which are an extension of traditional LSTMs, for its multitasking model, and features a version with attention that considerably improves the results in all tested datasets. Also using Bi-LSTM networks, Florez (Florez et al., 2019) differs from other authors in that it uses types of entities and the words of the entities being considered for a relation in addition to using information such as number of entities and distances, measured by the number of words and phrases between the pair of entities. The entry of the Bi-LSTM layer is concatenation of words and relations, with all words between the candidate entities (included), provided by a pre-trained interpolation layer. Yi (Yi and Hu, 2019) proposes to join a BERT language model and a Bidirectional Gated Recurrent Unit (Bi-GRU) network, which is a version of Bi-LSTM with a lower computational cost. Finally, they train their model based on a pre-trained BERT network, instead of training from the beginning, to speed up coverage.

Some works (Qin et al., 2017; GAN et al., 2019; Zhou and Zhang, 2018) use attention mechanisms to improve the performance of their neural network models. Such mechanisms assist in the automatic information filtering step that helps to find the most appropriate sentence section to distinguish named entities. Thus, it is possible that even in a very long sentence, and due to its size being considered complex, the model can capture the context information of each token in the sentence, being able to concentrate more in these terms the weights of influence. Pengda Qin (Qin et al., 2017) proposes a method using Bi-GRU with an attention mechanism that can automatically focus on valuable words, also using the pairs of entities and adding information related to them.

Tao Gan (GAN et al., 2019) also addresses RE with an attention method to capture important parts of the sentence and for that, it uses an LSTM attention network for entities at the subsequent level. In this way, he focuses more on important contextual information between two entities. Zhou (Zhou and Zhang, 2018) also implement a model based on RNN Bi-GRU with an attention mechanism to focus on the most important assumptions of the sentences for the financial market.

Despite having great importance, the financial domain, specifically, has been little explored in the literature. The authors at (Zhou and Zhang, 2018) created a corpus collecting 3000 sentence records manually from the main news sites, which was used to recognize the entity and extract relations such as learning and training as a whole.

Most studies present RE solutions for English texts, and, in this way, it is also possible to identify a larger number of data sets in this language. There are few data sets available in the Portuguese language, such as the Golden Collection HAREM, which is widely used in the literature (Chaves, 2008; Cardoso, 2008; Collovini et al., 2016). HAREM is a joint assessment event for the Portuguese language, organized by Linguateca

(Santos and Cardoso, 2007). Its objective is to evaluate recognizing systems of NE (Santos and Cabral, 2009). The Golden Collection (GC) is a subset of the HAREM collection, being used for the task of evaluating the systems that deal with Recognition of Named Entities.

The lack of this type of resource forces researchers to develop their own research corpus. In most cases, it is necessary to first create a set with the sentences and write them down when the classification is supervised to proceed with the RE task. Besides, the lack of public data sets also makes it difficult to fairly compare related work, as well as requires more time and effort from the researcher.

It is possible to observe that there are works that discuss the task of extracting relations between NE and that already employ machine learning techniques for this purpose. However, although we found some works for the RE task, few of them are suitable for the Portuguese language, and none of them are related to the financial context. Considering other languages, The work of Zhou (Zhou and Zhang, 2018) was the only one that came closest to our goals. However, there is a gap in the literature for works that address such tasks using deep learning techniques and Portuguese as the main language, especially in the financial-economic context as addressed in this work.

4 Architecture

In this section, we present our BERT-based model in detail. As shown in Figure 1, it contains three parts: (1) Input layer; (2) BERT layer; and (3) Output layer, which is composed of a Sigmoid activation function and two neurons that represent the classes to be predicted.

The input layer consists of a BERT encoder used for input sentence tokenization and produces a tuple of arrays (token, mask, sequence ids), which were used as input to the second layer that is the Portuguese BERT language model (Souza et al., 2020) [1] from Huggingface python package [2] (Wolf et al., 2020). Figure 2 illustrates the input layer of the proposed model. The entry consists of (1) the original sentence with the mentioned entities and (2) the entities to be verified concatenated. A special token [cls] and a token [sep] are added at the beginning and end of the input string respectively, as mentioned in the original BERT implementation (Devlin et al., 2018).

The third layer of the model architecture is identified as the output layer. This layer is fully connected with a tangent activation function. The output of this layer is propagated to a new fully connected layer, with a Sigmoid activation function, whose characteristic is the mapping of input values to 0 or 1. In this model, these values represent non-relation and relation, respectively. As shown in Figure 1, this layer still has two output neurons, which indicate the respective classes to be predicted by the model. In the end, we added a dropout layer with a 0.1 rate to avoid model overfitting, which happens when the model memorizes the training data and thereby loses the power of generalization.

5 Experiments

The purpose of this section is to verify the proposed model performance thought experiments on the financial domain corpus. The proposed study follows the classic methodology of Knowledge Discovery in Databases (KDD) (Fayyad et al., 1996), which contains 5 phases that range from data collection to the evaluation of the results.

The following subsections aim to indicate how each step of the methodology was applied in the context of our work. Subsection 5.1 refers to the Selection step and seeks to indicate what data will be used during the experiments for the RE task. Subsection 5.2 addresses the Pre-processing step, indicating procedures for quality checking, cleaning, correction, or removal of inconsistent or missing data. Subsection 5.3 reports the Transformation phase, where the transformation processes applied to the data set in the context of our work are explored. Subsection 5.4 brings the penultimate phase, of Mining, where the data mining process is presented. Finally, the last phase of the methodology is presented in the subsection 5.5, which consists of evaluating the performance of the model applied on top of the data that were not used in the training or mining phase.

5.1 Selection

As indicated in section 3, there was no evidence of open data sets in the context of extracting relations in the financial field for the Portuguese language. Therefore, for this work, a corpus was created with 3,288 tuples annotated manually. These tuples originate from more than 4,000 paragraphs of financial

[1] Available at `https://simpletransformers.ai/`

[2] Available at `https://github.com/huggingface/transformers`

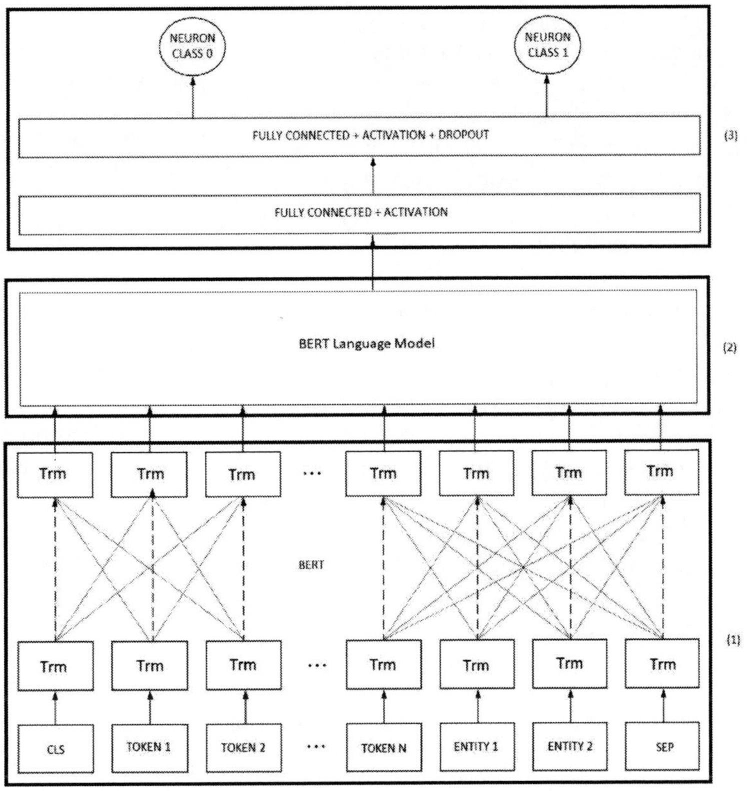

Figure 1: Complete model architecture with its 3 layers: (1) Input layer; (2) BERT layer; (3) Output layer.

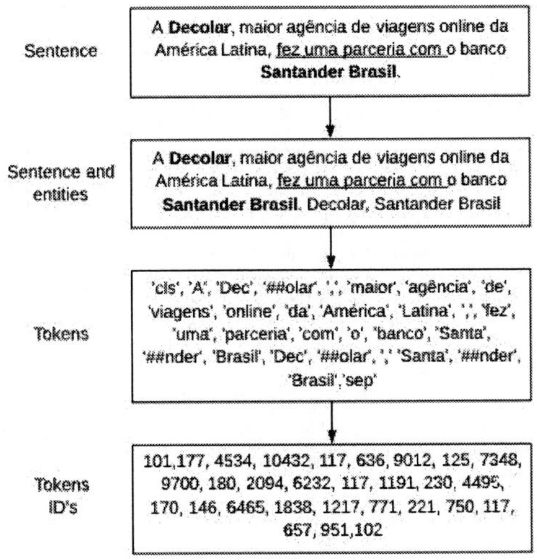

Figure 2: Examples of data transformations in the input layer of the model. The entities to be evaluated appear in bold, and the text that represents the semantic relation between them is underlined.

market news, provided by a partner company that collected them in various communication vehicles such as financial market websites, newspapers, and corporate balance sheets. Sentences that include co-referral are also removed because co-reference treatment would require additional processing.

5.2 Pre-processing

The next step concerns the data pre-processing and cleaning. This step occurs through the manual process of spelling correction of each sentence. Acronyms are also extended, as well as the standardization of different ways of indicating the same named entity.

The standardization can be done manually, but in a real work scenario, this task becomes massive and can be automated by creating a base of named entities and their acronyms. Thus, it is possible to elaborate a process that validates the acronyms contained in the sentence and replace them with their extensions or even with an approach that focuses on only a few specific entities informed by the CI analyst himself.

The data cleaning process is also done manually, where special characters and acronyms that follow the description itself are removed. Sentences containing less than 4 tokens will also be removed, as they can be considered irrelevant to the context of the approach. At the end of this cleaning step, just over 2500 sentences are filtered.

In this same phase, the identification of named entities will also occur, through a single NER tool, called SpaCy [3], ensuring that the same criterion was used for all sentences.

The named entities in question are those related to the categories person, location, and organization. The focal point is information about the organizations, as well as its relations with other organizations, persons, and locations.

After identifying all named entities, sentences that have less than 2 entities are discarded. At the end of this new disposal, the corpus consists of 1292 unique sentences that move on to the next stage.

5.3 Transformation

With the identification of the Named Entities in the previous phase, a combination of all the entities present in the sentence is made and a triple (sentence, entity, entity) is formed for each combination, which can generate several records for the same sentence. After this creation of records with the combination of entities, manual annotation of records that have a semantic relation between the highlighted named entities is made manually.

After the end of the manual annotation of the relations between the entities, the corpus consists of 3288 records. Of this total, 1485 (45%) are positive tuples, that is, it contains a relation between the highlighted entities, and 1803 (55%) are negative tuples, where there is no relation between the entities. Finally, the two named entities are concatenated at the end of the sentence. The data set is available at `https://github.com/DanielReeyes/relation-extraction-deep-learning`.

The relation annotating process did not consider the past defined classes or relations. A positive tuple is considered when there is any semantic relation between two named entities of the categories defined in 5.1. Here are some examples of positive annotated tuples that contain relation between named entities of type organization:

- A **Abraço** é uma **Instituição Particular de Solidariedade Social**.
- A **Caixa** é controladora do **Pan** , ao lado do BTG , com 32,8% do negócio.
- A **Havanna** fecha parceria com o **Santander** para inaugurar um novo modelo de negócios.
- A partir de agora , a **NET** está na **Claro**.

As sentences are naturally composed of words and characters, then the transformation step in the present study also consists of transforming the tokens into numerical representations by the BERT encoder. As stated in past sections, the special tokens [CLS] and [SEP] are also added and encoded properly on each sentence, finalizing the composition of the input layer.

5.4 Mining

The predictive task is characterized by the search for a behavioral pattern that can predict the behavior of a future entity (Fayyad et al., 1996). The corpus data are randomly divided into two parts, 80% of which are used for training the model and 20% for testing. The part for the test is still divided equally into 2, where they are used as validation and test sets to test the generalization of the model. The first set is used so that the algorithm can search for this particular pattern in the data concerning the relation label. Thus, after the training stage where the model can recognize this pattern, it is possible to apply it to the validation data and later on the test set, simulating a real environment. In this step, the original balance level is also maintained in all sets created, being able to rule out that the model contains any bias to learn a certain type of complexity.

The adjustment of hyper-parameters of the BERT used was due to the combination of all values indicated by Jacob Devlin in (Devlin et al., 2018), in addition to the standard values for the Simple Transformers library model. In this work, Jacob used most of the hyper-parameters with default values except for the lot size, learning rate, and the number of training epochs. The dropout rate was always maintained at 0.1. Thus, the values tested for this task were:

- **Batch Size:** 16, 32;

[3] `https://spacy.io/`

Hyper-parameter	Value
Batch Size	32
Learning Rate	5e-5
Epochs	4

Table 1: Combination of hyper-parameters that presented better results.

Set	Samples	Positive Class Distribution (%)	Positive Samples
Original	3288	45.16	1485
Training	2630	45.17	1188
Validation	329	45.28	149
Test	329	45.98	148

Table 2: Sample composition of each data set used in the experiments.

- **Learning Rate (AdamW):** 5e-5, 3e-5, 2e-5;
- **Epochs:** 2, 3, 4, 5.

In the end, we did a total of 24 experiments with all the possible combinations of the above described parameters. After analyzing the results, the model with the values was selected according to Table 1.

5.5 Evaluation

To evaluate the model, metrics such as Accuracy, Recall, Precision, and F1-Measure were provided. According to Table 2, each set maintained the original imbalance of the data set according to the target variable, in this case, indicating whether or not there is a relation between the entities assessed. In this way, the model is evaluated for the ability to indicate whether a given pair of entities contained in a sentence has a relation or not, configuring a binary classification problem, whose positive class refers to entities that have a semantic relation.

6 Results

After the training stage of the model, it was applied to the test data set. In this evaluation step, the model obtained reasonable results, achieving an overall accuracy and F-Measure of 86%. An important observation to make is that results are also good when it comes to the target class, that is, when the label is positive, as can be seen in Table 3.

As indicated in Section 3, the vast majority of studies present RE solutions for texts in English or a domain other than finance. Thus, it is difficult to compare the results of the proposed method with state-of-the-art approaches.

Metric	Positive	Negative	General
Recall	0,8993	0,8389	0,8662
Precision	0,8221	0,9096	0,8699
F-Measure	0,8590	0,8728	0,8665
Accuracy	-	-	0,8663

Table 3: Precision, Recall and F-Measure calculated for each class and Accuracy and general F-Measure of the model.

Nevertheless, it is shown that the proposed model was able to recognize patterns and indicate when two entities are semantically related in the same sentence in the financial domain.

The process of finding the best parameters for BERT is time-consuming as the predictions made by the network. The time might not be a constraint to using the RE task model applied to the context of the financial domain considering that this demand does not require the processing time to be real-time.

We believe that if the data set is increased with more samples, the model may have a performance gain. Also, we can notice that the data set has a small unbalanced distribution rate, with a greater number of negative samples.

This imbalance can help explain the difference in precision and F-measure between the positive and negative class indicated in Table 3, where it is possible to see that the model gets more right when the tested entities had no relation in the sentence.

Regarding Recall, the study indicates that, even with the imbalance of the data, the proposed model achieved a very good performance of approximately 90% when it comes to the positive class (it has a relation). That is, when it really belongs to the positive class, in approximately 90% of the cases, it identifies correctly.

It is also possible to carry out tests with adjustments of more hyper-parameters such as loss function, optimizers, among others. In addition to adjustments to the hyper-parameters of the approach, more contextual information of the samples can be added, such as the type of the named entity, whether it is an organization, person, or place, and scope adopted for the task being worked on. In this way, it is possible to delimit the types of relations between 2 entities, excluding, for example, an acquisition relation between two entities of the person type.

7 Conclusion and Future works

The present work proposed an approach to extract relations between named entities, in the financial-economic context, based on the Portuguese BERT language model, to our best knowledge, different from what is already in the literature. Thus, it provides an insight into the use of pre-trained deep language models for extracting relations for the Portuguese language financial market.

From the related work section, it is possible to verify that there is little research on the technology for extracting the relation between named entities for the financial domain, for the Portuguese language. This domain lacks practical solutions, given a large amount of information in the financial field, and manual analysis becomes difficult to meet the needs and make full use of that information.

A model of classification of relations between named entities based on BERT was proposed, which replaces explicit linguistic resources, required by previous methods. This approach uses the information from the sentence and the concatenated entity pair, which allows more than one entry to be sent since a sentence can have N pairs of named entities. Therefore, the adopted approach allows the sentence and the pair of entities to be inferred to be sent separately.

The results demonstrate that the approach used can bring satisfactory results, reaching an accuracy of 86%. During the discussion of results, some adjustments were made to try to improve accuracy, such as testing other combinations of hyper-parameters and also the increase in the corpus. However, the development of memory improvements and optimizations are still in need, especially in the training period, due to the complexity of the pre-trained BERT model.

As a natural continuation of this work, we will proceed with tests with other combinations of hyper-parameters as indicated in Section 6. To try to reduce the chance of the model being surprised with some non-standard samples, new data will be annotated and added to the research corpus. Thus, the model can be trained with a greater amount of data and a greater diversity of data patterns.

As a continuity, a second model will also be developed, with sequential classification, so that it is possible to highlight the parts of the sentences that represent or describe the relation between the named entities verified. To achieve this goal, this second model will be trained only with the tuples that contain the annotated relation. Thus, the output of the model proposed in this work will be the input of the sequential classifier model.

Acknowledgments

This work was partially funded by the Portuguese Foundation for Science and Technology, project UIDB/00057/2020.

References

Nuno Cardoso. 2008. Rembrandt-reconhecimento de entidades mencionadas baseado em relaçoes e análise detalhada do texto. *quot; Encontro do Segundo HAREM (Universidade de Aveiro Portugal 7 de Setembro de 2008).*

Marcírio Chaves. 2008. Geo-ontologias e padrões para reconhecimento de locais e de suas relações em textos: o sei-geo no segundo harem. *quot; In Cristina Mota; Diana Santos (ed) Desafios na avaliação conjunta do reconhecimento de entidades mencionadas: O Segundo HAREM Linguateca 2008.*

Sandra Collovini, Gabriel Machado, and Renata Vieira. 2016. A sequence model approach to relation extraction in portuguese. In *Proceedings of the Tenth International Conference on Language Resources and Evaluation (LREC'16)*, pages 1908–1912.

A Cvitaš. 2011. Relation extraction from text documents. In *2011 Proceedings of the 34th International Convention MIPRO*, pages 1565–1570. IEEE.

Jacob Devlin, Ming-Wei Chang, Kenton Lee, and Kristina Toutanova. 2018. Bert: Pre-training of deep bidirectional transformers for language understanding. *arXiv preprint arXiv:1810.04805.*

Usama Fayyad, Gregory Piatetsky-Shapiro, and Padhraic Smyth. 1996. From data mining to knowledge discovery in databases. *AI magazine*, 17(3):37. GS Search.

Edson Florez, Frederic Precioso, Romaric Pighetti, and Michel Riveill. 2019. Deep learning for identification of adverse drug reaction relations. In *Proceedings of the 2019 International Symposium on Signal Processing Systems*, pages 149–153.

TAO GAN, YUNQIANG GAN, and YANMIN HE. 2019. Subsequence-level entity attention lstm for relation extraction. In *2019 16th International Computer Conference on Wavelet Active Media Technology and Information Processing*, pages 262–265. IEEE.

Qingqing Li, Zhihao Yang, Ling Luo, Lei Wang, Yin Zhang, Hongfei Lin, Jian Wang, Liang Yang, Kan Xu, and Yijia Zhang. 2018. A multi-task learning based approach to biomedical entity relation extraction. In *2018 IEEE International Conference on*

Bioinformatics and Biomedicine (BIBM), pages 680–682. IEEE.

Chandra Pandey, Zina Ibrahim, Honghan Wu, Ehtesham Iqbal, and Richard Dobson. 2017. Improving rnn with attention and embedding for adverse drug reactions. In *Proceedings of the 2017 International Conference on Digital Health*, pages 67–71.

Pengda Qin, Weiran Xu, and Jun Guo. 2017. Designing an adaptive attention mechanism for relation classification. In *2017 International Joint Conference on Neural Networks (IJCNN)*, pages 4356–4362. IEEE.

Diana Santos and Luís Miguel Cabral. 2009. Gikiclef: Crosscultural issues in an international setting: asking non-english-centered questions to wikipedia. In *quot; In Francesca Borri; Alessandro Nardi; Carol Peters (ed) Cross Language Evaluation Forum: Working notes for CLEF 2009 (Corfu 30 Setembro-2 Outubro) Springer*. Springer.

Diana Santos and Nuno Cardoso. 2007. Reconhecimento de entidades mencionadas em português: Documentação e actas do harem, a primeira avaliação conjunta na área.

Sunita Sarawagi. 2008. *Information extraction*. Now Publishers Inc.

Fábio Souza, Rodrigo Nogueira, and Roberto Lotufo. 2020. BERTimbau: pretrained BERT models for Brazilian Portuguese. In *9th Brazilian Conference on Intelligent Systems, BRACIS, Rio Grande do Sul, Brazil, October 20-23 (to appear)*.

Thomas Wolf, Lysandre Debut, Victor Sanh, Julien Chaumond, Clement Delangue, Anthony Moi, Pierric Cistac, Tim Rault, Rémi Louf, Morgan Funtowicz, Joe Davison, Sam Shleifer, Patrick von Platen, Clara Ma, Yacine Jernite, Julien Plu, Canwen Xu, Teven Le Scao, Sylvain Gugger, Mariama Drame, Quentin Lhoest, and Alexander M. Rush. 2020. Transformers: State-of-the-art natural language processing. In *Proceedings of the 2020 Conference on Empirical Methods in Natural Language Processing: System Demonstrations*, pages 38–45, Online. Association for Computational Linguistics.

Shanchan Wu and Yifan He. 2019. Enriching pretrained language model with entity information for relation classification. In *Proceedings of the 28th ACM International Conference on Information and Knowledge Management*, pages 2361–2364.

Rongli Yi and Wenxin Hu. 2019. Pre-trained bert-gru model for relation extraction. In *Proceedings of the 2019 8th International Conference on Computing and Pattern Recognition*, pages 453–457.

Qin Zhang, Jianhua Liu, Ying Wang, and Zhixiong Zhang. 2017. A convolutional neural network method for relation classification. In *2017 International Conference on Progress in Informatics and Computing (PIC)*, pages 440–444. IEEE.

Zhenyu Zhou and Haiyang Zhang. 2018. Research on entity relationship extraction in financial and economic field based on deep learning. In *2018 IEEE 4th International Conference on Computer and Communications (ICCC)*, pages 2430–2435. IEEE.

BERT meets Shapley: Extending SHAP Explanations to Transformer-based Classifiers

Enja Kokalj
Jožef Stefan International Postgraduate School
Jožef Stefan Institute
enja.kokalj@ijs.si

Blaž Škrlj
Jožef Stefan International Postgraduate School
Jožef Stefan Institute

Nada Lavrač
Jožef Stefan International Postgraduate School
Jožef Stefan Institute

Senja Pollak
Jožef Stefan International Postgraduate School
Jožef Stefan Institute

Marko Robnik-Šikonja
Faculty for Computer and Information Science
Ljubljana

Abstract

Transformer-based neural networks offer very good classification performance across a wide range of domains, but do not provide explanations of their predictions. While several explanation methods, including SHAP, address the problem of interpreting deep learning models, they are not adapted to operate on state-of-the-art transformer-based neural networks such as BERT. Another shortcoming of these methods is that their visualization of explanations in the form of lists of most relevant words does not take into account the sequential and structurally dependent nature of text. This paper proposes the TransSHAP method that adapts SHAP to transformer models including BERT-based text classifiers. It advances SHAP visualizations by showing explanations in a sequential manner, assessed by human evaluators as competitive to state-of-the-art solutions.

1 Introduction

Recent wide spread use of deep neural networks (DNNs) has increased the need for their transparent classification, given that DNNs are black box models that do not offer introspection into their decision processes or provide explanations of their predictions and biases. Several methods that address the interpretability of machine learning models have been proposed. Model-agnostic explanation approaches are based on perturbations of inputs. The resulting changes in the outputs of the given model are the source of their explanations. The explanations of individual instances are commonly visualized in the form of histograms of the most impactful inputs. However, this is insufficient for text-based classifiers, where the inputs are sequential and structurally dependent.

We address the problem of incompatibility of modern explanation techniques, e.g., SHAP (Lundberg and Lee, 2017), and state-of-the-art pretrained transformer networks such as BERT (Devlin et al., 2019). Our contribution is twofold. First, we propose an adaptation of the SHAP method to BERT for text classification, called TransSHAP (Transformer-SHAP). Second, we present an improved approach to visualization of explanations that better reflects the sequential nature of input texts, referred to as the TransSHAP visualizer, which is implemented in the TransSHAP library.

The paper is structured as follows. We first present the background and motivation in Section 2. Section 3 introduces TransSHAP, an adapted method for explaining transformer language model such as BERT, which includes the TransSHAP visualizer for improved visualization of the generated explanations. Section 4 presents the results of an evaluation survey, followed by the discussion of results and the future work in Section 5.

2 Background and motivation

We first present the transformer-based language models, followed by an outline of perturbation-based explanation methods, in particular the SHAP method. We finish with the overview of visualizations for prediction explanations.

BERT (Devlin et al., 2019) is a large pretrained language model based on the transformer neural network architecture (Vaswani et al., 2017). Nowadays, BERT models exist in many mono- and multilingual variants. Fine-tuning BERT-like models to a specific task produces state-of-the-art results in many natural language processing tasks, such as text classification, question answering, POS-

Proceedings of the EACL Hackashop on News Media Content Analysis and Automated Report Generation, pages 16–21
April 19, 2021 © Association for Computational Linguistics

tagging, dependency parsing, inference, etc.

There are two types of explanation approaches, general and model specific. The general explanation approaches are applicable to any prediction model, since they perturb the inputs of a model and observe changes in the model's output. The second type of explanation approaches are specific to certain types of models, such as support vector machines or neural networks, and exploit the internal information available during training of these methods. We focus on general explanation methods and address their specific adaptations for use in text classification, more specifically, in text classification with transformer models such as BERT.

The most widely used perturbation-based explanation methods are IME (Štrumbelj and Kononenko, 2010), LIME (Ribeiro et al., 2016), and SHAP (Lundberg and Lee, 2017). Their key idea is that the contribution of a particular input value (or set of values) can be captured by 'hiding' the input and observing how the output of the model changes. In this work, we focus on the state-of-the-art explanation method SHAP (SHapley Additive exPlanations) that is based on the Shapley value approximation principle. Lundberg and Lee (2017) noted that several existing methods, including IME and LIME, can be regarded as special cases of this method.

We propose an adaptation of SHAP for BERT-like classifiers, but the same principles are trivially transferred to LIME and IME. To understand the behavior of a prediction model applied to a single instance, one should observe perturbations of all subsets of input features and their values, which results in exponential time complexity. Štrumbelj and Kononenko (2010) showed that the contribution of each variable corresponds to the Shapley value from the coalition game, where players correspond to input features, and the coalition game corresponds to the prediction of an individual instance. Shapley values can be approximated in time linear to the number of features.

The visualization approaches implemented in the explanation methods LIME and SHAP are primarily designed for explanations of tabular data and images. Although the visualization with LIME includes adjustments for text data, the resulting explanations are presented in the form of histograms that are sometimes hard to understand, as Figure 1 shows. The visualization with SHAP for the same sentence is illustrated in Figure 2. Here, the features with the strongest impact on the prediction correspond to longer arrows that point in the direction of the predicted class. For textual data this representation is non-intuitive.

Various approaches have been proposed to interpret neural text classifiers. Some of them focus on adapting existing SHAP based explanation methods by improving different aspects, e.g., the word masking (Chen and Ji, 2020), or reducing feature dimension (Zhao et al., 2020), while others explore the complex interactions between words (contextual decomposition) that are crucial when dealing with textual data but are ignored by other post-hoc explanation methods (Jin et al., 2019; Chen et al., 2020).

3 TransSHAP: The SHAP method adapted for BERT

Many modern deep neural networks, including transformer networks (Vaswani et al., 2017) such as BERT-like models, split the input text into subword tokens. However, perturbation-based explanation methods (such as IME, LIME, and SHAP) have problems with the text input and in particular subword input, as the credit for a given output cannot be simply assigned to clearly defined units such as words, phrases, or sentences. In this section, we first present the components of the new methodology and describe the implementation details required to make explanation method SHAP to work with state-of-the-art transformer prediction models such as BERT, followed by a brief description of the dataset used for training the model. Finally we introduce the TransSHAP visualizer, the proposed visualization method for text classification with neural networks. We demonstrate it using the SHAP method and the BERT model.

3.1 TransSHAP components

The model-agnostic implementation of the SHAP method, named Kernel SHAP[1], requires a classifier function that returns probabilities. Since SHAP contains no support for BERT-like models that use subword input, we implemented custom functions for preprocessing the input data for SHAP, to get the predictions from the BERT model, and to prepare data for the visualization.

Figure 3 shows the components required by SHAP in order to generate explanations for the

[1] We use the Kernel SHAP implementation of the SHAP method: `https://github.com/slundberg/shap`.

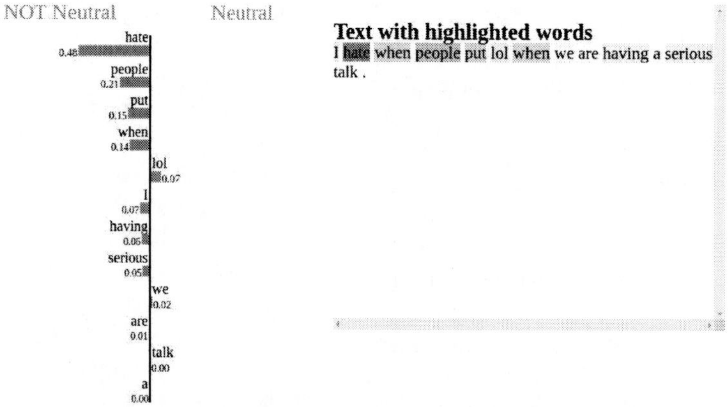

Figure 1: Visualization of prediction explanation with LIME.

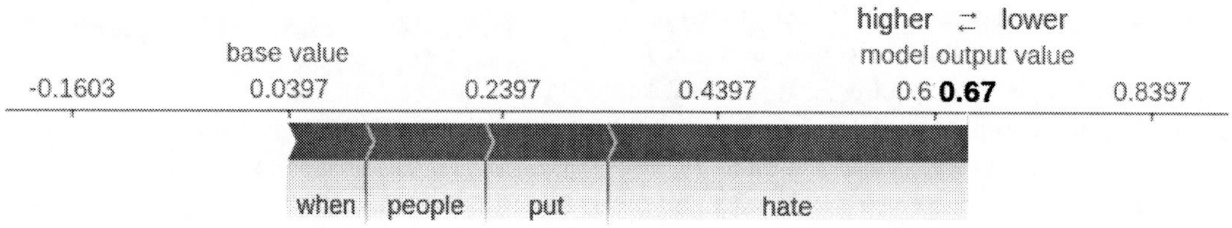

Figure 2: Visualization of prediction explanation with SHAP.

predictions made by the BERT model. The text data we want to interpret is used as an input to Kernel SHAP along with the special classifier function we constructed, which is necessary since SHAP requires numerical input in a tabular form.

To achieve this, we first convert the sentence into its numerical representation. This procedure consists of splitting the sentence into tokens and then preprocessing it. The preprocessing of different input texts is specific to their characteristics (e.g., tweets). The result is a list of sentence fragments (with words, selected punctuation marks and emojis), which serves as a basis for word perturbations (i.e. word masking). Each unique fragment is assigned a unique numerical key (i.e. index). We refer to a sentence, represented with indexes, as *an indexed instance*.

In summary, the TransSHAP's classifier function first converts each input instance into a word-level representation. Next, the representation is perturbed in order to generate new, locally similar instances which serve as a basis for the constructed explanation. This perturbation step is performed by the original SHAP. Then the perturbed versions of the sentence are processed with the BERT tokenizer that converts the sentence fragments to sub-word tokens. Finally, the predictions for the new locally generated instances are produced and returned to the Kernel SHAP explainer. With this modification, SHAP is able to compute the features' impact on the prediction (i.e. the explanation).

3.2 Datasets and models

We demonstrate our TransSHAP method on tweet sentiment classification. The dataset contains 87,428 English tweets with human annotated sentiment labels (positive, negative and neutral). For tweets we split input instances using the Tweet-Tokenizer function from NLTK library[2], we removed apostrophes, quotation marks and all punctuation marks except for exclamation and question marks. We fine-tuned the CroSloEngual BERT model (Ulčar and Robnik-Šikonja, 2020) on this classification task and the resulting model achieved the classification accuracy of 66.6%.

3.3 Visualization of a prediction explanation for the BERT model

To make a visualization of predictions better adapted to texts, we modified the histogram-based visualizations used in IME, LIME and SHAP for

[2]https://www.nltk.org

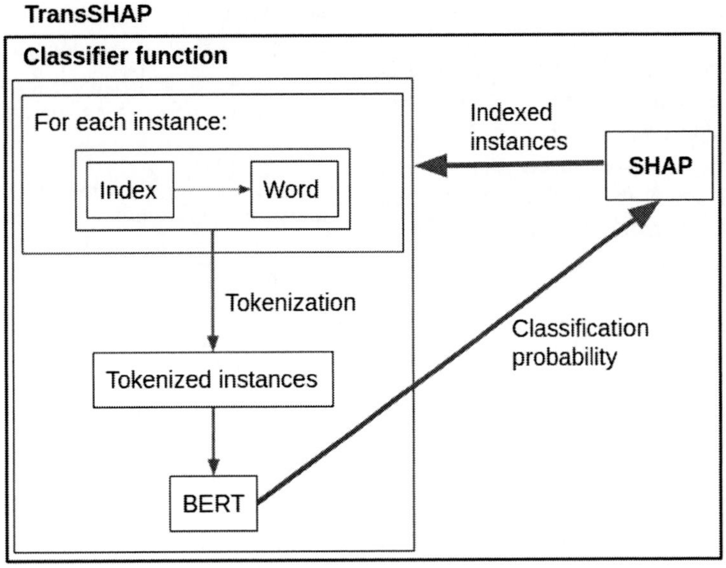

Figure 3: TransSHAP adaptation of SHAP to the BERT language model by introducing our classifier function.

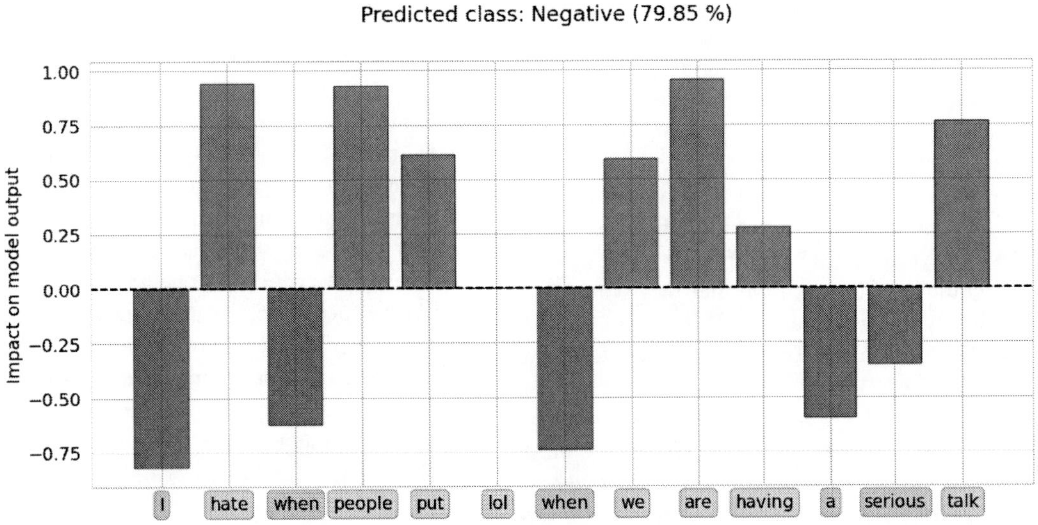

Figure 4: TransSHAP visualization of prediction explanations for negative sentiment. We obtained the features' contribution values with the SHAP method. It is evident that the word 'hate' strongly contributed to the negative sentiment classification, while the word 'lol' (laughing out loud) slightly opposed it.

tabular data. Figure 4 is an example of our visualization for explaining text classifications. It was inspired by the visualization used by the LIME method but we made some modifications with the aim of making it more intuitive and better adapted to sequences. Instead of the horizontal bar chart of features' impact on the prediction sorted in descending order of feature impact, we used the vertical bar chart and presented the features (i.e. words) in the order they appear in the original sentence. In this way, the graph allows the user to compare the direction of the impact (positive/negative) and also the magnitude of impact for individual words. The bottom text box representation of the sentence shows the words colored green if they significantly contributed to the prediction and red if they significantly opposed it.

4 Evaluation

We evaluated the novel visualization method using an online survey. The targeted respondents were researchers and PhD students not involved in the study that mostly had some previous experience with classifiers and/or their explanation methods. In the survey, the respondents were presented with three visualization methods on the same example: two visualizations were generated by existing libraries, LIME and SHAP, and the third one used our novel TransSHAP library. Respondents were asked to evaluate the quality of each visualization, suggest possible improvements, and rank the three methods.[3]

The results of 38 completed surveys are as follows. The most informative features of the visualization layout recognized by the users were the impact each word had on a prediction and the importance of the word contributions shown in a sequential view. The positioning of the visualization elements for each of the three methods was rated on the scale of 1 to 5. Our method achieved the highest average score of 3.66 (63.1% of the respondents rated it with a score of 4 or 5), second best was the LIME method with an average score of 3.13 (39.1% rated it with 4 or 5), and the SHAP method was rated as the worst with an average of 2.42 (81.5% rated it with 1 or 2). Regarding the question whether they would use each visualization method, LIME scored highest (44.7% voted "Yes"), TransSHAP closely followed (42.1% voted "Yes"), while SHAP was not praised (34.2% voted "Yes"). The overall ranking also corresponds to these results. LIME got the most votes (54.3%), TransSHAP was voted second best (40.0% of votes), and SHAP was the least desirable (5.7% of votes). In addition, we asked the participants to choose the preferred usage of the method out of the given options. The TransSHAP and SHAP methods were considered most useful for the purpose of debugging and bias detection, while the LIME method was also recognized as suitable for explaining a model to other researchers (usage in scientific articles).

5 Conclusion and further work

We presented the TransSHAP library, an extension of the SHAP explanation approach for transformer neural networks. TransSHAP offers a novel testing ground for better understanding of neural text classifiers, and will be freely accessible after acceptance of the paper (for review purposes available here: `https://bit.ly/2UVY2Dy`).

The explanations obtained by TransSHAP were quantitatively compared in a user survey, where we assessed the visualization capabilities, showing that the proposed TransSHAP's visualizations were simple, yet informative when compared to existing instance-based visualizations produced by LIME or SHAP. TransSHAP was scored better than SHAP, while LIME was scored slightly better in terms of overall user preference. However, in specific elements, such as positioning of the visualization elements, the visualization produced by TransSHAP is slightly better.

In further work, we plan to address problems of the perturbation-based explanation process when dealing with textual data. Currently, TransSHAP only supports random sampling from the word space, which may produce unintelligible and grammatically wrong sentences, and overall completely uninformative texts. We intend to take into account specific properties of text data and apply language models in the sampling step of the method. We plan to restrict the sampling candidates for each word based on their part of speech and general context of the sentence. We believe that better sampling will improve the speed of explanations and decrease the variance of explanations. Furthermore, the explanations could be additionally improved by expanding the features of explanations from individual words to larger textual units consisting of words that are grammatically and semantically linked.

Acknowledgements

We would like to acknowledge the Slovenian Research Agency (ARRS) for funding the first and the second author through young researcher grants and supporting other authors through the research program *Knowledge Technologies* (P2-0103) and the research project *Semantic Data Mining for Linked Open Data*. Further, we acknowledge the European Union's Horizon 2020 research and innovation programme under grant agreement No 825153, project EMBEDDIA (Cross-Lingual Embeddings for Cross-Lingual Embeddings for Less-Represented Languages in European News Media).

[3]The survey questions are available here: `https://forms.gle/icpYvHH78oE2TCJt7`.

References

Hanjie Chen and Yangfeng Ji. 2020. Learning variational word masks to improve the interpretability of neural text classifiers.

Hanjie Chen, Guangtao Zheng, and Yangfeng Ji. 2020. Generating hierarchical explanations on text classification via feature interaction detection.

Jacob Devlin, Ming-Wei Chang, Kenton Lee, and Kristina Toutanova. 2019. BERT: Pre-training of deep bidirectional transformers for language understanding. In *Proceedings of the 2019 Conference of the North American Chapter of the Association for Computational Linguistics: Human Language Technologies, Volume 1 (Long and Short Papers)*, pages 4171–4186, Minneapolis, Minnesota. Association for Computational Linguistics.

Xisen Jin, Junyi Du, Zhongyu Wei, Xiangyang Xue, and Xiang Ren. 2019. Towards hierarchical importance attribution: Explaining compositional semantics for neural sequence models.

Scott M. Lundberg and Su-In Lee. 2017. A unified approach to interpreting model predictions. In *Advances in Neural Information Processing Systems 30: Annual Conference on Neural Information Processing Systems 2017, December 4-9, 2017, Long Beach, CA, USA*, pages 4765–4774.

Marco Túlio Ribeiro, Sameer Singh, and Carlos Guestrin. 2016. "why should I trust you?": Explaining the predictions of any classifier. In *Proceedings of the 22nd ACM SIGKDD International Conference on Knowledge Discovery and Data Mining, San Francisco, CA, USA, August 13-17, 2016*, pages 1135–1144. ACM.

Matej Ulčar and Marko Robnik-Šikonja. 2020. FinEst BERT and CroSloEngual BERT: less is more in multilingual models. In *Proceedings of Text, Speech, and Dialogue, TSD 2020*. Accepted.

Ashish Vaswani, Noam Shazeer, Niki Parmar, Jakob Uszkoreit, Llion Jones, Aidan N. Gomez, Lukasz Kaiser, and Illia Polosukhin. 2017. Attention is all you need. In *Advances in Neural Information Processing Systems 30: Annual Conference on Neural Information Processing Systems 2017, December 4-9, 2017, Long Beach, CA, USA*, pages 5998–6008.

Erik Štrumbelj and Igor Kononenko. 2010. An efficient explanation of individual classifications using game theory. *Journal of Machine Learning Research*, 11(Jan):1–18.

Wei Zhao, Tarun Joshi, Vijayan Nair, and Agus Sudjianto. 2020. Shap values for explaining cnn-based text classification models.

Extending Neural Keyword Extraction with TF-IDF tagset matching

Boshko Koloski
Jožef Stefan Institute
Jožef Stefan IPS
Jamova 39, Ljubljana
boshko.koloski@ijs.si

Senja Pollak
Jožef Stefan Institute
Jamova 39, Ljubljana
senja.pollak@ijs.si

Blaž Škrlj
Jožef Stefan Institute
Jožef Stefan IPS
Jamova 39, Ljubljana
blaz.skrlj@ijs.si

Matej Martinc
Jožef Stefan Institute
Jamova 39, Ljubljana
matej.martinc@ijs.si

Abstract

Keyword extraction is the task of identifying words (or multi-word expressions) that best describe a given document and serve in news portals to link articles of similar topics. In this work, we develop and evaluate our methods on four novel data sets covering less-represented, morphologically-rich languages in European news media industry (Croatian, Estonian, Latvian, and Russian). First, we perform evaluation of two supervised neural transformer-based methods, Transformer-based Neural Tagger for Keyword Identification (TNT-KID) and Bidirectional Encoder Representations from Transformers (BERT) with an additional Bidirectional Long Short-Term Memory Conditional Random Fields (BiLSTM CRF) classification head, and compare them to a baseline Term Frequency - Inverse Document Frequency (TF-IDF) based unsupervised approach. Next, we show that by combining the keywords retrieved by both neural transformer-based methods and extending the final set of keywords with an unsupervised TF-IDF based technique, we can drastically improve the recall of the system, making it appropriate for usage as a recommendation system in the media house environment.

1 Introduction

Keywords are words (or multi-word expressions) that best describe the subject of a document, effectively summarise it and can also be used in several document categorization tasks. In online news portals, keywords help with efficient retrieval of articles when needed. Similar keywords characterise articles of similar topics, which can help editors to link related articles, journalists to find similar articles and readers to retrieve articles of interest when browsing the portals. For journalists manually assigning tags (keywords) to articles represents a demanding task, and high-quality automated keyword extraction shows to be one of components in news digitalization process that many media houses seek for.

The task of keyword extraction can generally be tackled in an unsupervised way, i.e., by relying on frequency based statistical measures (Campos et al., 2020) or graph statistics (Škrlj et al., 2019), or with a supervised keyword extraction tool, which requires a training set of sufficient size and from appropriate domain. While supervised methods tend to work better due to their ability to adapt to a specifics of the syntax, semantics, content, genre and keyword assignment regime of a specific text (Martinc et al., 2020a), their training for some less resource languages is problematic due to scarcity of large manually annotated resources. For this reason, studies about supervised keyword extraction conducted on less resourced languages are still very rare. To overcome this research gap, in this paper we focus on supervised keyword extraction on three less resourced languages, Croatian, Latvian, and Estonian, and one fairly well resourced language (Russian) and conduct experiments on data sets of media partners in the EMBEDDIA project[1]. The code for the experiments is made available on GitHub under the MIT license[2].

In media house environments, automatic keyword extraction systems are expected to return a diverse list of keyword candidates (of constant length), which is then inspected by a journalist who

[1] http://embeddia.eu/

[2] https://github.com/bkolosk1/Extending-Neural-Keyword-Extraction-with-TF-IDF-tagset-matching/

Proceedings of the EACL Hackashop on News Media Content Analysis and Automated Report Generation, pages 22–29
April 19, 2021 © Association for Computational Linguistics

manually selects appropriate candidates. While the state-of-the-art supervised approaches in most cases offer good enough precision for this type of usage as a recommendation system, the recall of these systems is nevertheless problematic. Supervised systems learn how many keywords should be returned for each news article on the gold standard train set, which generally contains only a small amount of manually approved candidates for each news article. For example, among the datasets used in our experiments (see Section 3), the Russian train set contains the most (on average 4.44) present keywords (i.e., keywords which appear in the text of the article and can be used for training of the supervised models) per article, while the Croatian test set contains only 1.19 keywords per article. This means that for Croatian, the model will learn to return around 1.19 keywords for each article, which is not enough.

To solve this problem we show that we can improve the recall of the existing supervised keyword extraction system by:

- Proposing an additional TF-IDF tagset matching technique, which finds additional keyword candidates by ranking the words in the news article that have appeared in the predefined keyword set containing words from the gold standard train set. The new hybrid system first checks how many keywords were returned by the supervised approach and if the number is smaller than needed, the list is expanded by the best ranked keywords returned by the TF-IDF based extraction system.

- Combining the outputs of several state-of-the-art supervised keyword extraction approaches.

The rest of this work is structured as follows: Section 2 presents the related work, while Section 3 describes the datasets on which we evaluate our method. Section 4 describes our proposed method with all corresponding steps. The experiment settings are described in Section 5 and the evaluation of the proposed methods is shown in Section 6. The conclusions and the proposed further work are presented in Section 7.

2 Related Work

Many different approaches have been developed to tackle the problem of extracting keywords. The early approaches, such as KP-MINER (El-Beltagy and Rafea, 2009) and RAKE (Rose et al., 2010) rely on unsupervised techniques which employ frequency based metrics for extraction of keywords from text. Formally, aforementioned approaches search for the words w from vocabulary $\mathcal{V}$ that maximize a given metric h for a given text t:

$$\mathrm{kw} = \underset{w \in \mathcal{V}}{\operatorname{argmax}}\, h(w, t).$$

In these approaches, frequency is of high relevance and it is assumed that the more frequent a given word, the more important the meaning this word carries for a given document. Most popular such metrics are the naïve frequency (word count) and the term frequency-inverse document frequency (TF-IDF) (Salton and McGill, 1986).

Most recent state-of-the-art statistical approaches, such as YAKE (Campos et al., 2020), also employ frequency based features, but combine them with other features such as casing, position, relatedness to context and dispersion of a specific term in order to derive a final score for each keyword candidate.

Another line of research models this problem by exploiting concepts from graph theory. Approaches, such as TextRank (Mihalcea and Tarau, 2004), Single Rank (Wan and Xiao, 2008), TopicRank (Bougouin et al., 2013) and Topical PageRank (Sterckx et al., 2015) build a graph G, i.e., a mathematical construct described by a set of vertexes V and a set of edges E connecting two vertices. In one of the most recent approaches called RaKUn (Škrlj et al., 2019), a directed graph is constructed from text, where vertexes V and two words w_i, w_{i+1} are linked if they appear following one another. Keywords are ranked by a shortest path-based metric from graph theory - the load centrality.

The task of keyword extraction can also be tackled in a supervised way. One of the first supervised approaches was an algorithm named KEA (Witten et al., 2005), which uses only TF-IDF and the term's position in the text as features for term identification. More recent neural approaches to keyword detection consider the problem as a sequence-to-sequence generation task (Meng et al., 2017) and employ a generative model for keyword prediction with a recurrent encoder-decoder framework and an attention mechanism capable of detecting keywords in the input text sequence whilst also potentially finding keywords that do not appear in the text.

Finally, the newest branch of models consider keyword extraction as a sequence labelling task and tackle keyword detection with transformers. Sahrawat et al. (2020) fed contextual embeddings generated by several transformer models (BERT (Devlin et al., 2018), RoBERTa (Liu et al., 2019), GPT-2 (Radford et al., 2019), etc.) into two types of neural architectures, a bidirectional Long short-term memory network (BiLSTM) and a BiLSTM network with an additional Conditional random fields layer (BiLSTM-CRF). Sun et al. (2020) on the other hand proposed BERT-JointKPE that employs a chunking network to identify phrases and a ranking network to learn their salience in the document. By training BERT jointly on the chunking and ranking tasks the model manages to establish balance between the estimation of keyphrase quality and salience.

Another state-of-the-art transformer based approach is TNT-KID (Transformer-based Neural Tagger for Keyword Identification) (Martinc et al., 2020a), which does not rely on pretrained language models such as BERT, but rather allows the user to train their own language model on the appropriate domain. The study shows that smaller unlabelled domain specific corpora can be successfully used for unsupervised pretraining, which makes the proposed approach easily transferable to low-resource languages. It also proposes several modifications to the transformer architecture in order to adapt it for a keyword extraction task and improve performance of the model.

3 Data Description

We conducted experiments on datasets containing news in four languages; Latvian, Estonian, Russian, and Croatian. Latvian, Estonian and Russian datasets contain news from the Ekspress Group, specifically from Estonian Ekspress Meedia (news in Estonian and Russian) and from Latvian Delfi (news in Latvian and Russian). The dataset statistics are presented in Table 2, and the datasets (Pollak et al., 2021) and their train/test splits[3] are publicly available. The media-houses provided news articles from 2015 up to the 2019. We divided them into training and test sets. For the Latvian, Estonian, and Russian training sets, we used the articles from 2018, while for the test set the articles from 2019 were used. For Croatian, the articles from 2019 are arranged by date and split into training and test (i.e., about 10% of the 2019 articles with the most recent date) set. In our study, we also use tagsets of keywords. Tagset corresponds either to a collection of keywords maintained by editors of a media house (see e.g. Estonian tagset), or to a tagset constructed from assigned keywords from articles available in the training set. The type of tagset and the number of unique tags for each language are listed in Table 1.

Dataset	Unique tags	Type of tags
Croatian	21,165	Constructed
Estonian	52,068	Provided
Russian	5,899	Provided
Latvian	4,015	Constructed

Table 1: Distribution of tags provided per language. The media houses provided tagsets for Estonian and Russian, while the tags for Latvian and Croatian were extracted from the train set.

4 Methodology

The recent supervised neural methods are very precise, but, as was already mentioned in Section 1, in same cases they do not return a sufficient number of keywords. This is due to the fact that the methods are trained on the training data with a low number of gold standard keywords (as it can be seen from Table 2). To meet the media partners' needs, we designed a method that complements state-of-the-art neural methods (the TNT-KID method (Martinc et al., 2020b) and the transformer-based method proposed by Sahrawat et al. (2020), which are both described in Section 2) by a tagset matching approach, returning constant number of keywords (k=10).

4.1 Transformer-based Keyword Extraction

Both supervised neural approaches employed in this study are based on the Transformer architecture (Vaswani et al., 2017), which was somewhat adapted for the specific task at hand. Both models are fed lowercased text consisting of the title and the body of the article. Tokenization is conducted by either using the default BERT tokenizer (when BERT is used) or by employing Sentencepiece tokenizer (Kudo and Richardson, 2018) (when TNT-KID is used). While the multilingual BERT model is already pretrained on a large corpus consisting of Wikipedias of about 100 languages (Devlin et al.,

[3]https://www.clarin.si/repository/xmlui/handle/11356/1403

			Avg. Train					Avg. Test				
Dataset	**Total docs**	**Total kw.**	**Total docs**	**Doc len**	**Kw.**	**% present kw.**	**present kw.**	**Total docs**	**Doc len**	**Kw.**	**% present kw.**	**Present kw.**
Croatian	35,805	126,684	32,223	438.50	3.54	0.32	1.19	3582	464.39	3.53	0.34	1.26
Estonian	18,497	59,242	10,750	395.24	3.81	0.65	2.77	7,747	411.59	4.09	0.69	3.12
Russian	25,306	5,953	13,831	392.82	5.66	0.76	4.44	11,475	335.93	5.43	0.79	4.33
Latvian	24,774	4,036	13,133	378.03	3.23	0.53	1.69	11,641	460.15	3.19	0.55	1.71

Table 2: Media partners' datasets used for empirical evaluation of keyword extraction algorithms.

2018), TNT-KID requires an additional language model pretraining on the domain specific corpus.

4.2 TF-IDF(tm) Tagset Matching

In our approach, we first take the keywords returned by a neural keyword extraction method and next complement the returned keyword list by adding the missing keywords to achieve the set goal of k keywords. The added keywords are selected by taking the top-ranked candidates from the TF-IDF tagset matching extraction conducted on the preprocessed news articles and keywords.

4.2.1 Preprocessing

First, we concatenate the body and the title of the article. After that we lowercase the text and remove stopwords. Finally, the text is tokenized and lemmatized with the Lemmagen3 lemmatizer (Juršič et al., 2010), which supports lemmatization for all the languages except Latvian. For Latvian we use the LatvianStemmer [4]. For the stopword removal we used the *Stopwords-ISO* [5] Python library which contained stopwords for all four languages. The final cleaned textual input consists of the concatenation of all of the preprocessed words from the document. We apply the same preprocessing procedure on the predetermined tagsets for each language. The preprocessing procedure is visualized in Figure 1.

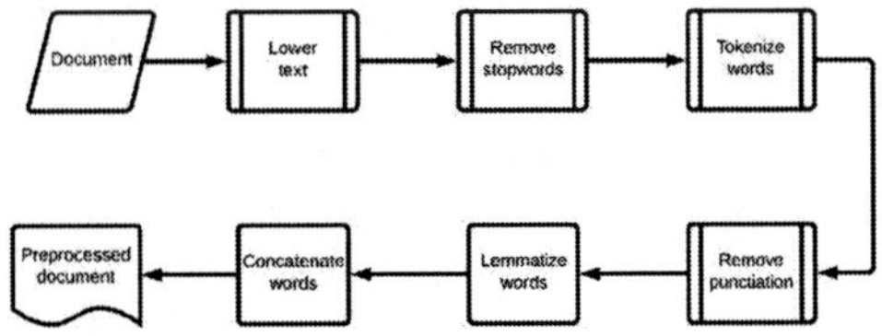

Figure 1: Preprocessing pipeline used for the document normalization and cleaning.

[4]https://github.com/rihardsk/LatvianStemmer

[5]https://github.com/stopwords-iso

4.2.2 TF-IDF Weighting Scheme

The TF-IDF weighting scheme (Salton and McGill, 1986) assigns each word its weight w based on the frequency of the word in the document (term frequency) and the number of documents the word appears in (inverse document frequency). More specifically, TF-IDF is calculated with the following equation:

$$TF-IDF_{\mathrm{i}} = tf_{\mathrm{i,j}} \cdot \log_e(\frac{|D|}{df_i})$$

The formula has two main components:

- *Term-frequency* (tf) that counts the number of appearances of a word in the document (in the equation above, $tf_{\mathrm{i,j}}$ denotes the number of occurrences of the word i in the document j)
- *Inverse-document-frequency* (idf) ensures that words appearing in more documents are assigned lower weights (in the formula above df_i is the number of documents containing word i and $|D|$ denotes the number of documents).

The assumption is that words with a higher TF-IDF value are more likely to be keywords.

4.3 Tagset Matching Keyword Expansion

For a given neural keyword extraction method *N*, and for each document *d*, we select *l* best ranked keywords according to the TF-IDF(tm), which appear in the keyword tagset for each specific dataset. Here, *l* corresponds to *k* - *m*, where $k = 10$ and *m* corresponds to the number of keywords returned by a neural method.

Since some of the keywords in the tagsets provided by the media partners were variations of the same root word (i.e., keywords are not lemmatized), we created a mapping from a root word (i.e., a word lemma or a stem) to a list of possible variations in the keyword dataset. For example, a word *'riigieksam'* (*'exam'*) appearing in the article, could be mapped to three tags in the tagset by the Estonian media house with the same root form *'riigieksam'*: *'riigieksamid'*, *'riigieksamide'* and *'riigieksam'*.

We tested several strategies for mapping the occurrence of a word in the news article to a specific tag in the tagset. For each lemma that mapped to multiple tags, we tested returning a random tag, a tag with minimal length and a tag of maximal length. In the final version, we opted to return the tag with the minimal length, since this tag corresponded to the lemma of the word most often.

5 Experimental Settings

We conducted experiments on the datasets described in Section 3. We evaluate the following methods and combinations of methods:

- **TF-IDF(tm):** Here, we employ the preprocessing and TF-IDF-based weighting of keywords described in Section 4 and select the top-ranked keywords that are present in the tagset.
- **TNT-KID** (Martinc et al., 2020b): For each dataset, we first pretrain the model with an autoregressive language model objective. After that, the model is fine-tuned on the same train set for the keyword extraction task. Sequence length was set to 256, embedding size to 512 and batch size to 8, and we employ the same preprocessing as in the original study (Martinc et al., 2020b).
- **BERT + BiLSTM-CRF** (Sahrawat et al., 2020): We employ an uncased multilingual BERT[6] model with an embedding size of 768 and 12 attention heads, with an additional BiLSTM-CRF token classification head, same as in Sahrawat et al. (2020).
- **TNT-KID & BERT + BiLSTM-CRF**: We extracted keywords with both of the methods and complemented the TNT-KID extracted keywords with the BERT + BiLSTM-CRF extracted keywords in order to retrieve more keywords. Duplicates (i.e., keywords extracted by both methods) are removed.
- **TNT-KID & TF-IDF**: If the keyword set extracted by TNT-KID contains less than 10 keywords, it is expanded with keywords retrieved with the proposed TF-IDF(tm) approach, i.e., best ranked keywords according to TF-IDF, which do not appear in the keyword set extracted by TNT-KID.
- **BERT + BiLSTM-CRF & TF-IDF**: If the keyword set extracted by BERT + BiLSTM-CRF contains less than 10 keywords, it is expanded with keywords retrieved with the proposed TF-IDF(tm) approach, i.e., best ranked keywords according to TF-IDF, which do not appear in the keyword set extracted by BERT + BiLSTM-CRF.
- **TNT-KID & BERT + BiLSTM-CRF & TF-IDF:** the keyword set extracted with the TNT-KID is complemented by keywords extracted with BERT + BiLSTM-CRF (duplicates are removed). If after the expansion the keyword set still contains less than 10 keywords, it is expanded again, this time with keywords retrieved by the TF-IDF(tm) approach.

For TNT-KID, which is the only model that requires language model pretraining, language models were trained on train sets in Table 2 for up to ten epochs. Next, TNT-KID and BERT + BiLSTM-CRF were fine-tuned on the training datasets, which were randomly split into 80 percent of documents used for training and 20 percent of documents used for validation. The documents containing more than 256 tokens are truncated, while the documents containing less than 256 tokens are padded with a special $< pad >$ token at the end. We fine-tuned each model for a maximum of 10 epochs and after each epoch the trained model was tested on the documents chosen for validation. The model that showed the best performance on this set of validation documents (in terms of F@10 score) was used for keyword detection on the test set.

6 Evaluation

For evaluation, we employ precision, recall and F1 score. While F1@10 and recall@10 are the most relevant metrics for the media partners, we also report precision@10, precision@5, recall@5 and F1@5. Only keywords which appear in a text (present keywords) were used as a gold standard, since we only evaluate approaches for keyword tagging that are not capable of finding keywords which do not appear in the text. Lowercasing and lemmatization (stemming in the case of Latvian) are performed on both the gold standard and the

[6]More specifically, we use the 'bert-base-multilingual-uncased' implementation of BERT from the Transformers library (`https://github.com/huggingface/transformers`).

Model	P@5	R@5	F1@5	P@10	R@10	F1@10
Croatian						
TF-IDF	0.2226	0.4543	0.2988	0.1466	0.5888	0.2347
TNT-KID	0.3296	0.5135	0.4015	0.3167	0.5359	0.3981
BERT + BiLSTM-CRF	**0.4607**	0.4672	**0.4640**	**0.4599**	0.4708	**0.4654**
TNT-KID & TF-IDF(tm)	0.2659	0.5670	0.3621	0.1688	0.6944	0.2716
BERT + BiLSTM-CRF & TF-IDF(tm)	0.2644	0.5656	0.3604	0.1549	0.6410	0.2495
TNT-KID & BERT + BiLSTM-CRF	0.2940	0.5447	0.3820	0.2659	0.5968	0.3679
TNT-KID & BERT + BiLSTM-CRF & TF-IDF(tm)	0.2648	**0.5681**	0.3612	0.1699	**0.7040**	0.2738
Estonian						
TF-IDF	0.0716	0.1488	0.0966	0.0496	0.1950	0.0790
TNT-KID	**0.5194**	0.5676	**0.5424**	**0.5098**	0.5942	**0.5942**
BERT + BiLSTM-CRF	0.5118	0.4617	0.4855	0.5078	0.4775	0.4922
TNT-KID & TF-IDF(tm)	0.3463	0.5997	0.4391	0.1978	0.6541	0.3037
BERT + BiLSTM-CRF & TF-IDF(tm)	0.3175	0.4978	0.3877	0.1789	0.5381	0.2686
TNT-KID & BERT + BiLSTM-CRF	0.4421	0.6014	0.5096	0.4028	0.6438	0.4956
TNT-KID & BERT + BiLSTM-CRF & TF-IDF(tm)	0.3588	**0.6206**	0.4547	0.2107	**0.6912**	0.3230
Russian						
TF-IDF	0.1764	0.2314	0.2002	0.1663	0.3350	0.2223
TNT-KID	**0.7108**	0.6007	**0.6512**	**0.7038**	0.6250	**0.6621**
BERT + BiLSTM-CRF	0.6901	0.5467	0.5467	0.6849	0.5643	0.6187
TNT-KID & TF-IDF(tm)	0.4519	0.6293	0.5261	0.2981	0.6946	0.4172
BERT + BiLSTM-CRF & TF-IDF(tm)	0.4157	0.5728	0.4818	0.2753	0.6378	0.3846
TNT-KID & BERT + BiLSTM-CRF	0.6226	0.6375	0.6300	0.5877	0.6707	0.6265
TNT-KID & BERT + BiLSTM-CRF & TF-IDF(tm)	0.4622	**0.6527**	0.5412	0.2965	**0.7213**	0.4203
Latvian						
TF-IDF	0.2258	0.5035	0.3118	0.1708	0.5965	0.2655
TNT-KID	0.6089	0.6887	**0.6464**	0.6054	0.6960	**0.6476**
BERT + BiLSTM-CRF	**0.6215**	0.6214	0.6214	**0.6204**	0.6243	0.6223
TNT-KID & TF-IDF(tm)	0.3402	**0.7934**	0.4762	0.2253	0.8653	0.3575
BERT + BiLSTM-CRF & TF-IDF(tm)	0.2985	0.6957	0.4178	0.1889	0.7427	0.3012
TNT-KID & BERT + BiLSTM-CRF	0.4545	0.7189	0.5569	0.4341	0.7297	0.5443
TNT-KID & BERT + BiLSTM-CRF & TF-IDF(tm)	0.3318	0.7852	0.4666	0.2124	**0.8672**	0.3414

Table 3: Results on the EMBEDDIA media partner datasets.

extracted keywords (keyphrases) during the evaluation. The results of the evaluation on all four languages are listed in Table 3.

Results suggest, that neural approaches, TNT-KID and BERT+BiLSTM-CRF offer comparable performance on all datasets but nevertheless achieve different results for different languages. TNT-KID outperforms BERT-BiLSTM-CRF model according to all the evaluation metrics on the Estonian and Russian news dataset. It also outperforms all other methods in terms of precision and F1 score. On the other hand, BERT+BiLSTM-CRF performs better on the Croatian dataset in terms of precision and F1-score. On Latvian TNT-KID achieves top results in terms of F1, while BERT+BiLSTM-CRF offers better precision.

Even though the TF-IDF tagset matching method performs poorly on its own, we can nevertheless drastically improve the recall@5 and the recall@10 of both neural systems, if we expand the keyword tag sets returned by the neural methods with the TF-IDF ranked keywords. The improvement is substantial and consistent for all datasets, but it nevertheless comes at the expanse of the lower precision and F1 score. This is not surprising, since the final expanded keyword set always returns 10 keywords, i.e., much more than the average number of present gold standard keywords in the media partner datasets (see Table 2), which badly affects the precision of the approach. Nevertheless, since for a journalist a manual inspection of 10 keyword candidates per article and manual selection of good candidates (e.g., by clicking on them) still requires less time than the manual selection of keywords from an article, we argue that the improvement of recall at the expanse of the precision is a good trade off, if the system is intended to be used as a recommendation system in the media house environment.

Combining keywords returned by TNT-KID and BERT + BiLSTM-CRF also consistently improves recall, but again at the expanse of lower precision and F1 score. Overall, for all four languages, the best performing method in terms of recall is the TNT-KID & BERT + BiLSTM-CRF & TF-IDF(tm).

7 Conclusion and Future Work

In this work, we tested two state-of-the-art neural approaches for keyword extraction, TNT-KID (Martinc et al., 2020a) and BERT BiLSTM-CRF (Sahrawat et al., 2020), on three less resourced European languages, Estonian, Latvian, Croatian, as well as on Russian. We also proposed a tagset based keyword expansion approach, which drastically improves the recall of the method, making it more suitable for the application in the media house environment.

Our study is one of the very few studies where supervised keyword extraction models were employed on several less resourced languages. The results suggest that these models perform well on languages other than English and could also be successfully leveraged for keyword extraction on morphologically rich languages.

The focus of the study was whether we can improve the recall of the supervised models, in order to make them more useful as recommendation systems in the media house environment. Our method manages to increase the number of retrieved keywords, which drastically improves the recall for all languages. For example, by combing all neural methods and the TF-IDF based approach, we improve on the recall@10 achieved by the best performing neural model, TNT-KID, by 16.81 percentage points for Croatian, 9.70 percentage points for Estonian, 9.63 percentage points for Russian and 17.12 percentage points for Latvian. The resulting method nevertheless offers lower precision, which we will try to improve in the future work.

In the future we also plan to perform a qualitative evaluation of our methods by journalists from the media houses. Next, we plan to explore how adding background knowledge from knowledge databases - lexical (e.g. Wordnet(Fellbaum, 1998)) or factual (e.g. WikiData(Vrandečić and Krötzsch, 2014)) would benefit the aforementioned methods. The assumption is that with the linkage of the text representation and the background knowledge we would achieve a more representative understanding of the articles and the concepts appearing in them, which would result in a more successful keyword extraction.

In traditional machine-learning setting a common practice of combining different classifier outputs to a single output is referred to as stacking. We propose further research on this topic by testing combinations of various keyword extraction models. Finally, we also plan to further improve our unsupervised TF-IDF based keyword extraction method. One way to to do this would be to add the notion of positional encoding, since some of the keywords in the news-media domain often can be found at the beginning of the article and the TF-IDF(tm) does not take this into account while applying the weighting on the matched terms.

8 Acknowledgements

This paper is supported by European Union's Horizon 2020 research and innovation programme under grant agreement No. 825153, project EMBEDDIA (Cross-Lingual Embeddings for Less-Represented Languages in European News Media). The third author was financed via young research ARRS grant. Finally, the authors acknowledge the financial support from the Slovenian Research Agency for research core funding for the programme Knowledge Technologies (No. P2-0103) and the project TermFrame - Terminology and Knowledge Frames across Languages (No. J6-9372).

References

Adrien Bougouin, Florian Boudin, and Béatrice Daille. 2013. Topicrank: Graph-based topic ranking for keyphrase extraction. In *International joint conference on natural language processing (IJCNLP)*, pages 543–551.

Ricardo Campos, Vítor Mangaravite, Arian Pasquali, Alípio Jorge, Célia Nunes, and Adam Jatowt. 2020. Yake! keyword extraction from single documents using multiple local features. *Information Sciences*, 509:257 – 289.

Jacob Devlin, Ming-Wei Chang, Kenton Lee, and Kristina Toutanova. 2018. Bert: Pre-training of deep bidirectional transformers for language understanding. *arXiv preprint arXiv:1810.04805*.

Samhaa R. El-Beltagy and Ahmed Rafea. 2009. Kp-miner: A keyphrase extraction system for english and arabic documents. *Inf. Syst.*, 34(1):132–144.

Christiane Fellbaum. 1998. *WordNet: An Electronic Lexical Database*. Bradford Books.

Matjaž Juršič, Igor Mozetič, Tomaž Erjavec, and Nada Lavrač. 2010. Lemmagen: Multilingual lemmatisation with induced ripple-down rules. *Journal of Universal Computer Science*, 16(9):1190–1214.

Taku Kudo and John Richardson. 2018. Sentencepiece: A simple and language independent subword tokenizer and detokenizer for neural text processing. *arXiv preprint arXiv:1808.06226*.

Yinhan Liu, Myle Ott, Naman Goyal, Jingfei Du, Mandar Joshi, Danqi Chen, Omer Levy, Mike Lewis, Luke Zettlemoyer, and Veselin Stoyanov. 2019. Roberta: A robustly optimized bert pretraining approach. *arXiv preprint arXiv:1907.11692*.

Matej Martinc, Blaž Škrlj, and Senja Pollak. 2020a. Tnt-kid: Transformer-based neural tagger for keyword identification. *arXiv preprint arXiv:2003.09166*.

Matej Martinc, Blaž Škrlj, and Senja Pollak. 2020b. Tnt-kid: Transformer-based neural tagger for keyword identification.

Rui Meng, Sanqiang Zhao, Shuguang Han, Daqing He, Peter Brusilovsky, and Yu Chi. 2017. Deep keyphrase generation. *arXiv preprint arXiv:1704.06879*.

Rada Mihalcea and Paul Tarau. 2004. Textrank: Bringing order into text. In *Proceedings of the 2004 conference on empirical methods in natural language processing*, pages 404–411.

Senja Pollak, Marko Robnik Šikonja, Matthew Purver, Michele Boggia, Ravi Shekhar, Marko Pranjić, Salla Salmela, Ivar Krustok, Tarmo Paju, Carl-Gustav Linden, Leo Leppänen, Elaine Zosa, Matej Ulčar, Linda Freienthal, Silver Traat, Luis Adrián Cabrera-Diego, Matej Martinc, Nada Lavrač, Blaž Škrlj, Martin Žnidaršič, Andraž Pelicon, Boshko Koloski, Vid Podpečan, Janez Kranjc, Shane Sheehan, Hannu Toivonen, Emanuela Boros, Jose Moreno, and Antoine Doucet. 2021. EMBEDDIA tools, datasets and challenges: Resources and hackathon contributions. In *Proceedings of the EACL Hackashop on News Media Content Analysis and Automated Report Generation*. Association for Computational Linguistics.

Alec Radford, Jeffrey Wu, Rewon Child, David Luan, Dario Amodei, and Ilya Sutskever. 2019. Language models are unsupervised multitask learners. Technical report, OpenAI.

Stuart Rose, Dave Engel, Nick Cramer, and Wendy Cowley. 2010. Automatic keyword extraction from individual documents. *Text mining: applications and theory*, 1:1–20.

Dhruva Sahrawat, Debanjan Mahata, Mayank Kulkarni, Haimin Zhang, Rakesh Gosangi, Amanda Stent, Agniv Sharma, Yaman Kumar, Rajiv Ratn Shah, and Roger Zimmermann. 2020. Keyphrase extraction from scholarly articles as sequence labeling using contextualized embeddings. In *Proceedings of European Conference on Information Retrieval (ECIR 2020)*, pages 328–335.

Gerard Salton and Michael J McGill. 1986. Introduction to modern information retrieval.

Blaž Škrlj, Andraž Repar, and Senja Pollak. 2019. Rakun: Rank-based keyword extraction via unsupervised learning and meta vertex aggregation. In *International Conference on Statistical Language and Speech Processing*, pages 311–323. Springer.

Lucas Sterckx, Thomas Demeester, Johannes Deleu, and Chris Develder. 2015. Topical word importance for fast keyphrase extraction. In *Proceedings of the 24th International Conference on World Wide Web*, pages 121–122.

Si Sun, Chenyan Xiong, Zhenghao Liu, Zhiyuan Liu, and Jie Bao. 2020. Joint keyphrase chunking and salience ranking with bert. *arXiv preprint arXiv:2004.13639*.

Ashish Vaswani, Noam Shazeer, Niki Parmar, Jakob Uszkoreit, Llion Jones, Aidan N Gomez, Lukasz Kaiser, and Illia Polosukhin. 2017. Attention is all you need. *arXiv preprint arXiv:1706.03762*.

Denny Vrandečić and Markus Krötzsch. 2014. Wikidata: A free collaborative knowledgebase. *Commun. ACM*, 57(10):78–85.

Xiaojun Wan and Jianguo Xiao. 2008. Single document keyphrase extraction using neighborhood knowledge. In *AAAI*, volume 8, pages 855–860.

Ian H Witten, Gordon W Paynter, Eibe Frank, Carl Gutwin, and Craig G Nevill-Manning. 2005. Kea: Practical automated keyphrase extraction. In *Design and Usability of Digital Libraries: Case Studies in the Asia Pacific*, pages 129–152. IGI global.

Zero-shot Cross-lingual Content Filtering: Offensive Language and Hate Speech Detection

Andraž Pelicon[1], **Ravi Shekhar**[3], **Matej Martinc**[1,2]
Blaž Škrlj[1,2], **Matthew Purver**[2,3], **Senja Pollak**[2]
[1]Jožef Stefan International Postgraduate School
[2]Jožef Stefan Institute, Ljubljana, Slovenia
[3]Computational Linguistics Lab, Queen Mary University of London, UK
{andraz.pelicon,matej.martinc,blaz.skrlj,senja.pollak}@ijs.si
{r.shekhar,m.purver}@qmul.ac.uk

Abstract

We present a system for zero-shot cross-lingual offensive language and hate speech classification. The system was trained on English datasets and tested on a task of detecting hate speech and offensive social media content in a number of languages without any additional training. Experiments show an impressive ability of both models to generalize from English to other languages. There is however an expected gap in performance between the tested cross-lingual models and the monolingual models. The best performing model (offensive content classifier) is available online as a REST API.

1 Introduction

Recent years have seen a dramatic improvement in natural language processing, with machine learning systems outperforming human performance on a number of benchmark language understanding tasks (Wang et al., 2019). This impressive achievement is somewhat tempered by the fact that a large majority of these systems work only for English, while other less-resourced languages are neglected due to a lack of training resources. On the other hand, another recent development is the introduction of systems capable of zero-shot cross-lingual transfer learning by leveraging multilingual embeddings (Artetxe and Schwenk, 2019). These systems can be trained on a language with available resources and employed on a less-resourced language without any additional language specific training.

In this study we present an offensive language classifier available through a REST API which leverages the cross-lingual capabilities of these systems. Due to the exponential growth of social media content, the amount of offensive language and hate speech has seen a steep increase and its identification and removal is no longer manageable by traditional manual inspection of the content (Schmidt and Wiegand, 2017). As a consequence, there is a need for a general model that could be used in content filtering systems to automatically detect such discourse.

Since the majority of research in the area of offensive language and hate speech detection is currently done in monolingual settings, we performed a preliminary study to assess the feasibility of the proposed zero-shot cross-lingual transfer for this task. Two approaches are tested in this study. The first uses multilingual Bidirectional Encoder Representations from Transformers (BERT, Devlin et al., 2019). The second uses Language-Agnostic SEntence Representations (LASER, Artetxe and Schwenk, 2019), a system built specifically for zero-shot cross-lingual transfer using multilingual sentence embeddings. Our best performing model is available online and can be used for detecting offensive content in less-resourced languages with no available training data.

2 Related work

The large majority of research on hate speech is monolingual, with English still the most popular language due to data availability (Wulczyn et al., 2017; Davidson et al., 2017), and a number of English-only shared tasks organized on the topic of hate or offensive speech (e.g., OffenseEval, Zampieri et al., 2019b). Lately, the focus has been shifting to other languages, with several shared tasks organized that cover other languages besides English, e.g. OffenseEval 2020 (Zampieri et al., 2020), EVALITA 2018 (Bai et al., 2018) and GermEval 2018 (Wiegand et al., 2018).

Proceedings of the EACL Hackashop on News Media Content Analysis and Automated Report Generation, pages 30–34
April 19, 2021 © Association for Computational Linguistics

For example, the EVALITA 2018 shared task (Bai et al., 2018) covered hate speech in Italian social media, the GermEval 2018 (Wiegand et al., 2018) shared tasks explored automatic identification of offensive German Tweets, and Semeval 2019 task 5 (Basile et al., 2019) covered detection of hate speech against immigrants and women in Spanish and English Twitter. Schmidt and Wiegand (2017); Poletto et al. (2020); Vidgen and Derczynski (2020) provide excellent surveys of recent hate speech related datasets.

Ousidhoum et al. (2019) conduct multilingual hate speech studies by testing a number of traditional bag-of-words and neural models on a multilingual dataset containing English, French and Arabic tweets that were manually labeled with six class hostility labels (abusive, hateful, offensive, disrespectful, fearful, normal). They report that multilingual models outperform monolingual models on some of the tasks. Shekhar et al. (2020) study multilingual comment filtering for newspaper comments in Croatian and Estonian.

Another multilingual approach was proposed by Schneider et al. (2018), who used multilingual MUSE embeddings (Lample et al., 2018) in order to extend the GermEval 2018 German train set with more English data. They report that no improvements in accuracy were achieved with this approach.

Cross-lingual hate speech identification is even less researched than the multilingual task. The so-called *bleaching* approach (van der Goot et al., 2018) was used by Basile and Rubagotti (2018) to conduct cross-lingual experiments between Italian and English at EVALITA 2018 misogyny identification task. The only other study we are aware of is a very recent study by Pamungkas and Patti (2019) proposing an LSTM joint-learning model with multilingual MUSE embeddings. Google Translate is used for translation in order to create a bilingual train and test input data. Bassignana et al. (2018) report that the use of a multilingual lexicon of hate words, HurtLex, slightly improves the performance of misogyny identification systems. Closest to our work is that of Glavaš et al. (2020), who propose a dataset called XHATE-999 to evaluate abusive language detection in a multi-domain and multilingual setting.

3 Dataset Description

As an English (EN) training set for *offensive language* classification, we used the training subset of the OLID dataset (Zampieri et al., 2019a). The trained models were evaluated on the test subset of the OLID dataset using their official gold labels and on the test subset of the GermEval 2018 dataset (Wiegand et al., 2018), which also contains manually labeled tweets. Both datasets use hierarchical annotation schemes for annotating hate speech content. For our purposes, we employed only the annotations on the first level which classify tweets into two classes, offensive and not offensive.

We trained the *hate speech* classifiers on the English training set from the HatEval dataset (Basile et al., 2019). For evaluation, we used the English and Spanish (ES) test sets from the HatEval competition, the German (DE) IGW hate speech dataset (Ross et al., 2016), an Indonesian (ID) hate speech dataset (Ibrohim and Budi, 2019) and the Arabic (AR) hate speech dataset LHSAB (Mulki et al., 2019). Each of the test datasets had binary labels that denoted the presence or absence of hate speech, except for the Arabic test set, which modeled hate speech as a three-class task, with labels denoting absence of hate speech, abusive language and hateful language. Since the authors themselves acknowledge there is a fine line between abusive and hateful language, we felt confident to join them into one class that denotes the presence of hate speech in a tweet. Tweets in the German IGW dataset included hate speech labels from two annotators and no common label, so we decided to evaluate only on those tweets where the two annotators agreed. The statistics of the datasets that were used in this study are reported in Table 1.

4 Classification models and methodology

Our models were trained and evaluated on two distinct albeit similar tasks, namely offensive language classification and hate speech detection, using two different approaches.

In the first approach, we tested the multilingual version of BERT to which we attached a classification layer with a softmax activation function. The model was fine-tuned on the chosen training datasets for 20 epochs. We limited the input sequence to 256 tokens and used a batch size of 32 and a learning rate of 2e-5. No additional hyperparameter tuning was performed.

Our second approach was using the pre-trained

	OLID (EN)	GermEval (DE)	HatEval (EN)	HatEval (ES)	IGW (DE)	ID	L-HSAB (AR)
# documents	14,100	8,541	13,000	6,600	541	13,169	5,846
Majority class	67%	66%	60%	60%	85%	57.77%	62.43%
Minority class	33%	34%	40%	40%	15%	43.23%	37.55%

Table 1: Dataset statistics.

LASER model and training a multilayer perceptron classifier with RELU activation function on top of that. To train the models we used the batch size of 32 and a learning rate of 0.001.

5 Results

The results for both tasks together with the majority baselines and the results reported in the literature are presented in Table 2. In the offensive language classification task, our best model (BERT) achieved an F1 score of 82.63 on the English test set, which is on par with the reported results achieved by monolingual classifiers (Zampieri et al., 2019b). When evaluated on the German dataset, we observe a considerable drop in performance compared to the reported results (Wiegand et al., 2018), however, it still achieves a solid F1 score of 70.67, which indicates its ability to generalize to languages it has not seen during training.

In the hate speech classification task, the two models are comparable, with LASER outperforming BERT on the Arabic and Spanish datasets. Overall, the scores for the hate speech classification task proved to be considerably lower for both models as well as lower than the reported results in the monolingual experiments (Basile et al., 2019; Ibrohim and Budi, 2019). Nevertheless, the results again indicate the ability of both models to generalize from English to other languages, as our models perform better than the majority baseline classifiers in terms of macro-averaged F1 score on all the datasets. It should be noted that the performance between our models and the reported performance on the Indonesian and Arabic datasets are not directly comparable as the original training and testing splits from the literature are not available. Therefore, our models were tested on different test splits.

6 Web API design

The best performing cross-lingual model, multilingual BERT for offensive language classification, was implemented as a REST web service in the Flask framework. The design of the web service allows us to easily update the current model with a new version trained on additional data in the future. The web service can be reached programmatically through the endpoint at `http://classify.ijs.si/ml_hate_speech/ml_bert` or through a demo browser-based interface at the URL `http://classify.ijs.si/embeddia/offensive_language_classifier`. The interface is designed for mobile devices and supports most popular screen sizes. It consists of an input area where users can input their sentence and submit it for classification. The classification results as well as the confidence score of the classifier are then displayed under the input area.

7 Conclusion and future work

In the course of this study, we tested the performance of two multilingual models, BERT and LASER, in zero-shot offensive language and hate speech detection. The results for the offensive language classification task show that even in the multilingual setting the BERT-based classifier achieves results comparable to the monolingual classifiers on English language data and solid performance on the German dataset. On the other hand, hate speech classification still proves to be a hard task for the multilingual classifiers as they achieve considerably lower scores on all languages compared to reported results. Nevertheless, both models show an impressive ability to generalize over languages they have not seen during fine-tuning. We implemented the best performing model, multilingual BERT for offensive language classification, as a REST web service. In the future, we plan to perform similar experiments with other multilingual language models, namely the XLM-R models (Conneau et al., 2019), which show increased performance in standard benchmark tasks compared to multilingual BERT, and the recently released CroSloEngual-BERT (Ulčar and Robnik-Šikonja, 2020).

While all datasets used in this study contain social media posts labeled for hate speech or of-

	Cross-lingual hate speech classification									
	Accuracy					F1-macro				
Model	EN	ES	DE	ID	AR	EN	ES	DE	ID	AR
LASER	**0.5241**	**0.6562**	0.5041	0.5755	**0.7013**	0.4994	0.6538	0.4630	**0.5172**	0.5500
BERT	0.5091	0.6313	**0.6369**	0.5823	0.6264	0.4341	0.5839	**0.6886**	0.4603	0.5033
Reported	/	/	/	**0.7353***	**0.9060***	**0.6510**	**0.7300**	/	/	**0.8930***
Majority	0.6000	0.6000	0.8500	0.5800	0.6200	0.3600	0.3700	0.4600	0.3700	0.3800
	Cross-lingual offensive language classification									
LASER	0.7500	/	0.7129	/	/	0.6823	/	0.6508	/	/
BERT	**0.8279**	/	**0.7148**	/	/	0.8263	/	0.7067	/	/
Reported	/	/	/	/	/	**0.829**	/	**0.7677**	/	/
Majority	0.6700	/	0.6600	/	/	0.4200	/	0.4000	/	/

Table 2: Results of the hate speech classification task (models trained on the English hatEval dataset) and offensive language classification task (models trained on the English OLID dataset) in comparison to the monolingual results as reported in the literature. The forward slash ('/') denotes results which are not reported in the literature. Figures marked with * denote results obtained on a different test split.

fensive language, there are still some differences in the way the data was labeled and collected, as each dataset was collected by a different research team. Therefore, some compromises had to be made in the course of this study to consolidate the datasets as best as possible. In order to better control for such variables, we would like to perform our experiment on the recently released XHate-999 dataset which contains instances in six diverse languages that were collected and annotated by the same research team using a unified annotation process. Given the fact we are working with relatively well-resourced languages, another future endeavour would be to also inspect the differences in cross-lingual model performance between zero-shot and few-shot testing scenarios. Finally, we plan on improving the performance of the model specifically on the task of hate speech classification, and update the existing web service.

8 Acknowledgements

This research is supported by the European Union's Horizon 2020 research and innovation programme under grant agreement No 825153, project EMBEDDIA (Cross-Lingual Embeddings for Less-Represented Languages in European News Media). The work of AP was funded also by the European Union's Rights, Equality and Citizenship Programme (2014-2020) project IMSyPP (Innovative Monitoring Systems and Prevention Policies of Online Hate Speech, grant no. 875263). The results of this publication reflect only the authors' views and the Commission is not responsible for any use that may be made of the information it contains. MP was also funded by the UK EPSRC under grant EP/S033564/1. We acknowledge also the funding by the Slovenian Research Agency (ARRS) core research programme Knowledge Technologies (P2-0103).

References

M. Artetxe and H. Schwenk. 2019. Massively multilingual sentence embeddings for zero-shot cross-lingual transfer and beyond. *Transactions of the ACL*, 7:597–610.

X. Bai, F. Merenda, C. Zaghi, T. Caselli, and M. Nissim. 2018. RuG@EVALITA 2018: Hate speech detection in Italian social media. *EVALITA Evaluation of NLP and Speech Tools for Italian*, 12:245.

A. Basile and C. Rubagotti. 2018. CrotoneMilano for AMI at Evalita2018. a performant, cross-lingual misogyny detection system. In *EVALITA@ CLiC-it*.

V. Basile, C. Bosco, E. Fersini, D. Nozza, V. Patti, F. M. Rangel Pardo, P. Rosso, and M. Sanguinetti. 2019. SemEval-2019 task 5: Multilingual detection of hate speech against immigrants and women in Twitter. In *Proc. SemEval*.

E. Bassignana, V. Basile, and V. Patti. 2018. Hurtlex: A multilingual lexicon of words to hurt. In *5th Italian Conference on Computational Linguistics, CLiC-it 2018*.

A. Conneau, K. Khandelwal, N. Goyal, V. Chaudhary, G. Wenzek, F. Guzmán, E. Grave, M. Ott, L. Zettlemoyer, and V. Stoyanov. 2019. Unsupervised cross-lingual representation learning at scale. *arXiv preprint arXiv:1911.02116*.

T. Davidson, D. Warmsley, M. Macy, and I. Weber. 2017. Automated hate speech detection and the problem of offensive language. In *Proc. ICWSM*.

J. Devlin, M.-W. Chang, K. Lee, and K. Toutanova. 2019. BERT: Pre-training of deep bidirectional transformers for language understanding. In *Proc. NAACL-HLT*.

G. Glavaš, M. Karan, and I. Vulić. 2020. XHate-999: Analyzing and detecting abusive language across domains and languages. In *Proceedings of the 28th International Conference on Computational Linguistics*.

R. van der Goot, N. Ljubešić, I. Matroos, M. Nissim, and B. Plank. 2018. Bleaching text: Abstract features for cross-lingual gender prediction. In *Proc. ACL*.

M. O. Ibrohim and I. Budi. 2019. Multi-label hate speech and abusive language detection in Indonesian Twitter. In *Proc. 3rd Workshop on Abusive Language Online*.

G. Lample, A. Conneau, L. Denoyer, and M. Ranzato. 2018. Unsupervised machine translation using monolingual corpora only. In *Proc. ICLR*.

H. Mulki, H. Haddad, C. Bechikh Ali, and H. Alshabani. 2019. L-HSAB: A Levantine Twitter dataset for hate speech and abusive language. In *Proc. 3rd Workshop on Abusive Language Online*.

N. Ousidhoum, Z. Lin, H. Zhang, Y. Song, and D.-Y. Yeung. 2019. Multilingual and multi-aspect hate speech analysis. In *Proc. EMNLP-IJCNLP*.

E. W. Pamungkas and V. Patti. 2019. Cross-domain and cross-lingual abusive language detection: A hybrid approach with deep learning and a multilingual lexicon. In *Proc. ACL Student Research Workshop*.

F. Poletto, V. Basile, M. Sanguinetti, C. Bosco, and V. Patti. 2020. Resources and benchmark corpora for hate speech detection: a systematic review. *Language Resources and Evaluation*, pages 1–47.

B. Ross, M. Rist, G. Carbonell, B. Cabrera, N. Kurowsky, and M. Wojatzki. 2016. Measuring the Reliability of Hate Speech Annotations: The Case of the European Refugee Crisis. In *Proc. NLP4CMC III: 3rd Workshop on Natural Language Processing for Computer-Mediated Communication*.

A. Schmidt and M. Wiegand. 2017. A survey on hate speech detection using natural language processing. In *Proc. 5th International Workshop on Natural Language Processing for Social Media*.

J. M. Schneider, R. Roller, P. Bourgonje, S. Hegele, and G. Rehm. 2018. Towards the automatic classification of offensive language and related phenomena in German tweets. In *14th Conference on Natural Language Processing KONVENS 2018*.

R. Shekhar, M. Pranjić, S. Pollak, A. Pelicon, and M. Purver. 2020. Automating News Comment Moderation with Limited Resources: Benchmarking in Croatian and Estonian. *Journal for Language Technology and Computational Linguistics (JLCL)*, 34(1).

M. Ulčar and M. Robnik-Šikonja. 2020. FinEst BERT and CroSloEngual BERT. In *International Conference on Text, Speech, and Dialogue*.

B. Vidgen and L. Derczynski. 2020. Directions in abusive language training data, a systematic review: Garbage in, garbage out. *Plos one*, 15(12):e0243300.

A. Wang, A. Singh, J. Michael, F. Hill, O. Levy, and S. R. Bowman. 2019. GLUE: A multi-task benchmark and analysis platform for natural language understanding. In *Proc. ICLR*.

M. Wiegand, M. Siegel, and J. Ruppenhofer. 2018. Overview of the GermEval 2018 shared task on the identification of offensive language.

E. Wulczyn, N. Thain, and L. Dixon. 2017. Ex machina: Personal attacks seen at scale. In *Proc. WWW*.

M. Zampieri, S. Malmasi, P. Nakov, S. Rosenthal, N. Farra, and R. Kumar. 2019a. Predicting the type and target of offensive posts in social media. In *Proc. NAACL-HLT*.

M. Zampieri, S. Malmasi, P. Nakov, S. Rosenthal, N. Farra, and R. Kumar. 2019b. SemEval-2019 task 6: Identifying and categorizing offensive language in social media (OffensEval). In *Proc. SemEval*.

M. Zampieri, P. Nakov, S. Rosenthal, P. Atanasova, G. Karadzhov, H. Mubarak, L. Derczynski, Z. Pitenis, and c. Çöltekin. 2020. SemEval-2020 Task 12: Multilingual Offensive Language Identification in Social Media (OffensEval 2020). In *Proceedings of SemEval*.

Exploring Linguistically-Lightweight Keyword Extraction Techniques for Indexing News Articles in a Multilingual Set-up

Jakub Piskorski
Institute for Computer Science
Polish Academy of Sciences
Warsaw, Poland
jpiskorski@gmail.com

Nicolas Stefanovitch
European Commission,
Joint Research Centre (JRC)
Ispra, Italy
nicolas.stefanovitch@ec.europa.eu

Guillaume Jacquet
European Commission,
Joint Research Centre (JRC)
Ispra, Italy
guillaume.jacquet@ec.europa.eu

Aldo Podavini
European Commission,
Joint Research Centre (JRC)
Ispra, Italy
aldo.podavini@ec.europa.eu

Abstract

This paper presents a study of state-of-the-art unsupervised and linguistically unsophisticated keyword extraction algorithms, based on statistic-, graph-, and embedding-based approaches, including, i.a., Total Keyword Frequency, TF-IDF, RAKE, KPMiner, YAKE, KeyBERT, and variants of TextRank-based keyword extraction algorithms.

The study was motivated by the need to select the most appropriate technique to extract keywords for indexing news articles in a real-world large-scale news analysis engine.

The algorithms were evaluated on a corpus of circa 330 news articles in 7 languages. The overall best F_1 scores for all languages on average were obtained using a combination of the recently introduced YAKE algorithm and KPMiner (20.1%, 46.6% and 47.2% for exact, partial and fuzzy matching resp.).

1 Introduction

Keyword Extraction (KE) is the task of automated extraction of single or multiple-token phrases from a textual document that best express all key aspects of its content and can be seen as automated generation of a short document summary. It constitutes an enabling technology for document indexing, clustering, classification, summarization, etc.

This paper presents a comparative study of the performance of some state-of-the-art unsupervised linguistically-lightweight keyword extraction methods and combinations thereof applied on news articles in seven languages. The main drive behind the reported work was to explore the usability of these methods for adding another level of indexing of news articles gathered and analysed by the Europe Media Monitor (EMM)[1] (Steinberger et al., 2017), a large-scale multilingual real-time news gathering and analysis system, which processes an average of 300,000 online news articles per day in up to 70 languages and is serving several EU institutions and international organisations.

While a vast bulk of research and tools for KE have been reported in the past, the specific focus of our research was to select the most suitable KE methods for indexing news articles taking specifically into account the operational, multilingual and real-time processing character of EMM. Hence, only unsupervised, scalable vis-a-vis multilinguality and robust algorithms that do not require any sophisticated linguistic resources and are capable of processing single news article in a time-efficient manner were considered.

Keyword extraction has been the subject of research for decades. Both unsupervised and supervised approaches exist, the unsupervised being particularly popular due to the scarcity of annotated data as well as their domain independence.

The unsupervised approaches are usually divided in three phases: (a) selection of candidate tokens that can constitute part of a keyword using some heuristics based on statistics and/or certain linguistic features (e.g., belonging to a specific part-of-speech or not being a stop word, etc.), (b) rank-

[1] https://emm.newsbrief.eu/

Proceedings of the EACL Hackashop on News Media Content Analysis and Automated Report Generation, pages 35–44
April 19, 2021 © Association for Computational Linguistics

ing the selected tokens, and (c) generating keywords out of the selected tokens, where the final rank is computed using the scores of the individual tokens. The unsupervised methods are divided into: statistics-, graph-, embeddings- and language model-based ones. The statistics-based methods exploit frequency, positional and co-occurrence statistics in the process of selecting candidate keywords. The graph-based methods create a graph from textual documents with nodes representing the candidate keywords and edges representing some relatedness to other candidate keywords, and then deploy graph ranking algorithms, e.g. PageRank, TextRank, to rank the final set of keywords. Recently, a third group of methods emerged which are based on word (Mikolov et al., 2013) and sentence embeddings (Pagliardini et al., 2018). Linguistic sophistication constitutes another dimension to look at the keyword extraction algorithms. Some of the methods use barely any language-specific resources, e.g., only stop word lists, whereas others exploit part-of-speech tagging or even syntactic parsing.

The supervised methods are simply divided into shallow and deep learning methods. The shallow methods exploit either binary classifiers to decide whether a token sequence is a keyword, linear regression-based models to rank the candidate keywords, and sequence labelling techniques. The deep learning methods exploit encoder-decoder and sequence-to-sequence labelling approaches. Most of the supervised machine-learning approaches reported in the literature deploy more linguistic sophistication (i.e., linguistic features) vis-a-vis unsupervised methods.

Extensive surveys on keyword extraction methods and comparison of their relative performance are provided in (Papagiannopoulou and Tsoumakas, 2020; Hasan and Ng, 2014; Kilic and Cetin, 2019; Alami Merrouni et al., 2019).

Since only a few monolingual corpora with keyword annotation of news articles exist (Marujo et al., 2013, 2012; Bougouin et al., 2013) that use different approaches to keyword annotation, we have created a new multilingual corpus of circa 330 news articles annotated with keywords covering 7 languages which is used for evaluation purposes in our study. We are not aware of any similar multilingual resource available for research purposes.

The paper is organized as follows. First, Section 2 introduces the Keyword Extraction task for news article indexing. Section 3 gives an overview of the methods explored. Next, Section 4 describes the creation of a multi-lingual data set and experiment results. Finally, we end up with conclusions and an outlook on future work in Section 5.

2 Keyword Extraction Task

The purpose of KE might vary depending on the domain in which it is deployed. In media monitoring and analysis the main objective is to capture from the text of each news article the main topics discussed therein, the key events reported, the entities involved in these events and what is the outcome, impact and significance thereof. For the sake of specifying what the expected output of KE should be, and in order to guide human annotators tasked to create test datasets, the following constraints on keyword selection were introduced (here in simplified form):

- a keyword can be a single word or a sequence of **up to 5 consecutive words** (unless it is a long proper name) **as they appear in the news article or the title** thereof,
- a **minimum of 5** and ideally **not more than 15** keywords (with ca 30% margin - to provide some flexibility) should be selected, however the set of selected keywords **may not** constitute more than 50% of the body of the news article,
- a single keyword **may not** include more than **one** entity,
- a keyword has to be either a **noun phrase**, **proper name**, **verb**, **adjective**, **phrasal verb**, or **part of a clause** (e.g., '*Trump died*'),
- a **stand-alone** adverb, conjunction, determiner, number, preposition or pronoun **may not** constitute a keyword,
- **a full sentence can never constitute a keyword,**
- keywords **should not** be converted into their corresponding base forms, disregarding the fact that a base form would appear more natural,
- if there are many candidate keywords to represent the same concept, only one of them should be selected.

3 Methods

Given the specific context of real-time media monitoring, our experiments imposed the following main selection criteria to the keyword extraction techniques to explore and evaluate:

- **efficiency:** ability to process a single news article within a fraction of a second,
- **multi-linguality:** ability to quickly adapt the method to the processing of many different languages,
- **robustness:** ability to process corrupted data without impacting performance.

Consequently, we have selected methods that: (a) do not require any language-specific resources except stop word lists and off-the-shelf pre-computed word embeddings, (b) exploit only information that can be computed in a time-efficient manner, e.g., frequency statistics, co-occurrence, positional information, string similarity, etc., (c) do not require any external text corpora (with one exception for a baseline method). The pool of methods (and variants thereof) explored includes:

Total Keyword Frequency (TKF) exploits only frequency information to rank candidate keywords, where candidates are 1-3 word n-grams from text that do not contain punctuation marks, and which neither start nor end with a stop word.

Term Frequency–Inverse Document Frequency (TF-IDF) constitutes the main baseline algorithm in our study. For the computation of TF-IDF scores a corpus consisting of 34.5M news articles gathered by EMM that span over the first 6 months of 2020 and covering ca. 70 languages was exploited.[2] A maximum of $\min(20, N/6)$ keywords with highest TF-IDF scores are returned for a news article, where N stands for the total number of tokens in the article.

Rapid Automatic Keyword Extraction (RAKE) exploits both frequency and co-occurrence information about tokens to score candidate keyword phrases (token sequences that do contain neither stop words nor phrase delimiters) (Rose et al., 2010). More specifically, the score for a candidate keyword phrase is computed as the sum of its member word scores. We explored three options for scoring words: (a) $s(w) = frequency(w)$ (RAKE-FREQ), (b) $s(w) = degree(w)$ (RAKE-DEG), which stands for the number of other content words that co-occurr with w in any candidate keyword phrase, and (c) $s(w) = degree(w)/frequency(w)$ (RAKE-DEGFREQ).

Keyphrase Miner (KP-Miner) exploits frequency and positional information about candidate keywords (word n-grams that do not contain punctuation marks, and which neither start nor end with a stop word) with some weighting of multi-token keywords (El-Beltagy and Rafea, 2009). More precisely, the score of a candidate keyword (in the case of single document scenario) is computed as:

$$s(k) = freq(k) \cdot \max(\frac{|K|}{\alpha \cdot |K_m|}, \omega) \cdot \frac{1}{AvgPos(k)}$$

where $freq(k)$, K, K_m denote frequency of k, the set of all candidate keywords and the set of all multi-token candidate keywords resp., whereas α and ω are two weight adjustment constants, and $AvgPos(k)$ denotes the average position of the keyword in a text in terms of regions separated by punctuations. KP-Miner also has a specific *cut-off* parameter, which determines the number of tokens after which if the keyword appears for the first time it is filtered out and discarded as a candidate. Our version of KP-Miner does not include stemming different from the original one (El-Beltagy and Rafea, 2009) due to our multilingual context and the specification of KE task (see Section 2). Finally, KP-Miner scans the top n ranking candidates and removes the ones which constitute sub-parts of others and adjusts the scores accordingly. Based on the empirical observations the specific parameters, namely, α, ω and *cut-off* were set to 1.0, 3.0 and 1000 resp.

Yet Another Keyword Extraction (Yake) exploits a wider range of features (Campos et al., 2020) vis-a-vis RAKE and KP-Miner in the process of scoring single tokens. Like the two algorithms introduced earlier, YAKE selects as candidate keywords word n-grams that do not contain punctuation marks, and which neither start nor end with a stop word. However, on top of this, an additional token classification step is then carried out in order to filter out additional tokens that should

[2]In particular, the pool of 34.5M news articles included: 11309K English, 6746K Spanish, 2322K French, 2001K Italian, 1431K German, 760K Romanian and 183K Polish articles, which covers the languages of the evaluation dataset (see Section 4.1).

not constitute part of a keyword (e.g. non alphanumeric character sequences, etc.). Single tokens are scored using the following formula:

$$Score(t) = \frac{T_{rel-context}(t) \cdot T_{position}(t)}{T_{case}(t) + \frac{T_{freq-norm}(t)+T_{sentence}(t)}{T_{rel-context}(t)}}$$

where: (a) $T_{case}(t)$ is a feature that reflects statistics on case information of all occurrences of t based on the assumption that uppercase tokens are more relevant than lowercase ones, (b) $T_{position}(t)$ is a feature that exploits positional information and boosts tokens that tend to appear at the beginning of a text, (c) $T_{freq-norm}$ is a feature that gives higher value to tokens appearing more than the mean and balanced by the span provided by standard deviation, (d) $T_{sentence}(t)$ is a feature that boosts significance of tokens that appear in many different sentences, and (e) $T_{rel-context}(t)$ is a *relatedness to context* indicator that 'downgrades' tokens that co-occur with higher number of unique tokens in a given window (see (Campos et al., 2020) for details). The score for a candidate keyword $k = t_1 t_2 \ldots t_n$ is then computed as:

$$Score(k) = \frac{\prod_{i=1}^{n} Score(t_i)}{frequency(k) \cdot (1 + \sum_{i=1}^{n} Score(t_i))}$$

Once the candidate keywords are ranked, potential duplicates are removed by adding them in relevance order. When a new keyword is added it is compared against all more relevant candidates in terms of semantic similarity, and if this similarity is below a specified threshold it is discarded. While the original YAKE algorithm exploits for this purpose the Levenshtein distance, our implementation uses *Weighted Logest Common Substrings* string distance metric (Piskorski et al., 2009) which favours overlap in the initial part of the strings compared.

Embedding-based Keyword Extraction (KEYEMB) exploits document embeddings and cosine similarity in order to identify candidate keywords. First, a document embedding is computed, then word n-grams of different sizes are generated, which are subsequently ranked along their similarity to the embedding of the document (Grootendorst, 2020).

We tested three different out-of-the-box transformer-based sentence embeddings. BERT-based ones are taken from (Reimers and Gurevych, 2020), which are both multilingual and fine-tuned on natural language inference and semantic text similarity tasks. One version uses a basic BERT model (KEYEMB-BERT-B) and the other a lightweight BERT model (KEYEMB-BERT-D). Finally, KEYEMB-LASER is based on LASER (Artetxe and Schwenk, 2019) embeddings. Contrary to BERT, they have not been fine-tuned on semantic similarity tasks, but for the task of aligning similar multilingual concepts to the same semantic space.

Filtering stop words without applying any of the different post-processing steps proposed in (Grootendorst, 2020) provided the best results and therefore is the setting we used in the evaluation and comparison against other methods.

Graph-based Keyword Extraction: (GRAPH) exploits properties of a graph whose nodes are substrings extracted from the text in order to identify which are the most important (Litvak and Last, 2008). This approach differs from TextRank (Mihalcea and Tarau, 2004), in two ways: firstly, the graph is constructed in a fundamentally different way yielding smaller graphs and therefore faster processing time; secondly, different lower-complexity graph measures are also explored, allowing even faster processing time.

A node of the graph corresponds either to a sentence, a phrase delimited by any punctuation marks or a token sequence delimited by stop words. Two nodes are connected only if they share at least 20% of words after removal of stop words.

The importance of the nodes can be defined in different ways. In this study we looked at: (a) *degree* (GRAPH-DEGREE), which measures the absolute number of related sentences in the text, (b) *centrality* (GRAPH-CENTR) which intuitively measures the extent to which a specific node serves as a bridge to connect any unrelated pieces of information, (c) *clustering* (GRAPH-CLUST) which measure the level of interconnection between the neighbours of a node and itself, and finally, (d) the sum of the centrality and clustering measure (GRAPH-CE&CL). Please refer to (Brandes, 2005) for further details on these graph measures.

Although more sophisticated linguistic processing resources such as POS taggers and dependency parsers are available for at least several languages we did not consider KE techniques that exploit them since the range of languages covered would be still far away from the ca. 70 languages covered by EMM. Furthermore, although the BERT-based approaches to KE (even without any tuning) are known to be orders of magnitudes slower than the other methods, we explored them given the wide range of languages covered in terms of off-the-shelf embeddings.

4 Experiments

4.1 Dataset

For the evaluation of the KE algorithms we created random samples of circa 50 news articles published in 2020 for 7 languages: English, French, German, Italian, Polish, Romanian and Spanish. The selection of the languages was motivated to cover all three main Indo-European language families: Germanic, Romance and Slavic languages.

The news articles were annotated with keywords by two human experts for each language in the following manner. Initially, all annotators were presented with the task definition, keyword selection guidelines, and annotated a couple of trial articles. Next, the annotators were tasked to select keywords for the proper set of 50 news articles for each language. The annotation was done by each annotator separately since we were interested to measure the discrepancies between annotators and differences between the languages. The final sets of documents used for evaluation for some of the languages contained less than 50 news articles due to some near duplicates encountered, etc.

Table 1 shows the differences in terms of keyword annotation distribution across languages. The average number of keywords per article varies from 8.68 for French to 13.20 for German. At the token level, the average ranges from 20.66 annotated tokens (French) per article to 30.24 (Romanian). The discrepancies between annotators differ significantly across languages, e.g., for Polish, only 9.37% of the keywords are shared between the two annotators, whereas for Romanian, they are 48.68%. However, when one measures the differences at the token level the discrepancies are significantly smaller, i.e., for Polish, 49.67% of the tokens are shared between the annotators, whereas for Romanian, 69.16%. This comparison between annotators is completed by computing the percentage of "fuzzy" common tokens (Table 1), corresponding to the common 4-gram characters. As expected, the percentage of "fuzzy" common tokens is higher than for exact common tokens for all languages. It increases by ca. 2 points for English, French, Italian, Spanish and more than 4 points for German, Polish and Romanian.

Based on the relatively high level of discrepancies between each pair of annotators per language (see Table 1) we decided to create the ground truth for evaluation by merging the respective keyword sets for each languages. The statistics of the resulting ground truth data are summarized in Table 2. We can observe that the average number of keywords per article for Italian and French is significantly lower than for the other languages. The average number of tokens per keyword is quite stable, from 2.33 (Spanish) to 2.79 (English), except for German, 1.75 tokens per keyword, due to the frequent use of compounds in this language.

4.2 Evaluation Methodology

We have used the classical *precision* (P), *recall* (R) and F_1 metrics for the evaluation purposes. The overall P, R and F_1 scores were computed as an average over the respective scores for single news articles.

We have computed the scores in three different ways. In the *exact matching* mode, we consider that an extracted keyword is matched correctly only if exactly the same keyword occurs in the ground truth (or vice versa).

In the *partial matching* mode, the match of a given keyword c vis-a-vis Ground Truth $GT = \{k_1, \ldots, k_n\}$ is computed as follows:

$$match(c) = \max_{k \in GT} \frac{2 \cdot commonTokens(c,k)}{|c|_T + |k|_T}$$

where $commonTokens(c,k)$ denotes the number of tokens that appear both in c and k, and $|c|_T$ ($|k|_T$) denote the number of tokens the keyword c (k) consists of. The value of $match(c)$ is between 0 and 1.

Analogously, in the *fuzzy matching* mode, the match of a given keyword c vis-a-vis Ground Truth $GT = \{k_1, \ldots, k_n\}$ is computed as follows:

$$match(c) = \max_{k \in GT} Similarity(c,k)$$

where $Similarity(c,k)$ is computed using *Longest Common Substring* similarity metric (Bergroth et al., 2000), whose value is between

Language	average number of annotated keywords per article	percentage of common keywords	average number of annotated tokens per article	percentage of exact common tokens	percentage of fuzzy common tokens
English	11.63	17.35%	28.95	53.08%	53.77%
French	8.68	42.97%	20.66	63.95%	65.00%
German	13.20	44.10%	22.37	62.91%	67.56%
Italian	9.81	43.86%	21.87	63.94%	64.74%
Polish	11.01	9.37%	27.77	49.67%	55.28%
Romanian	12.72	48.68%	30.24	69.16%	72.19%
Spanish	12.72	24.13%	26.71	58.06%	59.19%

Table 1: Exact and fuzzy overlap of keywords and tokens for annotator pairs for each language.

Language	#articles	avg. nb of keywords per article	avg. nb of tokens per keyword
English	50	22.04	2.79
French	47	14.34	2.70
German	50	21.36	1.75
Italian	50	16.16	2.34
Polish	39	21.18	2.67
Romanian	49	20.61	2.62
Spanish	48	22.75	2.33

Table 2: Ground Truth statistics.

0 and 1. Both P and R are computed analogously using the concept of partial and fuzzy matching.

The main rationale behind using the partial and fuzzy matching mode was the fact that exact matching is simply too strict in terms of penalisation of automatically extracted keywords which do have strong overlap with keywords in the ground truth.

Finally, we have also computed standard deviation (SD) for all metrics in order to observe whether any of the algorithms is prone to producing response outliers.

4.3 Results

We have evaluated all the algorithms described in Section 3 with the following settings, unless specified elsewhere differently: (a) the max. number of tokens per keyword is 3, whereas the minimum (maximum) number of characters is set to 2 (80), (b) keywords can neither start nor end with a stop word, (c) keywords cannot contain tokens composed only of non-alphanumeric characters, and (d) the default maximum number of keywords to return is 15. The main drive behind setting the maximum number of keywords to 15 is based on empirical observation, optimizing both F_1 score and not returning too long list of keywords.

The overall performance of each algorithm averaged across languages, in term of P, R and F_1 scores is listed in Table 3, respectively for exact, partial and fuzzy matching. In general, only the results for the best settings per algorithm type are provided except for YAKE and KPMINER, which performed overall best. More specifically, the table contains results of some additional variants of YAKE and its combinations with KPMiner, namely: (a) YAKE-15 and YAKE-20 which return 15 and 20 keywords resp., (b) YAKE-KPMINER-I (intersection) which returns the intersection of the results returned by YAKE-15 and KP-Miner, (c) YAKE-KPMINER-U (union) which merges up to 10 top keywords returned by YAKE and KP-Miner output, and (d) YAKE-KPMINER-R (re-ranking) which sums the ranks of the keywords returned by YAKE-15 and KPMINER and selects top 15 keywords after the re-ranking.

Across the three types of matching, the list of algorithms obtaining good results is quite stable (cf. Table 3). YAKE-KPMINER-R constantly obtaining the best F_1, respectively 20.1%, 46.6% and 47.2% for the exact, partial and fuzzy matching, followed or equaled by the YAKE-KPMINER-U.

YAKE-KPMINER-I obtained the best precision, respectively 28.5%, 55.9% and 57.2%. In terms of standard deviation (SD), YAKE-KPMINER-I appears to be the most unstable since it is constantly the algorithm with the highest SD, for P, R and F_1, and for all types of matching.

As expected, the results obtained with partial and fuzzy matching are better than with exact matching. More interestingly, the fuzzy matching also allows to smooth the discrepancy between languages. Figure 1 highlights for YAKE-KPMINER-R algorithm how some languages like Polish, a highly inflected language, have a poor F_1 for exact matching, but are close to the all-language average for fuzzy matching. Figure 2 aims at comparing the results obtained in each language with a selection of algorithms for the fuzzy matching. The KPMINER algorithm appears to be best suited for the French language, whereas German the group of YAKE algorithms appears to be a better choice. There are some other language specific aspects according to the different algorithms, but less significant. As a matter of fact, the observations on YAKE and KPMINER strengths when applying on texts in specific languages were the main drive to introduce the various variants of combining these KE algorithms.

One can also conclude from the evaluation figures that YAKE-KP-MINER-R appears to be the best "all-rounder" algorithm. In this context it is also important to emphasize that the performance of the various algorithms relies on the quality and coverage of the stop word lists, which are used by almost all algorithms compared here. In particular, the respective algorithms used identical stop word lists, covering: English (583 words), French (464), German (604), Italian (397), Polish (355), Romanian (282), and Spanish (352).

KEYEMB-based approaches tend to focus only on the most important sentence in the news article. As such, frequently, several 3-grams candidates originating from the same sentence are returned, where most of them are redundant. Interestingly, as regards fuzzy matching KEYEMB-LASER performs better than BERT-based ones despite not being specially trained on similarity tasks, while KEYEMB-BERT-D performs overall best out of the three. It is worth mentioning that this approach is by far the slowest of the reported approaches in terms of time efficiency.

GRAPH-based approaches suffer from a similar focusing bias: they tend to focus on the most important concepts, as such they are always present but so are some variations thereof, e.g. reporting most frequent words within all the different contexts they appear in, therefore generating redundant keywords. Among this family of algorithms, the GRAPH-DEGREE performed best, meaning that a high co-occurrence count is a good indicator of relevance for KE.

Embedding and graph-based approaches overfocus on the key concepts of a text. The fact that they are based on an indirect form of counting the most important words, without any further post-processing, may in part explain why their performance is comparable to TF-IDF, which relies directly on frequency count. An advantage of graph-based approaches compared to embedding-based ones and TF-IDF is that they don't need to be trained in advance on any corpora.

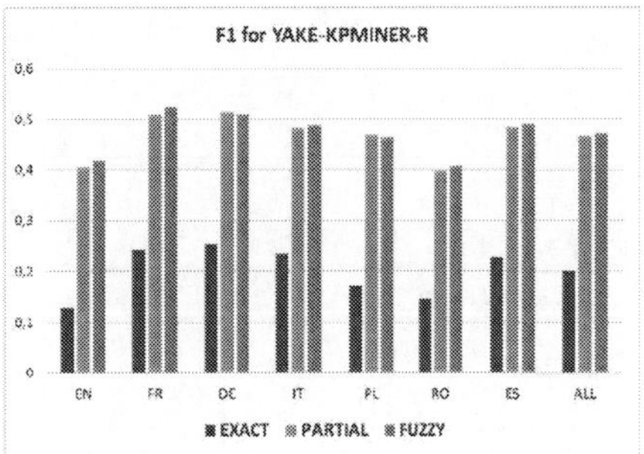

Figure 1: F_1 scores for exact, partial and fuzzy matching for YAKE-KPMINER-R.

4.3.1 Deduplication

Based on the results presented in the previous Section we carried out some additional experiments in order to explore whether the best performing algorithm, namely, YAKE-KPMINER-R, could be improved. In particular, given that this algorithm combines merging of keywords of two different algorithms, we have added an additional deduplication step. To be more precise, all keyword candidates that are properly included in other keyword candidates are discarded. We evaluated this new variant with different settings as regards the maximum allowed number of keywords returned. While we have not observed significant improvements in terms of the F_1 score when increasing the number of keywords returned by the algorithms described in the previous Section, the evaluation of YAKE-KPMINER-R with deduplication revealed that increasing this parameter yields some gains. Figure 3 and 4 provide P, R and F_1 curves for fuzzy matching according to the maximum number of keywords allowed to be returned for the English and German subcorpus.

One can observe that shifting the maximum number of keywords to ca. 25 results in some improvement for F_1 and R. While these findings pave the way for some future explorations on parameter tuning to improve F_1 figures, one needs to emphasize here that increasing the number of keywords, even if resulting in some small gains in F_1 is not a desired feature from an application point of view, where analysts expect and prefer to 'see less than more'.

4.4 Time efficiency performance

We have carried out a small comparison of the runtime behaviour of the algorithms with respect to the time needed to process a collection of 16983

	Exact (%)				Partial (%)				Fuzzy (%)			
Algorithm	P	R	F_1	SD	P	R	F_1	SD	P	R	F_1	SD
TF-IDF	14.2	12.1	12.6	09.2	33.5	30.7	31.2	10.1	34.0	31.1	31.6	10.8
KPMINER	17.8	15.4	15.9	08.6	49.4	38.1	41.9	12.3	51.3	37.2	41.7	14.5
RAKE-DEG	13.1	11.9	12.0	09.0	45.9	33.3	37.1	14.8	47.5	30.6	35.0	18.3
RAKE-DEGFREQ	10.4	09.5	09.5	09.3	37.6	30.5	32.6	13.4	35.2	27.0	29.2	16.1
RAKE-FREQ	14.0	12.6	12.8	09.4	46.8	34.1	38.0	14.3	49.2	31.6	36.3	18.2
KTF	16.8	14.5	14.8	09.6	39.4	30.7	33.5	12.2	43.3	31.5	35.3	13.6
KEYEMB-BERT-D	08.1	08.1	07.6	07.0	38.6	24.5	28.6	16.0	40.3	27.5	31.7	13.9
KEYEMB-BERT-B	04.5	05.0	04.5	05.8	22.6	17.2	18.6	10.7	36.2	27.1	29.9	12.1
KEYEMB-LASER	02.9	03.5	03.0	05.6	18.8	15.1	16.1	11.2	39.4	29.0	32.4	13.2
GRAPH-CENTR	03.2	04.0	03.7	05.9	17.7	12.1	14.3	12.2	29.1	20.0	22.9	12.6
GRAPH-CLUST	04.1	03.8	03.8	**05.4**	17.2	13.0	14.2	**09.2**	29.0	24.6	25.9	10.7
GRAPH-CE&CL	03.9	03.9	03.8	05.5	19.1	13.4	14.7	10.4	31.4	24.8	26.7	12.2
GRAPH-DEGREE	04.2	04.4	04.1	05.9	21.2	15.3	16.8	11.2	34.5	27.3	29.4	11.6
YAKE-15	22.0	17.8	19.1	10.3	45.9	42.3	43.1	10.6	46.6	42.9	43.5	11.3
YAKE-20	19.2	20.3	19.2	09.1	41.9	**47.2**	43.6	09.5	42.1	**48.3**	44.0	**10.0**
YAKE-KPMINER-I	**28.5**	08.8	12.6	18.3	**55.9**	24.3	32.2	26.4	**57.2**	23.5	31.3	28.7
YAKE-KPMINER-R	19.9	**21.9**	**20.1**	08.5	48.2	47.1	**46.6**	09.4	49.8	47.2	**47.2**	10.6
YAKE-KPMINER-U	19.4	21.7	19.8	08.6	48.7	46.6	**46.6**	09.6	50.4	46.4	47.0	11.0

Table 3: Overall performance overview: exact, partial and fuzzy matching.

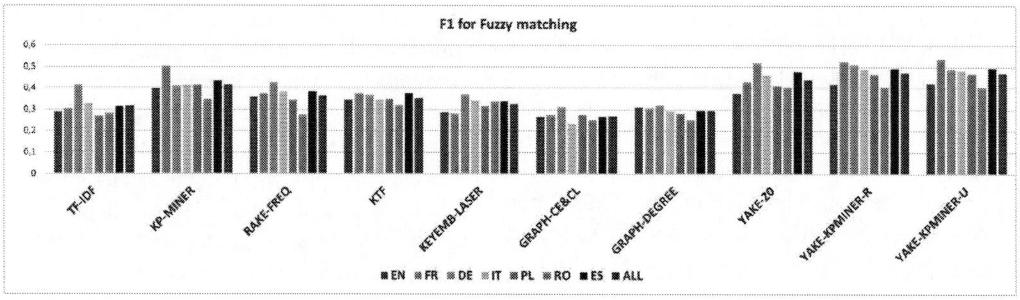

Figure 2: F_1 fuzzy matching figures for a selection of algorithms and all languages.

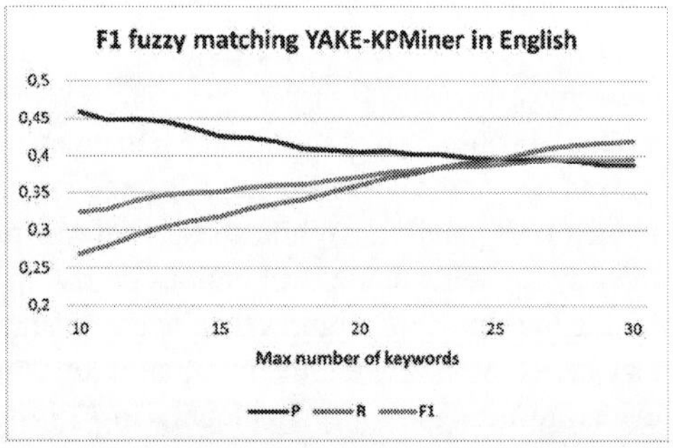

Figure 3: P, R and F_1 curves for fuzzy matching for the varying number of maximum number of keywords returned for the English subcorpus.

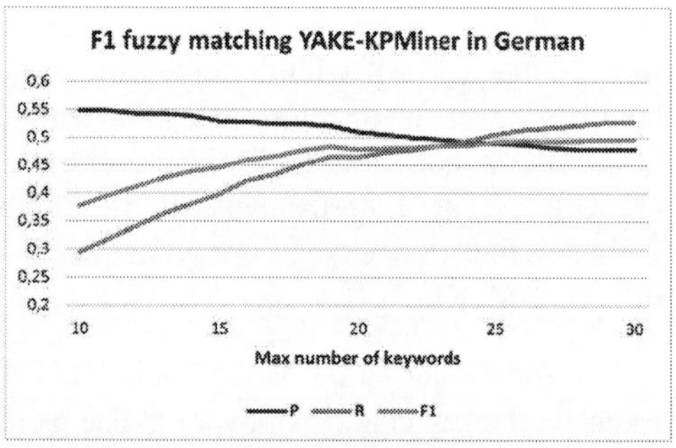

Figure 4: P, R and F_1 curves based on varying number of maximum number of keywords returned for the German news subcorpus.

Algorithm	time (seconds)
KTF	12.13
RAKE-DEG	9.36
RAKE-FREQ	9.33
RAKE-DEGFREQ	9.37
KPMINER	21.12
YAKE-15	21.04
YAKE-KPMINER-R	42.56

Table 4: Time efficiency comparison on a set of circa 17K news articles in English on Covid-19.

news articles on Covid-19 in English (84.9 MB of space on disk). The time given in seconds to run KTF, Rake, KPMiner, Yake and some variants thereof are provided in Table 4. All the aforementioned algorithms have been implemented in Java and optimized in term of efficient data structures used that correspond to the upper bounds of the respective time complexity of these algorithms. Both embedding- and graph-based algorithms explored in our study were implemented in Python, using some existing libraries, and were not optimized for speed. For these reasons, it is not meaningful to report their exact time performance. As before, on a given CPU, embedding-based approaches run an order of magnitude slower than graph based algorithms, which themselves run a magnitude slower than the simpler algorithms, whose performance is reported in Table 4.

5 Conclusions and Outlook

This paper presented the results of a small comparative study of the performance of some state-of-the-art knowledge-lightweight keyword extraction methods in the context of indexing news articles in various languages with keywords. The best performing method, namely, a combination of Yake and KPMiner algorithms, obtained F_1 score of 20.1%, 46.6% and 47.2% for the exact, partial and fuzzy matching respectively. Since both of these algorithms exploit neither any language-specific (except stop word lists) nor other external resources like domain-specific corpora, this solution can be easily adapted to the processing of many languages and constitutes a strong baseline for further explorations.

The comparison presented in this paper is not exhaustive, other linguistically-lightweight unsupervised approaches could be explored, e.g., the graph-centric approach presented in (Skrlj et al., 2019), and some post-processing filters to merge redundant keywords going beyond exploiting string similarity metrics, and simultaneously, techniques to improve diversification of the keywords returned.

Extending the approaches explored in this study, e.g., through use of part-of-speech-based patterns to filter out implausible keywords (e.g., imposing constraints to include only adjectives and nouns as elements of keywords), use of more elaborated graph-based keyword ranking methods (e.g. Page Rank), integration of semantics (e.g., linking semantic meaning to text sequences through using knowledge bases and semantic networks (Papagiannopoulou and Tsoumakas, 2020; Hasan and Ng, 2014; Kilic and Cetin, 2019; Alami Merrouni et al., 2019)) would potentially allow to improve the performance. However, these extensions would require significantly more linguistic sophistication, and consequently would be more difficult to port across languages.

For matters related to accessing the ground truth dataset created for the sake of carrying out the evaluation presented in this paper please contact the authors.

Acknowledgments

We are greatly indebted to Stefano Bucci, Florentina Ciltu, Corrado Mirra, Monica De Paola, Teófilio Garcia, Camelia Ignat, Jens Linge, Manuel Marker, Małgorzata Piskorska, Camille Schaeffer, Jessica Scornavacche and Beatriz Torighelli for helping us with the keyword annotation of news articles in various languages. We are also thankful to Martin Atkinson who contributed to the work presented in this report, and to Charles MacMillan for proofreading the paper.

References

Zakariae Alami Merrouni, Bouchra Frikh, and Brahim Ouhbi. 2019. Automatic keyphrase extraction: a survey and trends. *Journal of Intelligent Information Systems*, 54.

Mikel Artetxe and Holger Schwenk. 2019. Massively multilingual sentence embeddings for zero-shot cross-lingual transfer and beyond. *Transactions of the Association for Computational Linguistics*, 7:597–610.

Lasse Bergroth, H. Hakonen, and T. Raita. 2000. A survey of longest common subsequence algorithms. pages 39–48.

Adrien Bougouin, Florian Boudin, and Béatrice Daille. 2013. TopicRank: Graph-based topic ranking for keyphrase extraction. In *Proceedings of the* 6th *International Joint Conference on NLP*, pages 543–551, Nagoya, Japan.

Ulrik Brandes. 2005. *Network analysis: methodological foundations*, volume 3418. Springer Science & Business Media.

Ricardo Campos, Vítor Mangaravite, Arian Pasquali, A. Jorge, C. Nunes, and Adam Jatowt. 2020. Yake! keyword extraction from single documents using multiple local features. *Inf. Sci.*, 509:257–289.

Samhaa R. El-Beltagy and Ahmed A. Rafea. 2009. Kp-miner: A keyphrase extraction system for english and arabic documents. *Inf. Syst.*, 34(1):132–144.

Maarten Grootendorst. 2020. Keybert: Minimal keyword extraction with bert.

Kazi Saidul Hasan and Vincent Ng. 2014. Automatic keyphrase extraction: A survey of the state of the art. In *Proceedings of the* 52nd *ACL Conference*, pages 1262–1273, Baltimore, Maryland. ACL.

Ozlem Kilic and Aydın Cetin. 2019. A survey on keyword and key phrase extraction with deep learning. pages 1–6.

Marina Litvak and Mark Last. 2008. Graph-based keyword extraction for single-document summarization. In *Coling 2008: Proceedings of the workshop Multi-source Multilingual Information Extraction and Summarization*, pages 17–24.

Luís Marujo, Anatole Gershman, G. Jaime Carbonell, E. Robert Frederking, and Paulo João Neto. 2012. Supervised topical key phrase extraction of news stories using crowdsourcing, light filtering and coreference normalization. *Language Resources and Evaluation*, pages 399–403.

Luís Marujo, Márcio Viveiros, and João Neto. 2013. Keyphrase cloud generation of broadcast news. *Proceedings of INTERSPEECH 2013*.

Rada Mihalcea and Paul Tarau. 2004. Textrank: Bringing order into text. In *Proceedings of the 2004 conference on empirical methods in natural language processing*, pages 404–411.

Tomas Mikolov, Ilya Sutskever, Kai Chen, Greg S Corrado, and Jeff Dean. 2013. Distributed representations of words and phrases and their compositionality. In *NIPS*, pages 3111–3119. Curran Associates, Inc.

Matteo Pagliardini, Prakhar Gupta, and Martin Jaggi. 2018. Unsupervised learning of sentence embeddings using compositional n-gram features. In *Proceedings of NAACL 2018*, pages 528–540, New Orleans, Louisiana. ACL.

Eirini Papagiannopoulou and Grigorios Tsoumakas. 2020. A review of keyphrase extraction. *Wiley Interdisciplinary Reviews: Data Mining and Knowledge Discovery*, 10.

Jakub Piskorski, Karol Wieloch, and Marcin Sydow. 2009. On knowledge-poor methods for person name matching and lemmatization for highly inflectional languages. *Information Retrieval*, 12(3):275–299.

Nils Reimers and Iryna Gurevych. 2020. Making monolingual sentence embeddings multilingual using knowledge distillation. In *Proceedings of the 2020 Conference on Empirical Methods in Natural Language Processing*. Association for Computational Linguistics.

Stuart Rose, Dave Engel, Nick Cramer, and Wendy Cowley. 2010. Automatic keyword extraction from individual documents. In Michael W. Berry and Jacob Kogan, editors, *Text Mining. Applications and Theory*, pages 1–20. John Wiley and Sons, Ltd.

Blaz Skrlj, Andraz Repar, and Senja Pollak. 2019. Rakun: Rank-based keyword extraction via unsupervised learning and meta vertex aggregation. In *SLSP*.

Ralf Steinberger, Martin Atkinson, Teofilo Garcia, Erik van der Goot, Jens Linge, Charles Macmillan, Hristo Tanev, Marco Verile, and Gerhard Wagner. 2017. EMM: Supporting the analyst by turning multilingual text into structured data. In *Transparenz Aus Verantwortung: Neue Herausforderungen Für Die Digitale Datenanalyse*. Erich Schmidt Verlag.

No NLP Task Should be an Island: Multi-disciplinarity for Diversity in News Recommender Systems

Myrthe Reuver[♡] **Antske Fokkens**[♡♣] **Suzan Verberne**[◇]

♡ CLTL, Dept. of Language, Literature & Communication, Vrije Universiteit Amsterdam

♣ Dept. of Mathematics and Computer Science, Eindhoven University of Technology

◇ Leiden Institute of Advanced Computer Science, Leiden University

{myrthe.reuver,antske.fokkens}@vu.nl,
s.verberne@liacs.leidenuniv.nl

Abstract

Natural Language Processing (NLP) is defined by specific, separate tasks, with each their own literature, benchmark datasets, and definitions. In this position paper, we argue that for a complex problem such as the threat to democracy by non-diverse news recommender systems, it is important to take into account a higher-order, normative goal and its implications. Experts in ethics, political science and media studies have suggested that news recommendation systems could be used to support a deliberative democracy. We reflect on the role of NLP in recommendation systems with this specific goal in mind and show that this theory of democracy helps to identify which NLP tasks and techniques can support this goal, and what work still needs to be done. This leads to recommendations for NLP researchers working on this specific problem as well as researchers working on other complex multidisciplinary problems.

1 Introduction

The field of Natural Language Processing (NLP) uses specific, self-defined definitions for separate tasks – each with their own leaderboards, benchmark datasets, and performance metrics. When dealing with complex, societal problems, it may however be better to take into account a broader view, starting from the actual needs to solve the overall societal problem. In particular, this paper addresses the complex issue of non-diverse news recommenders potentially threatening democracy (Helberger, 2019). We focus on a theory of democracy and its role in news recommendation, as described in Helberger (2019), and reflect on which NLP tasks may help address this issue. In doing so, we consider work by experts on the problem and domain, such as political scientists, recommender system experts, philosophers and media and communication experts.

News recommender systems play an increasingly important role in online news consumption (Karimi et al., 2018). Such systems recommend several news articles from a large pool of possible articles whenever the user wishes to read news. Recommender systems usually attempt to make the recommended articles increase the user's interaction and engagement. In a news recommender system, this typically means optimizing for the individual user's "clicks" or "reading time" (Zhou et al., 2010). These measures are considered a proxy for reader interest and engagement, but other metrics could also be used, including the time spent on a page or article ratings.

Recommender systems are tailored to individual user interests. For other types of recommender systems, e.g. entertainment systems (recommending music or movies), this is less of a problem. However, *news* recommendation is connected to society and democracy, because news plays an important role in keeping citizens informed on recent societal issues and debates (Helberger, 2019). Personalization to user interest in the news recommendation domain can lead to a situation where users are increasingly unaware of different ideas or perspectives on current issues. The dangers of such news 'filter bubbles' (Pariser, 2011) and online 'echo chambers' (Jamieson and Cappella, 2008) due to online (over)personalization have been pointed out before (Bozdag, 2013; Sunstein, 2018).

Political theory provides several models of democracy, which each also imply different roles for news recommendation. We follow the deliberative model of democracy, which states citizens of a functioning democracy need to get access to different ideas and viewpoints, and engage with these and with each other (Manin, 1987; Helberger, 2019) (a further explanation of this model is given in Section 2). A uniform news diet and personalization to only personal interests can, in theory if not

Proceedings of the EACL Hackashop on News Media Content Analysis and Automated Report Generation, pages 45–55
April 19, 2021 © Association for Computational Linguistics

in practice, lead to a narrow view on current issues and a lack of deliberation in democracy. When considering this model, it becomes clear that news personalization on user interest alone is potentially harmful for democracy. The normative goal of a recommender system then becomes: supporting a deliberative democracy by showing a diverse set of views to users. NLP can play a role here, by automatically identifying viewpoints, arguments, or claims in news texts. Output of such trained models can help recommend articles that show a diverse set of views and arguments, and thus support a deliberative democracy.

The explicit goals and underlying values of democracy expressed in the model of deliberative democracy can help in defining what NLP tasks and analyses are relevant for tackling the potential harmful effects of news recommendation. This can increase the societal impact of relevant NLP tasks. We believe considering such theories and normative models can also help work on other complex concepts and societal problems where NLP plays a role. In this paper, we outline societal challenges and a theoretical model of the role of non-diverse news recommenders in democracy, as developed by experts such as political scientists and media experts. We then argue that argument mining, viewpoint detection, and related NLP tasks can make a valuable contribution to the effort in diversifying news recommendation and thereby supporting a deliberative democracy.

This position paper provides the following contributions to the discussion: We argue that taking normative and/or societal goals into account can provide insights in the usefulness of specific NLP tasks for complex societal problems. As such, we believe that approaching such problems from an interdisciplinary point of view can help define NLP tasks better and/or increase their impact. In particular, we outline the normative and societal goals for diversifying news recommendation systems and illustrate how these goals relate to various NLP tasks. This results in a discussion on how, on the one hand, news recommendation can make better use of NLP and, on the other hand, how the goal of diversifying news provides inspiration for improving existing tasks or developing new ones.

This paper is structured as follows: We first describe the problem that personalized news recommendation could pose for democracy, as well as the importance of an interdisciplinary approach to solving this problem in Section 2. Section 3 provides an overview of literature tackling diversity in news recommendation as a solution to this problem, and points out remaining gaps in these efforts, specifically connected to the idea of a deliberative democracy. Section 4 outlines several related NLP tasks and their connection to this overarching normative goal. In Section 5, we discuss what we think the NLP community should take away from this reflection, and in Section 6 we will conclude our paper.

2 Personalization in the News, Theories of Democracy, and Interdisciplinarity

The online news domain has increasingly moved towards personalization (Karimi et al., 2018). In the news domain, such personalization comes with specific issues and challenges. A combination of personalizaton and (political) news can lead to polarization, Filter Bubbles (Pariser, 2011), and Echo Chambers (Jamieson and Cappella, 2008). This trend to personalize leads to shared internet spaces becoming much more tailored to the individual user rather than being a shared, public space (Papacharissi, 2002). Such phenomena could negatively impact a citizen's rights to information and right to not be discriminated (Eskens et al., 2017; Wachter, 2020). Evidence for filter bubbles is under discussion (Borgesius et al., 2016; Bruns, 2019), but empirical work does indicate that especially fringe groups holding extreme political or ideological opinions may end up into such a conceptual bubble (Boutyline and Willer, 2017).

Helberger (2019) points out that a lack of diversity in news recommendation can also harm democracy. This clearly holds for the *deliberative* model of democracy. This model assumes that democracy functions on deliberation, and the exchange of points of view. A fundamental assumption in this model is that individuals need access to diverse and conflicting viewpoints and argumentation to participate in these discussions (Manin, 1987). News recommendations supporting a deliberative democracy should then play a role in providing access to these different viewpoints, ideas, and issues in the news (Helberger, 2019).

The threat to democracy of non-diverse news recommenders is a complex problem. It requires input from different academic disciplines, from media studies and computer science to political science and philosophy (Bernstein et al., 2020). Political theory can provide a framework that helps define what is needed from more empirical and technical researchers to address this problem. In the next section, we will discuss recent work in diversity in news recommendation. We point out remaining gaps in these efforts, specifically connected to the idea of a deliberative democracy.

3 Diversity in News Recommendation

3.1 Recent Diversity Efforts

Previous work on diversity in news recommender systems has mainly focused on assessing the current state of diversity in news recommendation (Möller et al., 2018), or on assessing diversity especially at the end of a computational pipeline, in the form of (evaluation) metrics (Vrijenhoek et al., 2021; Kaminskas and Bridge, 2016), or on computational implementations of diversity (Lu et al., 2020). Less attention has been given to defining and identifying the viewpoints, entities, or perspectives that are being diversified, or to the underlying values and goals of diversification.

Within the recommender systems field, there are several ideas and concepts related to diversity, especially where it concerns evaluation or optimization metrics. Diversity, serendipity, and unexpectedness all are metrics used in the recommender systems literature that go beyond mere click accuracy (Kaminskas and Bridge, 2016). There are two gaps we see in many of these earlier metrics. Firstly, these metrics rarely focus on linguistic or conceptual features or representations of (aspects of) diversity in the news articles. Or, when they do, the NLP approaches are simplified (e.g. topic models in Draws et al. (2020b)) to centralize the recommendation algorithm and its optimization. Secondly, such "beyond user interest" optimization in recommender systems is usually not connected to normative goals and societal gains, but still geared towards user interest and the idea that users react positively to unexpected or previously unseen items. However, several fairly recent works (Lu et al., 2020; Vrijenhoek et al., 2021) have attempted to go beyond "click accuracy" for user interest and tackle the diversity in news recommendation problem while also explicitly considering normative values.

Lu et al. (2020) discuss how to implement "editorial values" in a news recommender for a Dutch online newspaper. Editorial values were defined as journalistic missions or ideals found important by the newspaper's editors and journalists. One of these values is diversity, but their case-study concerns implementing and optimizing for "dynamism" – a diversity-related metric the authors define as "how much a list changes between updates". The authors note the computational difficulty of measuring and optimizing for diversity, and propose a proxy. They define "intra-list diversity" as the inverse of the similarity of a recommendation set. This similarity is calculated over pre-defined news categories of the articles, such as 'sports' and 'finance', as well as over different authors. Viewpoints or perspectives are not mentioned. Lu et al. (2020)'s "editorial values" seem to correspond to the public values mentioned in Bernstein et al. (2020), and implicitly also relate to the democratic values described by Helberger (2019). Both mention diversity as a central important aspect, but Lu et al. (2020) still centralize the user's satisfaction, rather than public values or democracy.

Vrijenhoek et al. (2021) connect several democratic models to computational evaluative metrics of news recommender diversity. The paper discusses several metrics that could be used as optimization and evaluation functions for diversity for news recommender systems supporting a deliberative democracy, such as one to measure and optimize for the "representation" of different societal opinions and voices, and another to measure the "fragmentation": whether different users receive different news story chains. These evaluation metrics are, to our knowledge, the first to explicitly consider normative values and models of democracy in news recommender system design. However, this work does not discuss how to *represent* or *identify* different voices in news articles. The NLP-related components discussed are limited to annotating different named entities.

We argue that the inclusion of more fine-grained and state-of-the-art NLP methods allows more precise identification of different "voices" and viewpoints in support of diverse news recommender systems. The connection of these NLP tasks to diversifying news recommendation is as follows. We compare the building of diverse news recommenders in support of a deliberative democracy to building a tower, with the identification of the different voices or viewpoints as the base of that tower. When an approach can reliably and consistently identify different viewpoints or arguments, we can also diversify these viewpoints in recommendations. A solid definition of viewpoints and reliable methods to detect them thus form the foundation of our diverse news recommendation tower, and builds it towards the goal of a functioning deliberative democracy.

3.2 Technical and Conceptual Challenges

The news is a specific domain for recommender systems, with much faster-changing content than for instance movie or e-commerce recommendation. This leads to a number of unique technical challenges.

Two specific technical and conceptual challenges to a (diverse) news recommendation have been addressed in previous work. The first is the cold start problem (Zhou et al., 2010), which occurs when a news recommender needs data on articles to decide whether to recommend the article to a (new) user. Recommendation, in news as well as in other domains, often uses the interaction data of similar users to recommend data to new users, such as in the method "collaborative filtering". Such data is missing on the large volumes of new articles added in the news domain every day, which makes such approaches less useful in this domain. This leads to other recommendation techniques being more common in the news recommendendation domain.

The second challenge specific to our problem is the continuous addition of new and many different topics, issues, and entities in public discussion and in the news. This makes detecting viewpoints with one automated, single model and one set of training data difficult. Previous work often explores one well-known publicly debated topic, such as abortion (Draws et al., 2020a) or misinformation related to COVID-19 (Hossain et al., 2020). However, in an ideal solution we would also be able to continuously identify all kinds of new debates and related views.

We believe that a combination of state-of-the-art NLP techniques such as neural language models can help address this problem without resorting to manual or unsupervised techniques. A possible interesting research direction is zero-shot or one-shot learning as in Allaway and McKeown (2020), where a model with the help of large(-scale) language models learns to identify new debates and viewpoints not seen at training time. In our case, this would mean identifying new debates and new viewpoints without explicit training on these when training for our task. We elaborate on potentially useful NLP tasks to focus on for our problem in the following section.

4 Relevant NLP Tasks

Within the NLP, text mining, and recommender systems literature, there are several (related) tasks that deal with identifying viewpoints, perspectives, and arguments in written language. We define a task in NLP as a clearly defined problem such as "stance detection", with each task having connected methods, benchmark datasets, leaderboards and literature. The literature is currently fragmented in different related tasks and also definitions of viewpoint, argument or claim, and perspective. Researchers also use different datasets and content-types (tweets and microblogs, internet discussions on websites like debate.org, or news texts).

In this section we discuss NLP tasks that are related to viewpoint and argumentation diversity as defined in relation to the normative goal of a healthy deliberative democracy. Recall that a deliberative model assumes that participants of a democracy need access to a variety of (conflicting) viewpoints and lines of argumentation. As such, we focus on NLP tasks that help identify what claims, stances, and argumentation are present in news articles, and how specific items in the news are presented or framed.

An important distinction that needs to be made is the one between *stance* and *sentiment*: a negative sentiment does not necessarily mean a negative stance or viewpoint on an issue, and vice versa. An example would be someone who supports the use of mouth masks as COVID-19 regulation (positive stance), and expresses negative sentiment towards the topic by criticizing the shortage of mouth masks available for caregivers. In this paper, we concern ourselves with stance *on* issues (being in favor of masks) rather than with sentiment expressed *about* such issues (being negative about their shortage).

The remainder of this section is structured as follows. We first describe work on recommender systems that explicitly refers to detecting viewpoints. We then address three relatively established NLP tasks: argumentation mining, stance detection and polarization, frames & propaganda. We then briefly address work that refers to 'perspectives'.

4.1 Viewpoint Detection and Diversity

The recommender systems literature specifically uses the term 'viewpoint' in relation to diversifying recommendation. In these viewpoint-based papers, we notice a systems-focused tendency. Defining a viewpoint is less of a concern, nor is evaluating the viewpoint detection. Instead, researchers centralize viewpoint *presentation* to users, or how these respond to more diverse news, as in Lu et al. (2020) and Tintarev (2017). As a result, there is no standard definition of 'viewpoint' and the concept is operationalized differently by various authors.

Draws et al. (2020a) use topic models to extract and find viewpoints in news texts with an unsupervised method, with the explicit goal to diversify a news recommender. They explicitly connect different *sentiments* to different *viewpoints or perspectives*. For this study, they use clearly argumentative text on abortion from a debating website. The words 'viewpoint' and 'perspective' are used interchangeably in this study.

Carlebach et al. (2020) also address what they call "diverse viewpoint identification". Here as well, we see a wide range of definitions and terms related to viewpoints and perspectives (e.g. 'claim', 'hypothesis', 'entailment'). The authors use state-of-the-art methods including large neural language models, but the study does not seem to consider carefully defining their task, term definitions, and the needs of the problem. As such, it is unclear what they detect exactly. This is mainly due to the detection itself not being the main focus of their paper.

With the more NLP-based tasks and definitions in the following sections, we explore how NLP tasks relate to this 'viewpoints' idea from the recommender systems community, and see what ideas and techniques these other tasks can add to diversity in news recommendation.

4.2 Argument Mining

Argument Mining is the automatic extraction and analysis of specific units of argumentative text. It usually involves user-generated texts, such as comments, tweets, or blogposts. Such content is often highly argumentative by design, with high sentiment scores. In some studies, arguments are related to stances, as in the Dagstuhl ArgQuality Corpus (Wachsmuth et al., 2017), where 320 arguments cover 16 (political or societal) topics, and are balanced for different stances on the same topic. These arguments are from websites specifically aimed at debating.

Stab and Gurevych (2017) identify the different sub-tasks in argumentation mining, and use essays as the argumented texts in question. For instance, one sub-task is separating argumentative from non-argumentative text units. Then, their pipeline involves classifying argument components into claims and premises, and finally it involves identifying argument relations. This first sub-task is also sometimes called *claim detection*, and is related to detecting stances and viewpoints when connecting claims to issues.

For a deliberative democracy, the work on distinguishing argumentative from non-argumentative text in argument mining is useful, since our goal requires the highlighting of deliberations and arguments, and not statements on facts. Identifying this distinction might enable us to identify viewpoints in news texts. The precise identification of claims and premises may also prove valuable, because supporting a deliberative democracy requires the detection of different deliberations and arguments in news texts.

4.3 Stance Detection

Stance detection is the computational task of detecting "whether the author of the text is in favor of, against, or neutral towards a proposition or target" (Mohammad et al., 2017, p. 1). This task usually involves social media texts and, once again, user-generated content. Commonly, these are shorts texts such as tweets. For instance, Mohammad et al. (2017) provide a frequently used Twitter dataset that strongly connects stances with sentiment and/or emotional scores of the text. Another common trend in stance detection is to use text explicitly written in the context of an (online) debate, such as the website debate.org and social media discussions.

A recent study on Dutch social media comments highlights the difficulties in annotating stances on vaccination (Bauwelinck and Lefever, 2020). The authors identify the need to annotate topics, but also topic aspects and whether units are expressing an argument or not. Getting to good inter-annotator agreement (IAA) is difficult, showing that these concepts related to debate and stance are not uniform to all annotators even after extensive training. The same is found by Morante et al. (2020): Annotating Dutch social media text as well as other debate text on the vaccination debate, they find obtaining a high IAA is no easy task.

Other work related to stance detection is more related to the news domain. The Fake News Classification Task (Hanselowski et al., 2018b) has a sub-task that concerns itself with predicting the stance of a news article towards the news headline. In their setup stances can be 'Unrelated', 'Discuss', 'Agree' or 'Disagree'. The Fake News Classification tasks also introduces *claim verification* as a sub-task. This task is also related to the claim detection task: in order to verify claims, one needs to detect them first.

Several papers specifically aim at stance detection in the news domain. Conforti et al. (2020) note that different types of news events, from wars to economic issues, might lead to stance classes that are not uniform across events. As a response, they decide to annotate stance on one specific type of news event: company acquisitions. The authors explicitly note here that textual entailment and sentiment analysis are different tasks from stance detection, but acknowledge that all these tasks are related. However, as stated before, in the news domain new topics or issues occur constantly. Data on only one type of news event is less representative of all texts in the news domain. Some recent work aims to address this through one-shot or zero-shot learning for detecting issues and viewpoints on issues (Allaway and McKeown, 2020). In such an approach, unseen topics or viewpoints would be detected even when they are very different from what is annotated or seen at training time.

Based on the above, there are three challenges involved in applying previous approaches on stance detection for diversifying news: First, most work on stance detection aims at short, high-sentiment user-generated texts with one specific stance. News articles are more complex. News texts might highlight a debate with several viewpoints of different people, with the emphasis on one rather than the other. Secondly, the authors of news articles generally do not express opinions explicitly, unlike authors of tweets or blogs. News articles can express viewpoints in more subtle ways, in the way a story is told or framed. Additionally, training data that does come from the news domain may not generalize well to new topics.

We conclude that stance detection is, in principle, a relevant task when aiming to ensure news recommendation supports a deliberative democracy, but the challenges generalizing to new topics and dealing with more subtle ways of expressing viewpoints must be addressed. One shot learning may provide means to deal with new topics in the every-changing news landscape. The focus on longer, less explicitly argumentative text is helpful for our goal, and exists in for instance the first subtasks of fake news detection (Hanselowski et al., 2018a) and other recent news-focused datasets and papers (Conforti et al., 2020; Allaway and McKeown, 2020).

4.4 Polarization, Frames, and Propaganda

Some work already explicitly takes into account the more complex political dimension of news texts when defining an NLP task. This work is often interdisciplinary in nature, with NLP researchers working with political scientists or media scholars. The idea of (political) perspectives is prominent in these papers, though researchers in this subfield use different definitions and names for similar tasks.

'Frames', 'propaganda', and 'polarization' are loaded terms, with less nuance than terms such as 'stance' and 'argument'. Terms like 'polarization' are (ironically) more polarizing due to their political connotations. An explicitly political aspect in the task definition can be useful for our societal problem – as stated, the deliberative democracy goal is also inherently connected to political debates. However, it can also lead to a confusion of terminology or the use of (accidentally) loaded terminology, for instance terms that are controversial in related disciplines such as communication science or media studies.

An example is a recent shared task on Propaganda techniques (Da San Martino et al., 2019). It distinguishes 18 classes of what the authors call 'rhetorical strategies' that are not synonymous with, but related to, propaganda. These include 'whataboutism', 'bandwagon', and 'appeal to fear and prejudice', as well as 'Hitler-comparisons'. These terms are, incidentally, also known as cognitive biases (the bandwagon effect) or framing (appeal to fear) and argumentation flaws (Hitler-comparisons, on the internet known as Godwin's Law). Such confusion of terminology, especially in a politically sensitive context, makes it less straightforward to see how this task can be used for viewpoint diversification in support of a deliberative democracy.

Sometimes, the task of identifying different viewpoints on an issue or event in the news is translated to 'political bias'. In such work, the viewpoints are related to a certain ideology or political party (Roy and Goldwasser, 2020) or 'media frames'. However, we would argue that a viewpoint in the public debate does not have to be a political standpoint related to a specific political ideology. Limiting ourselves only to detecting debates and viewpoints explicitly related to political parties would also limit the view on public debate and deliberative democracy, and thus would not support our normative goal to its full extent.

Other NLP work that addresses the political nature of news texts and perspectives is Fokkens et al. (2018). In this work, stereotypes on Muslims are detected with a self-defined method known as 'micro-portrait extraction'. This paper is an example of work where other disciplines (communication and media experts) are heavily involved in task definition and execution, aiding clear and careful definitions and aiding to the problem and the societal complex issue (stereotypes in the news) at hand.

'Fake news' related tasks are also connected to the political content of news. The Fake News Classification Task (Hanselowski et al., 2018b) has the explicit goal to identify fake news. It consists of several sub-tasks related to argument mining and stance detection. The debate on (fake) news has recently shifted away from the simple label 'fake news', since it is not only the simple distinction between fake and true that is interesting. This again shows the importance of multi-disciplinary work: computational tasks are often aimed at a simple classification such as 'true' versus 'false', while social scientists and media experts call for different labels not directly related to the truth of an entire article or claim, such as 'false news', 'misleading news', 'junk news' (Burger et al., 2019), or 'clickbait'. All these are terms for a media diet with lower quality (or with less 'editorial values' to use the term from Lu et al. (2020)).

It can be useful for a deliberative democracy-supporting diverse news recommender when tasks already incorporate the political dimension of news texts. However, it can also be harmful when the political or social science definitions are not clear and uniform, or when the political dimension actually narrows what a deliberative democracy is by only considering explicitly political viewpoints, or only views tied to political parties or ideologies.

4.5 Perspectives

In NLP, definitions of 'perspective' range from 'a relation between the source of a statement (i.e. the author or another entity introduced in the text) and a target in that statement (i.e. an entity, event, or (micro-)proposition)' (Van Son et al., 2016) to stances to specific (political) claims in text (Roy and Goldwasser, 2020). These definitions are similar to those seen in the Stance Detection literature. Sometimes, it is unclear what the difference is between a stance and a perspective.

Common debate content used for analysis and task definition of perspectives is political elections (Van Son et al., 2016), vaccination (Morante et al., 2020), and also societally debated topics like abortion. Perspectives are especially useful for our goal, since they assume different groups in society are seeing one issue from different angles. This allows us to identify an active debate in society, which explicitly supports a deliberative democracy.

5 Discussion

In the previous section, we have outlined a number of relevant NLP tasks, and made their possible contribution to the support of a deliberative democracy through diverse news recommendation explicit. In the following section, we discuss the implications and considerations following from these separate tasks for diversity in news recommendations, and provide some advice for NLP researchers.

5.1 Evaluation

There has been a general push in NLP evaluation to go "beyond accuracy" (Ribeiro et al., 2020) and in recommender systems to go "beyond click accuracy" (Lu et al., 2020; Zhou et al., 2010) in evaluation and optimization. We believe that going beyond these evaluations might also mean looking at normative, societal goals and values, and the implications for the task and its effect on these goals and values. A possible advantage of a higher-level evaluation with a normative goal is that it allows the measurement of real-world impact. One explicit problem however is how to evaluate whether support of a deliberative democracy has been achieved.

Recent work by Vrijenhoek et al. (2021) has identified evaluation metrics to evaluate whether a recommender system supports specific models of democracy, one of which is the deliberative model. They propose a number of evaluation metrics for recommender system diversity that are explicitly connected to different models of democracy. These metrics could be used to evaluate different aspects of diversity related to a (deliberative) democracy. The aspects discussed are the representation of different groups in the news, whether alternative voices from minority groups are represented in the recommendations, whether the recommendations activate users to take action, and the degree of fragmentation between different users.

However, Vrijenhoek et al. (2021) does not address the evaluation of the NLP tasks involved. Where specific, clearly defined NLP tasks can generally be evaluated through hand-labelled evaluation sets, such sets do not provide the necessary insights to determine their role in supporting a deliberative democracy. In the end, we need to find a way to connect accuracy of NLP technologies to the overall increased diversity of news offers. Ideally, we would then also measure the ultimate impact on the users of a diverse recommender system diversifying viewpoints or stances with an NLP method. Such an evaluation is highly complex and clearly requires expertise from various fields (including technology, user studies and methods for investigating social behavior). It could for instance involve longitudinal studies on user knowledge of issues and viewpoints.

5.2 No NLP Task is An Island

We argue that NLP tasks have a clear role in the development of diverse recommender systems. Especially recent developments in the field, such as the use of pre-trained language models and neural models, could be used to obtain a reliable and useful representations of issues in the news, as well as viewpoints and perspectives on these issues. Such approaches are possibly more fine-grained and can be more reliable than the now commonly used unsupervised methods such as topic models.

Benchmarking with separate datasets, definitions, and shared tasks and challenges has brought our field far, and much progress has been achieved in this manner. However, we feel complex societal issues should be aimed at achieving a societal goal rather than evaluated on task-specific benchmarking dataset. When considering issues such as diversity in news recommendation and its effects on democracy and public debate, we are at the limit of what separate NLP tasks could bring us. We should dare to look past the limits of separate tasks, and attempt to oversee the over-arching normative goals and tasks related to such problems, especially when working on real-world impact.

As discussed in Section 4, the NLP field has many related tasks that seem to be relevant to the problem of news recommender diversity and especially the support of a deliberative democracy. However, we note that NLP tends to use their own definitions, and not consider other fields or even sub-fields, when designing these tasks. This means the field covers a wide array of different implementations and definitions related to perspectives and viewpoints in the news. We therefore urge NLP researchers to not only consider and evaluate their systems on their own definitions and tasks, but also consider the wider societal and normative goals their task connects to, and what other related tasks could be used to achieve the same or similar goals.

5.3 NLP and Other Disciplines

NLP, especially NLP working on societal real-world problems, should involve other fields, and expertise in other fields. This is especially true when working on complex problems like viewpoint diversity in news recommendation. This recommendation has also been made at the Dagstuhl perspectives workshop "Diversity, fairness, and data-driven personalization in (news) recommender systems" (Bernstein et al., 2020), but we would like to emphasize it more specifically for the NLP field.

One example where a lack of interdisciplinary seems to sometimes to lead to issues for our problem is in the Polarization, Frames, and Propaganda set of NLP tasks outlined in Section 4.4. Definitions used of 'frame', 'propaganda', and 'polarization' are sometimes seemingly made without consulting relevant experts, or without considering earlier theoretical work defining these terms. This leads to definitions that are easy to computationally measure with existing NLP techniques, such as classification. However, these definitions do not necessarily do justice to the complex problem the model or task is aimed at. Such work also does not consult earlier theoretical and empirical considerations of these terms and definitions.

We argue for the inclusion of experts from the social sciences and humanities in every step of the process – designing the tasks and definitions, evaluation of task success and usefulness, and tying the result to broader implications. For diversity in news recommenders, this means discussing and engaging with experts on political theory and philosophy, ethics of technology, and media studies and communication science (Bernstein et al., 2020).

5.4 Ethical and Normative Considerations

When our goal is to foster a healthy democratic debate, we should consider whether we should highlight or recommend content with fringe opinions that might be dangerous to individuals or the debate itself, e.g. the anti-vaxxing argument in the vaccination debate, conspiracy theories on the state of democracy, or inherently violent arguments. The deliberative model of democracy values rational and calm debate, not emotional or affective language. While this is a question of whether to *recommend* such views, not whether to *detect* them, we find it important to stress such considerations here. In a complex problem with a high-level normative goal, it is important to make such considerations explicit, as these also influence whether we are actually fostering a healthy deliberative debate. This means a simple computational solution, e.g. *maximize diversity of viewpoints and debates*, might not always be the best manner to reach the normative goal (e.g. *foster a healthy deliberative democracy*).

Such more nuanced and complex issues come to light when we consider public values such as diversity and the normative goal of a deliberative democracy. They are less explicit when only considering the NLP task as a separate task, which only needs to be evaluated by its performance on a benchmark dataset. However, questions such as these are especially important when considering that NLP and its technology is contributing to the solution of a societal problem. The attention to an over-arching normative goal helps NLP researchers to consider their responsibility and the implications of their work when it is used in real-world settings. This has been argued before by researchers in the NLP community (Fokkens et al., 2014; Bender et al., 2021), and we think it is a positive development when NLP researchers consider the wider ethical and normative considerations of their tasks and goals.

6 Conclusion

In this paper, we have provided an overview of several separate NLP tasks related to news recommender system diversity, especially considering the normative goal of a deliberative democracy. An explicit incorporation of such over-arching normative goals is currently missing in these tasks, while this is conceptually very useful and societally relevant. As such, taking this end goal into account can help improve social relevance of NLP and support NLP researchers in defining specific goals and next steps in their research.

Research on recommendation systems could benefit from more specific work that operationalizes the theoretical concepts in democratic theory. Such operationalizations should start with the groundwork laid by NLP tasks such as stance detection, argumentation mining and tasks aiming at detecting frames, propaganda and polarization. However, current NLP tasks do not address problems related to viewpoint diversity in news recommendation in its full complexity yet. NLP should take the complexities of news and the news recommendation domain into account. News texts often contain more than one stance or argument, and they tend to have more implicitly expressed viewpoints than other texts. Moreover, news comes with the challenge that new topics constantly appear and training data on detecting viewpoints in some issues may not generalize well to new data on other topics or issues.

This leads us to the following two concrete steps for future work, specifically in NLP: (1) researchers should further advance methods that aim to identify more subtle ways in which viewpoints occur in real-world news text; (2) methods should address the issue of constant changes in data, with one possible solution being one-shot learning. Last but not least, in order to find out how these tasks can truly be used to improve a deliberative democracy, we face the challenge of evaluating beyond assigning correct labels to pieces of text. This brings us back to the main message of this paper: Answering this question goes beyond the expertise of NLP researchers. In order to maximize the impact of our technologies for addressing this complex problem, we need expertise from other disciplines.

Acknowledgments

This research is funded through Open Competition Digitalization Humanities and Social Science grant nr 406.D1.19.073 awarded by the Netherlands Organization of Scientific Research (NWO). We would like to thank our interdisciplinary team members, and the anonymous reviewers whose comments helped improve the paper. All opinions and remaining errors are our own.

References

Emily Allaway and Kathleen McKeown. 2020. Zero-shot stance detection: A dataset and model using generalized topic representations. In *Proceedings of the 2020 Conference on Empirical Methods in Natural Language Processing (EMNLP)*, pages 8913–8931.

Nina Bauwelinck and Els Lefever. 2020. Annotating topics, stance, argumentativeness and claims in dutch social media comments: A pilot study. In *Proceedings of the 7th Workshop on Argument Mining*, pages 8–18.

Emily M Bender, Timnit Gebru, Angelina McMillan-Major, and Shmargaret Shmitchell. 2021. On the dangers of stochastic parrots: Can language models be too big. *Proceedings of FAccT*.

Abraham Bernstein, Claes De Vreese, Natali Helberger, Wolfgang Schulz, and Katharina A Zweig. 2020. Diversity, fairness, and data-driven personalization in (news) recommender system (dagstuhl perspectives workshop 19482).

Frederik J Zuiderveen Borgesius, Damian Trilling, Judith Moller, Balázs Bodó, Claes H De Vreese, and Natali Helberger. 2016. Should we worry about filter bubbles? *Internet Policy Review*, 5(1).

Andrei Boutyline and Robb Willer. 2017. The social structure of political echo chambers: Variation in ideological homophily in online networks. *Political psychology*, 38(3):551–569.

Engin Bozdag. 2013. Bias in algorithmic filtering and personalization. *Ethics and information technology*, 15(3):209–227.

Axel Bruns. 2019. *Are filter bubbles real?* John Wiley & Sons.

Peter Burger, Soeradj Kanhai, Alexander Pleijter, and Suzan Verberne. 2019. The reach of commercially motivated junk news on facebook. *PloS one*, 14(8):e0220446.

Mark Carlebach, Ria Cheruvu, Brandon Walker, Cesar Ilharco Magalhaes, and Sylvain Jaume. 2020. News aggregation with diverse viewpoint identification using neural embeddings and semantic understanding models. In *Proceedings of the 7th Workshop on Argument Mining*, pages 59–66.

Costanza Conforti, Jakob Berndt, Mohammad Taher Pilehvar, Chryssi Giannitsarou, Flavio Toxvaerd, and Nigel Collier. 2020. Stander: An expert-annotated dataset for news stance detection and evidence retrieval. In *Proceedings of the 2020 Conference on Empirical Methods in Natural Language Processing: Findings*, pages 4086–4101.

Giovanni Da San Martino, Alberto Barrón-Cedeño, and Preslav Nakov. 2019. Findings of the NLP4IF-2019 shared task on fine-grained propaganda detection. In *Proceedings of the Second Workshop on Natural Language Processing for Internet Freedom: Censorship, Disinformation, and Propaganda*, pages 162–170, Hong Kong. Association for Computational Linguistics.

Tim Draws, Jody Liu, and Nava Tintarev. 2020a. Helping users discover perspectives: Enhancing opinion mining with joint topic models. In *Proceedings of SENTIRE'20*.

Tim Draws, Nava Tintarev, Ujwal Gadiraju, Alessandro Bozzon, and Benjamin Timmermans. 2020b. Assessing viewpoint diversity in search results using ranking fairness metrics. In *Informal Proceedings of the Bias and Fairness in AI Workshop at ECML-PKDD (BIAS 2020)*.

Sarah Eskens, Natali Helberger, and Judith Moeller. 2017. Challenged by news personalisation: five perspectives on the right to receive information. *Journal of Media Law*, 9(2):259–284.

Antske Fokkens, Serge ter Braake, Niels Ockeloen, Piek Vossen, Susan Legêne, and Guus Schreiber. 2014. Biographynet: Methodological issues when nlp supports historical research. In *Proceedings of the Ninth International Conference on Language Resources and Evaluation (LREC'14)*, pages 3728–3735.

Antske Fokkens, Nel Ruigrok, Camiel Beukeboom, Sarah Gagestein, and Wouter van Atteveldt. 2018. Studying muslim stereotyping through microportrait extraction. In *Proceedings of the Eleventh International Conference on Language Resources and Evaluation (LREC 2018)*.

Andreas Hanselowski, PVS Avinesh, Benjamin Schiller, Felix Caspelherr, Debanjan Chaudhuri, Christian M Meyer, and Iryna Gurevych. 2018a. A retrospective analysis of the fake news challenge stance-detection task. In *Proceedings of the 27th International Conference on Computational Linguistics*, pages 1859–1874.

Andreas Hanselowski, Avinesh PVS, Benjamin Schiller, Felix Caspelherr, Debanjan Chaudhuri, Christian M. Meyer, and Iryna Gurevych. 2018b. A retrospective analysis of the fake news challenge stance-detection task. In *Proceedings of the 27th International Conference on Computational Linguistics*, pages 1859–1874, Santa Fe, New Mexico, USA. Association for Computational Linguistics.

Natali Helberger. 2019. On the democratic role of news recommenders. *Digital Journalism*, 7(8):993–1012.

Tamanna Hossain, Robert L Logan IV, Arjuna Ugarte, Yoshitomo Matsubara, Sean Young, and Sameer Singh. 2020. Covidlies: Detecting covid-19 misinformation on social media. In *Proceedings of the 1st Workshop on NLP for COVID-19 (Part 2) at EMNLP 2020*.

Kathleen Hall Jamieson and Joseph N Cappella. 2008. *Echo chamber: Rush Limbaugh and the conservative media establishment*. Oxford University Press.

Marius Kaminskas and Derek Bridge. 2016. Diversity, serendipity, novelty, and coverage: a survey and empirical analysis of beyond-accuracy objectives in recommender systems. *ACM Transactions on Interactive Intelligent Systems (TiiS)*, 7(1):1–42.

Mozhgan Karimi, Dietmar Jannach, and Michael Jugovac. 2018. News recommender systems–survey and roads ahead. *Information Processing & Management*, 54(6):1203–1227.

Feng Lu, Anca Dumitrache, and David Graus. 2020. Beyond optimizing for clicks: Incorporating editorial values in news recommendation. In *Proceedings of the 28th ACM Conference on User Modeling, Adaptation and Personalization*, pages 145–153.

Bernard Manin. 1987. On legitimacy and political deliberation. *Political theory*, 15(3):338–368.

Saif M Mohammad, Parinaz Sobhani, and Svetlana Kiritchenko. 2017. Stance and sentiment in tweets. *ACM Transactions on Internet Technology (TOIT)*, 17(3):1–23.

Judith Möller, Damian Trilling, Natali Helberger, and Bram van Es. 2018. Do not blame it on the algorithm: an empirical assessment of multiple recommender systems and their impact on content diversity. *Information, Communication & Society*, 21(7):959–977.

Roser Morante, Chantal Van Son, Isa Maks, and Piek Vossen. 2020. Annotating perspectives on vaccination. In *Proceedings of The 12th Language Resources and Evaluation Conference*, pages 4964–4973.

Zizi Papacharissi. 2002. The virtual sphere: The internet as a public sphere. *New media & society*, 4(1):9–27.

Eli Pariser. 2011. *The filter bubble: What the Internet is hiding from you*. Penguin UK.

Marco Tulio Ribeiro, Tongshuang Wu, Carlos Guestrin, and Sameer Singh. 2020. Beyond accuracy: Behavioral testing of NLP models with CheckList. In *Proceedings of the 58th Annual Meeting of the Association for Computational Linguistics*, pages 4902–4912, Online. Association for Computational Linguistics.

Shamik Roy and Dan Goldwasser. 2020. Weakly supervised learning of nuanced frames for analyzing polarization in news media. *EMNLP Findings*.

Christian Stab and Iryna Gurevych. 2017. Parsing argumentation structures in persuasive essays. *Computational Linguistics*, 43(3):619–659.

Cass R Sunstein. 2018. *# Republic: Divided democracy in the age of social media*. Princeton University Press.

Nava Tintarev. 2017. Presenting diversity aware recommendations: Making challenging news acceptable. In *The FATREC Workshop on Responsible Recommendation*.

Chantal Van Son, Tommaso Caselli, Antske Fokkens, Isa Maks, Roser Morante, Lora Aroyo, and Piek Vossen. 2016. GRaSP: A multilayered annotation scheme for perspectives. In *Proceedings of the Tenth International Conference on Language Resources and Evaluation (LREC'16)*, pages 1177–1184.

Sanne Vrijenhoek, Mesut Kaya, Nadia Metoui, Judith Möller, Daan Odijk, and Natali Helberger. 2021. Recommenders with a mission: assessing diversity in news recommendations. In *SIGIR Conference on Human Information Interaction and Retrieval (CHIIR) Proceedings*.

Henning Wachsmuth, Nona Naderi, Yufang Hou, Yonatan Bilu, Vinodkumar Prabhakaran, Tim Alberdingk Thijm, Graeme Hirst, and Benno Stein. 2017. Computational argumentation quality assessment in natural language. In *Proceedings of the 15th Conference of the European Chapter of the Association for Computational Linguistics: Volume 1, Long Papers*, pages 176–187.

Sandra Wachter. 2020. Affinity profiling and discrimination by association in online behavioural advertising. *Berkeley Technology Law Journal*, 35(2).

Tao Zhou, Zoltán Kuscsik, Jian-Guo Liu, Matúš Medo, Joseph Rushton Wakeling, and Yi-Cheng Zhang. 2010. Solving the apparent diversity-accuracy dilemma of recommender systems. *Proceedings of the National Academy of Sciences*, 107(10):4511–4515.

TeMoTopic: Temporal Mosaic Visualization of Topic Distribution, Keywords, and Context

Shane Sheehan, Saturnino Luz
University of Edinburgh
United Kingdom
shane.sheehan@ed.ac.uk
s.luz@ed.ac.uk

Masood Masoodian
Aalto University
Finland
masood.masoodian@aalto.fi

Abstract

In this paper we present *TeMoTopic*, a visualization component for temporal exploration of topics in text corpora. *TeMoTopic* uses the temporal mosaic metaphor to present topics as a timeline of stacked bars along with related keywords for each topic. The visualization serves as an overview of the temporal distribution of topics, along with the keyword contents of the topics, which collectively support detail-on-demand interactions with the source text of the corpora. Through these interactions and the use of keyword highlighting, the content related to each topic and its change over time can be explored.

1 Introduction

Many text corpora, such as news articles, are temporal in nature, with the individual documents distributed across a span of time. As the size and availability of text corpora have continued to increase in recent years, effective analysis of the content of corpora has become challenging. Taking the temporal nature of most corpora into account when analysing the text makes it more difficult to describe the corpora and to interpret intuitively the results of analysis.

Topic modeling techniques, such as Latent Dirichlet Allocation (LDA) (Blei et al., 2003), have been used to automatically generate topic groups in text corpora. These topics can help in understanding the contents of a corpus by using keywords and topic association probabilities generated by the topic modelling technique. However, interpreting the results of the techniques is not always easy, and the results can seem counter-intuitive when looking only at the weighted keyword lists. Therefore, visualization techniques have been used extensively to help with the interpretation of the large number of topics generated by these models. The same is true of temporal topic modeling techniques, such as Dynamic Topic Modeling (Blei and Lafferty, 2006), which require additional visualization techniques to aid intuitive understanding of the temporal segmentation of the topics and their related keywords.

In this paper, we propose *TeMoTopic* as a contribution to the collection of visualization techniques for exploring the temporal distribution of topics in text corpora through the use of temporal mosaics. *TeMoTopic* adopts a space-filling approach to show topic distribution over time, and presents keywords related to each topic at the overview level of the visualization. The visualization is interactive and, in contrast to many other techniques, enables direct investigation of the source documents associated with individual topics and keywords. This allows the user to get a general sense of the meaning of a topic through its associated keywords, as well as providing the ability to dive into the details of the related documents.

2 Related Work

2.1 Temporal Topic Visualization

Topic visualization systems are an active research area, with a variety of approaches for visualizing different aspects of topic model outputs, topic hierarchies, and topic evolution. In this paper, we only focus on related work in the area of temporal topic evolution and topic visualization of text corpora. While some methods address the temporal structuring of topics in short texts in the context of meetings and dialogues (Luz and Masoodian, 2005; Sheehan et al., 2019), in recent years, visualization of temporal topic evolution for larger text collections has been based on flow diagrams. An early example of such an approach is *ThemeRiver* (Havre et al., 2002), with later additions such as *TextFlow* (Cui et al., 2011), *TopicFlow* (Malik et al., 2013), *ThemeDelta* (Gad et al., 2015) and *RoseRiver* (Cui et al., 2014).

While *TeMoTopic* and flow-based temporal topic visualizations are similar, we expect they could

Proceedings of the EACL Hackashop on News Media Content Analysis and Automated Report Generation, pages 56–61
April 19, 2021

Task	Description
Visualize Topics	Visualize topic in terms of extracted keywords
Overview of Document - Topic Relations	View documents related to a topic
Remove Topics from the visualization	Topic removal from overview
Filtering Documents	View a subset of documents for a topic
Perform Set Operations	Enable exclusion/inclusion of documents in the corpus
Show and Cluster Similar Topics	Enable identification of similar topics
Perform Cluster Operations	Enable grouping of similar topics
Annotating Topics	Allow for labelling of the topics
Visualize Topic Change	View topic distribution and keywords over time

Table 1: Visualization tasks for topic model exploration.

form complementary components used in model assessment tools that are used to evaluate model quality. Flow diagrams are, for instance, useful for getting a high-level overview of many topics across long spans of text. *TeMoTopic*, on the other hand, aims to provide support for detailed viewing of a subset of topics and shorter timeslices, which are not possible in a flow diagram. As such, we envisage that other existing visualization tools which include a flow diagram component – such as *LDA-Explore* (Ganesan et al., 2015), *VISTopic* (Yang et al., 2017), *ParallelTopics* (Dou et al., 2011) and *TIARA* (Wei et al., 2010) – could be further expanded to include a temporal mosaic visualization, in the style of *TeMoTopic*. The largest benefit to this integration would come from enabling intuitive interactive filtering of the source documents based on the temporal topic and keyword distribution.

2.2 Topic Visualization Tasks

The design of a visualization tool should clearly be motivated by concrete tasks relevant to the end-users of the intended tool. Munzner's *nested model for visualization design and validation* (Munzner, 2009) describes steps that can be taken to mitigate threats to the validity of a visualization design. The first of the four levels of this design model is the characterization of domain specific tasks which should be supported by the visual encoding.

Ganesan et al. (2015) identify key tasks, in the design description of *LDAExplore*, which should be supported by visualizations that aim to help users explore the results of Latent Dirichlet Allocation (LDA). Since LDA is one of the most commonly used topic modelling techniques for text corpora, these key tasks could be generalized to other techniques where a corpus is also split into topics, and keywords associated with those topics are extracted.

In addition, Ganesan et al. (2015) argue that the results of LDA can be counter-intuitive, and that the ability to explore and interact with the document set should make the topic and word distributions more intuitive and insightful. Table 1 shows the eight tasks identified by Ganesan et al. (2015), as well as one additional task which we consider to be important for visualizing temporal topics. The table also includes a brief description of the tasks which are fully described by Ganesan et al. (2015).

Theses tasks describe a need for topic overview with document detail available on-demand, this follows the well-known visual information seeking mantra proposed by Shneiderman (1996). Interactions around viewing, filtering, removing, and combining topics and documents should also be supported. Finally, we include an additional task for visualizing topic changes over time. This modifies the *Visualize Topics* task, such that the change in distribution and keywords across is available to explore.

3 TeMoTopic: Temporal Mosaic Topic visualization

Figure 1 shows the *TeMoTopic* visualization tool. It consists of two juxtaposed views (Javed and Elmqvist, 2012): the temporal mosaic (left), and the document view (right). The design of the temporal mosaic is based on a visualization proposed by Luz and Masoodian (2007), and further expanded in our previous temporal mosaic visualizations *TeMoCo* visualization (Sheehan et al., 2019) and *TeMoCo-Doc* visualization (Sheehan et al., 2020), which have been used to link transcripts of meetings to document reports in a medical context.

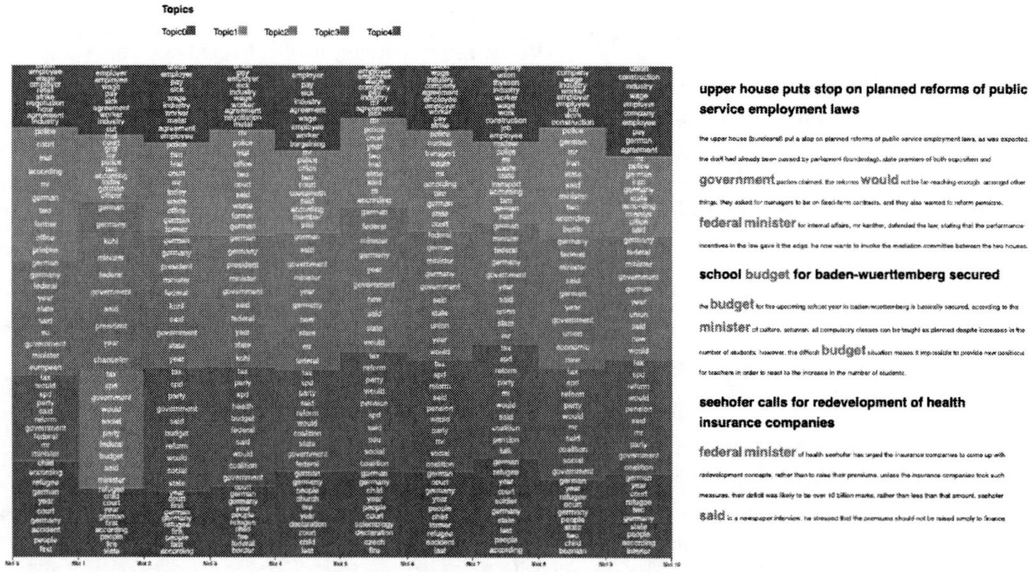

Figure 1: *TeMoTopic* visualization, showing the temporal mosaic view (left) and the document view (right), showing the selected keywords for the red topic in the second timeslice (red tile on the bottom left).

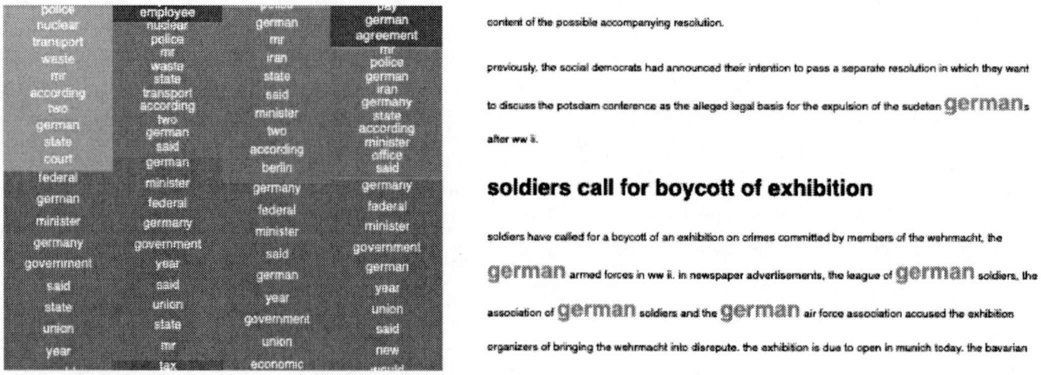

Figure 2: *TeMoTopic* visualization, showing the temporal mosaic view (left) and the filtered document view (right), with the word "german" selected from a temporal topic timeslice (orange tile on the top left).

3.1 Prototype

The temporal mosaic encoding was designed using Mackinlay's ranking (Mackinlay, 1986) of visual variables (Bertin, 1983), such that the visualization uses a perceptually efficient static encoding of the key data attributes. Horizontal position is used to emphasize the temporal order of the topics, and topic distribution per timeslice is encoded using vertical length. Each tile in the mosaic represents a single combination of topic and timeslice. The height of each tile represents its topic weight in that timeslice.

The top ten keywords which describe the associated temporal topic are placed within the tile, and can be scaled to encode the keyword topic probability, using area in a manner similar to keyword scaling in text visualizations such as word clouds (Viegas et al., 2009). Although the keywords are currently presented in order of descending topic probability, in future work alternative keyword presentation styles such as alphabetized lists and word clouds will be compared in terms of their effectiveness for comparison between the tiles. The categorical topics are encoded using color, allowing topics weights and keyword changes to be examined across the span of timeslices.

The mosaic visualization provides an overview of the topic distribution and associated keywords over time. However, as the number of topics and

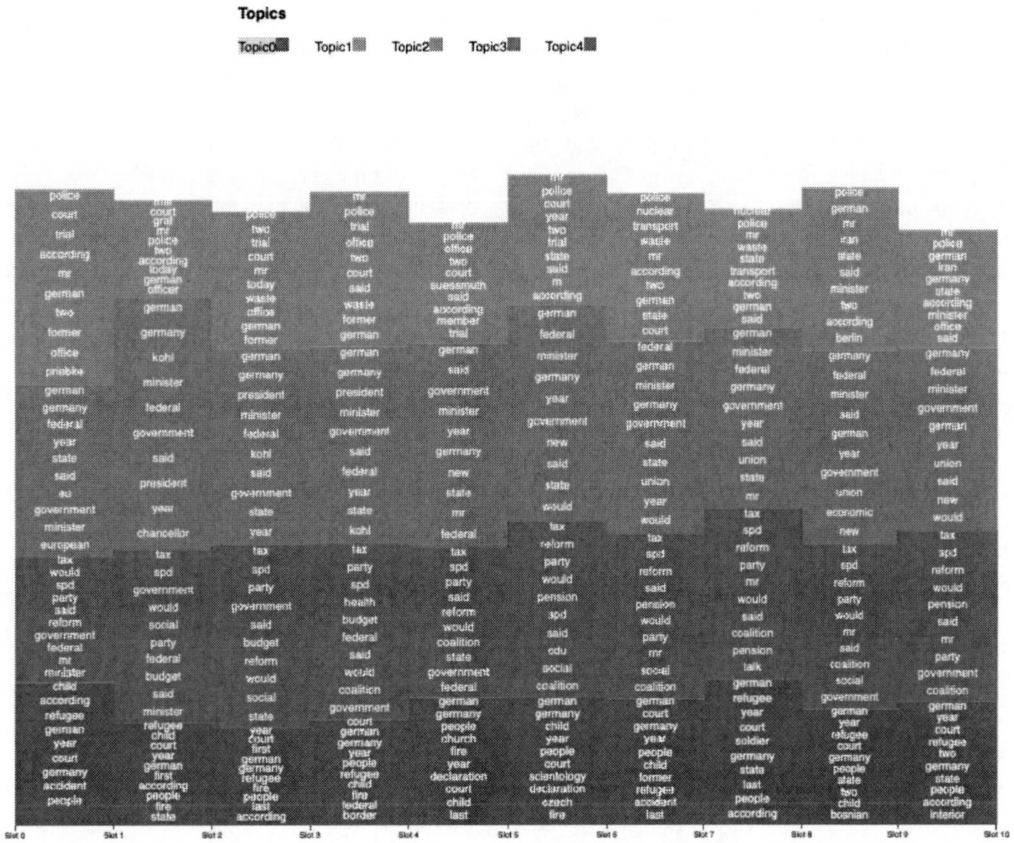

Figure 3: *TeMoTopic* filtered temporal mosaic view after the blue topic was selected for removal via clicking on the legend.

timeslices increase, if the visualization area is kept at a fixed size, the overview would become more abstract, cluttered, and difficult to examine for individual tiles and keywords. To maintain readability, the visualization can extend both horizontally and vertically to accommodate more topics and timeslices. The user can pan and zoom to get the detailed views of topics and keywords, or a higher-level view of the entire temporal topic space. The removal interaction is particularly useful when the number of topics is large, since filtering out topics that are not relevant to the current analysis allows for more of the detail to be presented on a single screen.

The temporal mosaic, as currently described, addresses two of the tasks from Table 1, namely *Visualize Topics* and *Visualize Topic Change*. To facilitate *Overview of Document - Topic Relations*, the document view (Figure 1, right) was created and linked, via click interactions, to the temporal mosaic (Figure 1, left). The document view is used to display the documents associated with a temporal topic tile. When a coloured tile is selected in the temporal mosaic, the related articles are presented in a scroll box and, the keywords from the topic tile are highlighted in the text. If keyword weights (or probabilities) are provided, the highlighted words are scaled accordingly. This dual combination of views and described interactions, support the user in investigating the meaning of a topic, and by investigating the differences between the topic timeslices, temporal document similarities and differences can be revealed.

Although it is useful to view the entirety of a topic, *Filtering Documents* is a task that was also identified as important to facilitate. One simple and intuitive way to do this with the temporal mosaic is by clicking on individual keywords rather than on the entire topic tile. This will cause the document view to display only documents from the related topic timeslice which contain the selected keywords, as shown in Figure 2. Selection from multiple topics is also possible, and the keywords are highlighted in the related topic colour to differentiate between topics.

The final interaction supported by this version of *TeMoTopic* is the removal of topics from the temporal mosaic. To do this, a topic can be selected from the legend shown above the temporal mosaic (Figure 3, top). Alternatively right-clicking on a topic removes all the other topics except the selected one. In the example shown in Figure 3, the blue topic has been removed from the temporal mosaic. When topics are removed, the temporal mosaic no longer fills the entire vertical space of the visualization. This interaction is useful when dealing with a large number of topics of which only a few are of interest for the analysis.

3.2 Implementation

The visualization tool[1] is implemented as a single-page web application using the *D3.js* framework (Bostock et al., 2011) . It takes two JavaScript Object Notation (JSON) files as input: the first file contains topic, keyword, timeslice, weights, and associated filenames, and the second input file is simply a JSON structure containing the documents with filename used as the retrieval key. Sample Python scripts are provided for generating topics and keywords on the sample dataset and for preparing the visualization input files from the model output.

The current version of *TeMoTopic* was designed to be model agnostic, and can even be used for tasks unrelated to topic model exploration. For example, metadata attributes such as the source of the news articles or their author could be used in place of topics. Keywords could be extracted using any available technique, including simple frequency lists. The visualization could also be used for corpus comparison and even cross-lingual analysis using entire corpora as replacements for the topics.

However, in our implementation we make use of dynamic topic modelling (Blei and Lafferty, 2006) to identify temporal topics and keywords in a subset of the *de-news*[2] corpus of German-English parallel news. The dataset consists of transcribed German radio broadcasts which were manually translated into English. Between 1996 and 2000 volunteers selected and transcribed five to ten of these news broadcasts per day and added them to the dataset. In the examples of *TeMoTopic*, shown in Figures 2, 1 and 3, we selected a ten month span of the dataset and presented the four largest topics. The choice of time span and topic number was only for presentation and to exemplify the interface features. We did not attempt to choose a time period or number of topics based on prior knowledge of the news relevant at the time in Germany. We present our examples to describe the interface and interactions, rather than as an analysis of the dataset, and we choose to draw no conclusions about the dataset contents and topics.

4 Conclusions

While many other temporal visualization techniques, such as ThemeRiver (Havre et al., 2002), offer some of the functionality for temporal visualization of topics or visualization of content changes, they do not feature implicit linking between the visualization and the underlying content documents. We consider this to be the main contribution of *TeMoTopic* visualization and its distinguishing feature with regards to the state of the art. As such, determining the necessity and validity of this approach in the identified domain is an important step before further development of the visualization prototype. Future work will, therefore, include evaluating the usability of a future iteration of the system with domain experts in both news analysis and topic modelling.

Acknowledgments

The work of the first and second authors is supported by European Union's Horizon 2020 research and innovation programme under grant agreement No 825153, project EMBEDDIA (Cross-Lingual Embeddings for Less-Represented Languages in European News Media). The results of this paper reflects only the authors' view and the Commission is not responsible for any use that may be made of the information it contains.

References

Jacques Bertin. 1983. *Semiology of Graphics*. University of Wisconsin Press.

David M Blei and John D Lafferty. 2006. Dynamic topic models. In *Proceedings of the 23rd international conference on Machine learning*, pages 113–120.

[1]The software and working example are available at `https://github.com/sfermoy/TeMoCo`.

[2]`http://homepages.inf.ed.ac.uk/pkoehn/publications/de-news/`

David M. Blei, Andrew Y. Ng, and Michael I. Jordan. 2003. Latent dirichlet allocation. *J. Mach. Learn. Res.*, 3(null):993–1022.

Michael Bostock, Vadim Ogievetsky, and Jeffrey Heer. 2011. D3 data-driven documents. *IEEE Transactions on Visualization and Computer Graphics*, 17(12):2301–2309.

W. Cui, S. Liu, L. Tan, C. Shi, Y. Song, Z. Gao, H. Qu, and X. Tong. 2011. Textflow: Towards better understanding of evolving topics in text. *IEEE Transactions on Visualization and Computer Graphics*, 17(12):2412–2421.

W. Cui, S. Liu, Z. Wu, and H. Wei. 2014. How hierarchical topics evolve in large text corpora. *IEEE Transactions on Visualization and Computer Graphics*, 20(12):2281–2290.

Wenwen Dou, Xiaoyu Wang, Remco Chang, and William Ribarsky. 2011. Paralleltopics: A probabilistic approach to exploring document collections. In *2011 IEEE conference on visual analytics science and technology (VAST)*, pages 231–240. IEEE.

Samah Gad, Waqas Javed, Sohaib Ghani, Niklas Elmqvist, Tom Ewing, Keith N Hampton, and Naren Ramakrishnan. 2015. Themedelta: Dynamic segmentations over temporal topic models. *IEEE transactions on visualization and computer graphics*, 21(5):672–685.

Ashwinkumar Ganesan, Kiante Brantley, Shimei Pan, and Jian Chen. 2015. Ldaexplore: Visualizing topic models generated using latent dirichlet allocation. *arXiv preprint arXiv:1507.06593*.

S. Havre, E. Hetzler, P. Whitney, and L. Nowell. 2002. Themeriver: visualizing thematic changes in large document collections. *IEEE Transactions on Visualization and Computer Graphics*, 8(1):9–20.

Waqas Javed and Niklas Elmqvist. 2012. Exploring the design space of composite visualization. In *Pacific Visualization Symposium (PacificVis), 2012 IEEE*, pages 1–8.

Saturnino Luz and Masood Masoodian. 2005. A model for meeting content storage and retrieval. In *Proceedings of the 11th International Multimedia Modelling Conference*, MMM '05, pages 392–398.

Saturnino Luz and Masood Masoodian. 2007. Visualisation of parallel data streams with temporal mosaics. In *Proceedings of the 11th International Conference Information Visualization*, IV '07, pages 197–202.

Jock Mackinlay. 1986. Automating the design of graphical presentations of relational information. *ACM Transactions on Graphics*, 5(2):110–141.

Sana Malik, Alison Smith, Timothy Hawes, Panagis Papadatos, Jianyu Li, Cody Dunne, and Ben Shneiderman. 2013. Topicflow: Visualizing topic alignment of twitter data over time. In *Proceedings of the 2013 IEEE/ACM international conference on advances in social networks analysis and mining*, pages 720–726.

T. Munzner. 2009. A nested model for visualization design and validation. *IEEE Transactions on Visualization and Computer Graphics*, 15(6):921–928.

Shane Sheehan, Pierre Albert, Masood Masoodian, and Saturnino Luz. 2019. Temoco: A visualization tool for temporal analysis of multi-party dialogues in clinical settings. In *2019 IEEE 32nd International Symposium on Computer-Based Medical Systems (CBMS)*, pages 690–695. IEEE.

Shane Sheehan, Saturnino Luz, Pierre Albert, and Masood Masoodian. 2020. Temoco-doc: A visualization for supporting temporal and contextual analysis of dialogues and associated documents. In *Proceedings of the International Conference on Advanced Visual Interfaces*, AVI '20, New York, NY, USA. Association for Computing Machinery.

Ben Shneiderman. 1996. The eyes have it: a task by data type taxonomy for information visualizations. In *Proceedings the IEEE Symposium on Visual Languages*, pages 336–343.

Fernanda B. Viegas, Martin Wattenberg, and Jonathan Feinberg. 2009. Participatory visualization with wordle. *IEEE Transactions on Visualization and Computer Graphics*, 15(6):1137–1144.

Furu Wei, Shixia Liu, Yangqiu Song, Shimei Pan, Michelle X Zhou, Weihong Qian, Lei Shi, Li Tan, and Qiang Zhang. 2010. Tiara: a visual exploratory text analytic system. In *Proceedings of the 16th ACM SIGKDD international conference on Knowledge discovery and data mining*, pages 153–162.

Yi Yang, Quanming Yao, and Huamin Qu. 2017. Vistopic: A visual analytics system for making sense of large document collections using hierarchical topic modeling. *Visual Informatics*, 1(1):40–47.

Using contextual and cross-lingual word embeddings to improve variety in template-based NLG for automated journalism

Miia Rämö
University of Helsinki
Department of Computer Science
miia.ramo@helsinki.fi

Leo Leppänen
University of Helsinki
Department of Computer Science
leo.leppanen@helsinki.fi

Abstract

In this work, we describe our efforts in improving the variety of language generated from a rule-based NLG system for automated journalism. We present two approaches: one based on inserting completely new words into sentences generated from templates, and another based on replacing words with synonyms. Our initial results from a human evaluation conducted in English indicate that these approaches successfully improve the variety of the language without significantly modifying sentence meaning. We also present variations of the methods applicable to low-resource languages, simulated here using Finnish, where cross-lingual aligned embeddings are harnessed to make use of linguistic resources in a high-resource language. A human evaluation indicates that while proposed methods show potential in the low-resource case, additional work is needed to improve their performance.

1 Introduction

The use of automation to help journalists in news production is of great interest to many newsrooms across the world (Fanta, 2017; Sirén-Heikel et al., 2019). *Natural Language Generation* (NLG) methods have previously been employed, for example, to produce soccer reports (Chen and Mooney, 2008), financial reports (Plachouras et al., 2016) and weather forecasts (Goldberg et al., 1994). Such 'automated journalism' (Carlson, 2015; Graefe, 2016) or 'news automation' (Sirén-Heikel et al., 2019) imposes restrictions on system aspects such as transparency, accuracy, modifiability, transferability and output's fluency (Leppänen et al., 2017). Likely as a consequence of these requirements, news industry applications of NLG have traditionally employed the 'classical' rule-based approaches to NLG, rather than the more recent neural methods increasingly seen in recent academic literature (Sirén-Heikel et al., 2019). A major downside of these rule-based systems, however, is that their output often lacks variety. Adding variety by increasing the amount of templates is possible, but this would significantly increase the cost of system creation and limits reuse potential. As users of automated journalism already find the difficulty of reuse limiting (Linden, 2017), this is not a sustainable solution.

In this paper, we extend a modular rule-based NLG system – used for automated journalism in the domain of statistical news – with a dedicated component for varying the produced language in a controlled manner. The proposed extension enables two methods of inducing further variation: in *insertion*, new words are introduced into the generated text, whereas in *replacement* certain words in the original sentence are replaced with synonyms. To accomplish these tasks, we employ a combination of traditional language resources (e.g. synonym dictionaries) as well as recent neural processing models (i.e. word embeddings). These resources complement each other, enabling us to harness the power of statistical NLP tools while retaining control via the classical linguistic resources. We also experiment with using these methods in the context of a *low-resource* language which lacks linguistic resources such as synonym dictionaries. For this case, we propose to use cross-lingual aligned word embeddings to utilize a high-resource language's resources even within said low-resource language.

In the next section, we briefly describe some related previous works and further motivate our approach. Section 3 describes our proposed variation induction methods for both the high-resource and the low-resource contexts. Sections 4 and 5, respectively, introduce our human evaluation method and the results obtained. Sections 6 provides some additional thoughts on these results, while Section 7 concludes the paper.

Proceedings of the EACL Hackashop on News Media Content Analysis and Automated Report Generation, pages 62–70
April 19, 2021 © Association for Computational Linguistics

2 Background

Natural language generation has been associated with news production from the early years of the field, with some of the earliest industry applications of the NLG methods being in the domain of weather report production (Goldberg et al., 1994). Interest in applying NLG to news production has only increased since, with many media houses experimenting with the technology (Fanta, 2017; Sirén-Heikel et al., 2019). Still, adoption of automated journalism methods has been slow. According to news media insiders, rule-based, classical, NLG system such as those described by Reiter and Dale (2000), are costly to create and difficult to reuse (Linden, 2017). At the same time, even the most recent neural (end-to-end) approaches to NLG are not fit for customer needs as they limit the ability to "customise, configure, and control the content and terminology" (Reiter, 2019). Another major problem is the fact they suffer from a form of overfitting known as 'hallucination', where ungrounded output text is produced. This is catastrophic in automated journalism.

Concurrently with works on improved neural NLG methods, others have investigated increasingly modular rule-based approaches with the intent of addressing the reusability problem described by Linden (2017). For example, Leppänen et al. (2017) describe a modular rule-based system for automated journalism that seeks to separate text domain specific processing from language specific processing to allow for easier transfer of the system to new text domains. While such rule-based approaches produce output that is grammatically and factually correct (Gatt and Krahmer, 2017), they often suffer from a lack of variety in language. This is especially true for systems that are based on some type of *templates*, or fragmentary language resources that are combined to form larger segments of text and into which content dependent on system input is embedded. Using such templates (or hand-crafted grammars) is costly, especially when a large number is required for varied output.

As template (or grammar) production can be costly, automated variation induction methods that could be integrated into rule-based systems are very interesting. One trivial approach to inducing variation would be to employ a synonym dictionary, such as is available in WordNet (Miller, 1995), to replace words within the generated text with their synonyms. This approach, however, suffers from some major problems. First, simply looking up all synonyms for all meanings of a token is not feasible due to polysemy and homonymy. At the same time, incorporating knowledge of which semantic meaning of a token is correct in each case significantly slows down template and grammar generation. Furthermore, even within a certain semantic meaning, the various (near) synonyms might not be equally suitable for a given context. Finally, such linguistic resources are not available for many low-resource languages.

An alternative approach, more suited to generation within medium and low-resource languages where there are no available synonym dictionaries, but large text corpora can be collected, would be to use word embeddings (E.g. Rumelhart et al., 1986; Bengio et al., 2003; Mikolov et al., 2013) to identify words that are semantically close to the words in the template. This approach, however, suffers from the fact that both synonyms and antonyms of a word reside close to it in the word embedding space. While potential solutions have been proposed (E.g. Nguyen et al., 2016), they are not foolproof.

3 Variety Induction Algorithms

As described above, naïve methods based on either classical linguistic resources or word embeddings alone are not suitable for variation induction. To this end, we are interested in identifying a simple variety induction method that combines the positive sides of both the classical linguistic resources (such as synonym dictionaries) with those of statistical resources such as word embeddings. Optimally, the method should also function for a wide variety of languages, including low-resource languages where costly resources such as comprehensive synonym dictionaries are not readily available.

In this work, we introduce variety into the generated language using two distinct methods: by introducing completely new words into sentences, and by replacing existing words. We will use the terms *insertion* and *replacement* to distinguish between the two approaches, respectively.

3.1 Introducing Variety with Insertion

In our insertion method, new words are introduced to sentences at locations where placeholder tokens are defined in templates. We use a combination of a part-of-speech (POS) tagger and a contextual language model to control the process. A simplified

Algorithm 1 Pseudocode describing the insertion approach. The parameters are a single sentence, a desired POS tag, some value of k, and finally min and max number of `[MASK]` tokens inserted. The approach is tailored for high-resource languages, such as English, and uses additional linguistic resources (here, a part of speech tagger) to conduct further filtering.

function HIGHRESOURCEINSERTION($Sentence, PoS, k, minMasked, maxMasked$)
  $WordsAndScores \leftarrow \emptyset$
  for $n \in [minMasked, maxMasked]$ **do**
    $MaskedSentence \leftarrow$ Sentence with n `[MASK]` tokens inserted
    $Words, Scores \leftarrow$ MASKEDLM.TOPKPREDICTIONS($MaskedSentence, k$)
    $WordsAndScores \leftarrow WordAndScores \cup \{(w, s) | w \in Words$ **and** $s \in Scores\}$
  end for
  return SAMPLE($\{w | (w, s) \in WordsAndScores,$ POSTAG$(w) = PoS, s >= Threshold\}$)
end function

Step 1: In Austria in 2018 75 year old or older females {*empty, pos=RB*} received median equivalised net income of 22234 €.

Step 2: In Austria in 2018 75 year old or older females *still* received median equivalised net income of 22234 €.

Figure 1: The general idea of sentence modification using the insertion method. Step 1 represents the intermediate step between a template and the final modified sentence presented in Step 2.

example of the general idea is shown in Figure 1.

During variety induction, a contextual language model with a masked language modeling head (In this case, FinEstBert by Ulčar and Robnik-Šikonja, 2020) is used to predict suitable content to replace the placeholder token. This is achieved by replacing the placeholder token with one or more `[MASK]` tokens in the sentence. Multiple `[MASK]` tokens are required where the language model uses subword tokens. The language model is then queried for the k most likely (subword) token sequences to replace the sequence of `[MASK]` tokens. This results in a selection of potential tokens ('proposals', each consisting of one or more subword tokens) to replace the original placeholder.

As an additional method for control, we associate the original placeholder token with a certain POS tag, and filter the generated proposals to those matching this POS tag. In addition, we use a threshold likelihood value so that each proposal has to reach a minimal language model score. This is required for cases wherein a certain length sequence of mask tokens results in no believable proposals in the top-k selection. Finally, we sample one of the filtered proposals and replace the original placeholder token with it. In cases where there are no suitable proposals, the placeholder value is simply removed. This method is described in pseudocode in Algorithm 1.

Naturally, this approach is dependent on the availability of two linguistic resources: the contextual word embeddings and a POS tagging model. While word embeddings/language models are relatively easily trainable as long as there are any available text corpora, high-quality POS tagging models are less common outside of the most widely spoken languages. To extend this approach to such low-resource languages that have available corpora for training language models such as BERT, but lack POS tagging models, cross-lingual aligned word embeddings can be utilized.

Once a low-resource language proposal has been obtained using the method described above, an aligned cross-lingual word embeddings model – in our case, FastText embeddings (Bojanowski et al., 2016) aligned using VecMap (Artetxe et al., 2018) – between the low-resource language and some high-resource language (e.g. English) can be used to obtain the closest high-resource language token in the aligned embedding space. The retrieved high-reasource language token is, in theory, the closest semantic high-resource language equivalent to the low-resource token. We then apply a POS tagging model *for the high-resource language* to the high-resource 'translation', and use that POS tag as the low-resource token's POS tag for the purposes of filtering the proposals. This approach is described as pseudocode in Algorithm 2.

Algorithm 2 Pseudocode describing how the language resources, here a POS tagger, are utilized for a low-resource language with cross-lingual word embeddings. In other words, when working with a low-resource language, insertion is done as in Algorithm 1, but the POS tagging phase utilises this algorithm. The FINDVECTOR method finds the word embedding vector for the low resource word, and the CLOSESTWORD method is then used for finding the closest match for that vector from the aligned high-resource language embedding space. The algorithm parameters are the low-resource original word to be replaced, and the pairwise aligned low- and high-resource word embeddings.

```
function POSTAGLOWRESOURCELANGUAGE(LowResWord, LowResEmbeddings, HighResEmbeddings)
    LowResVector ← FINDVECTOR(LowResWord, LowResEmbeddings)
    HighResWord ← CLOSESTWORD(LowResVector, HighResEmbeddings)
    LowResTagged ← (LowResWord, POSTAG(HighResWord))
    return LowResTagged
end function
```

Step 1: In Finland in 2016 households' total {*expenditure, replace=True*} on healthcare was 20.35 %.

Step 2: In Finland in 2016 households' total *spending* on healthcare was 20.35 %.

Figure 2: The general idea of sentence modification using the replacement method. Step 1 represents the intermediate step between a template and the final modified sentence presented in Step 2.

3.2 Inducing Variety with Replacement

In addition to insertion of completely new words, variety can also be induced by replacing existing content, so that previously lexicalized words within the text are replaced by suitable alternatives. We propose to use a combination of a synonym dictionary and a contextual language model to do this in a controlled fashion. A simplified example of this approach is shown in Figure 2.

On a high level, we mark certain words within the template fragments used by our system as potential candidates for replacement. This provides us with further control, allowing us to limit the variety induction to relatively 'safe' words such as those not referring to values in the underlying data.

During variation induction, the synonym dictionary is first queried for synonyms of the marked word. To account for homonymy, polynymy, as well as the contextual fit of the proposed synonyms, we then use the contextual word embeddings (with a masked language model head) to score the proposed words. To score the word, it needs to be tokenized. In cases where the word is not part of BERT's fixed size vocabulary, it is tokenized as multiple subword tokens. To account for this we use the mean score of the (subword) tokens as the score of the complete word.

As above, a threshold is used to ensure that only candidates that are sufficiently good fits are retained in the pool of proposed replacements. The final word is sampled from the filtered pool of proposals. If the pool of proposed words is empty after filtering, the sentence is not modified. The original word is also explicitly retained in the proposals. This procedure is shown in Algorithm 3.

We emphasize that the use of the synonym dictionary is required to avoid predicting antonyms, as both antonyms and synonyms reside close to the original word in the word embedding space. While an antonym such as 'increase' for the verb 'decrease' would be a good replacement in terms of language modeling score, such antonymous replacement would change the sentence meaning tremendously and must be prevented.

The modification of the replacement approach for low-resource languages (where no synonym dictionary is available) is similar to that presented above for insertion: We conduct a round-trip via a high-resource language using the cross-lingual embeddings when retrieving synonyms. The low-resource language words are 'translated' to the high-resource language using the cross-lingual embeddings, after which synonyms for these translations are retrieved from the synonym dictionary available in the high-resource language. The synonyms are then 'translated' back to the low-resource language using the same cross-lingual embeddings. This approach is shown in Algorithm 4.

Algorithm 3 Pseudocode describing a method for replacement using a combination of a masked language model (based on contextual word embeddings) and a synonym dictionary, such as provided by WordNet. The parameters are the original word marked to be replaced in the input sentence ('expenditure' in Figure 2), and the input sentence for context.

```
function HIGHRESOURCEREPLACEMENT(OriginalWord, Sentence)
    WordsAndScores ← ∅
    Synonyms ← GETSYNONYMS(OriginalWord)
    for w ∈ Synonyms do
        CandidateSentence ← Sentence with w replacing the original word
        CandidateScore ← MASKEDLM.SCORE(CandidateSentence, w)
        WordsAndScores ← WordsAndScores ∪ (w, CandidateScore)
    end for
    return SAMPLE({w|(w, s) ∈ WordsAndScores, s >= Threshold})
end function
```

Algorithm 4 Pseudocode describing how synonyms are retrieved for a low-resource language by utilizing cross-lingual word embeddings. Low-resource variant of replacement is as Algorithm 3, but this algorithm is used to retrieve synonyms. The FINDVECTOR method finds the correct word embedding vector for the low resource word, and the CLOSESTWORD method is then used for finding the closest match for that vector from the aligned high-resource language embedding space. The algorithm parameters are the low-resource original word to be replaced, and the pairwise aligned low- and high-resource word embeddings.

```
function SYNONYMSFORLOWRESOURCELANGUAGE(LowResWord, LowResEmbeddings,
HighResEmbeddings)
    LowResVector ← FINDVECTOR(LowResWord, LowResEmbeddings)
    HighResWord ← CLOSESTWORD(LowResVector, HighResEmbeddings)
    HighResSynonyms ← GETSYNONYMS(HighResWord)
    LowResSynonyms ← ∅
    for w ∈ HighResSynonyms do
        HighResVector ← FINDVECTOR(w, HighResEmbeddings)
        LowResWord ← CLOSESTWORD(HighResVector, LowResEmbeddings)
        LowResSynonyms ← LowResSynonyms ∪ {LowResWord}
    end for
    return LowResSynonyms
end function
```

As we conduct our case study using Finnish as the (simulated) low-resource language, words need to be lemmatized before synonym lookup. We apply UralicNLP (Hämäläinen, 2019) to analyze and lemmatize the original word and reinflect the retrieved synonyms after lookup. A difficulty is presented by the fact that oftentimes, a specific token can have multiple plausible grammatical analyses and lemmas. In our approach, synonyms are retrieved for all of the plausible lemmas, and the algorithm regenerates all morphologies proposed by UralicNLP for all synonyms. While this results in some ungrammatical or contextually incorrect tokens, we rely on the language model to score these as unlikely.

4 Evaluation

We have implemented the above algorithms within a multi-lingual (Finnish and English) natural language generation system that conducts automated journalism from time-series data provided by Eurostat (the statistical office of the European Union). The system is derived from the template-based modular architecture presented by Leppänen et al. (2017). It produces text describing the most salient factors of the input data in several languages in a technically accurate manner using only a few templates, but the resulting language is very stiff, and the sentences are very alike. This makes the final report very repetitive and thus a good candidate for variety induction.

For all of the algorithms described, we utilise the same trilingual BERT model: FinEst BERT (Ulčar and Robnik-Šikonja, 2020). The FinEst BERT model is trained with monolingual corpora for English, Finnish and Estonian from a mixture of news articles and a general web crawl. In addition to the BERT model, the low-resource language variants of the algorithms utilize cross-lingual pairwise aligned word embeddings for word 'translations'. We use monolingual FastText (Bojanowski et al., 2016) word embeddings mapped with VecMap (Artetxe et al., 2018) to form the cross-lingual embeddings. POS tagging is done with NLTK (Bird et al., 2009) and the lexical database used as a synonym dictionary is WordNet (Miller, 1995).

A human evaluation of our methods was conducted following the best practices proposed by van der Lee et al. (2019). In the evaluation setting, judges were first presented with three statements about a sentence pair. Sentence 1 of the pair was an original sentence, generated by the NLG system without variation induction. Sentence 2 of the pair was the same sentence with a variation induction procedure applied. Cases where the sentence would remain unchanged, or where no insertion/replacement candidates were identified, were ruled out from the evaluation set. The part of the sentence to be modified was marked in the original sentence and the inserted/replaced word highlighted.

The judges were asked to evaluate the following statements on a Likert scale ranging from 1 ('Strongly Disagree') to 4 ('Neither Agree nor Disagree') to 7 ('Strongly Agree'):

Q1: Sentence 1 is a good quality sentence in the target language.

Q2: Sentence 2 is a good quality sentence in the target language.

Q3: Sentences 1 and 2 have essentially the same meaning.

In addition to the two sentences, the judges were presented with two groups of words to examine if using the scores by BERT would correctly distinguish suitable words from unsuitable words. Group 1 contained the words scored as acceptable by BERT while group 2 contained the words ruled out due to a low score. All words in both groups met the criteria of being synonyms (in the case of replacement) or being the correct POS (in the case of insertion). The judges were asked to evaluate the following questions on a 5-point Likert scale ranging from 1 ('None of the words') to 3 ('Half of the words') to 5 ('All of the words'):

Q4: How many of the words in word group 1 could be used in the marked place in sentence 1 so that the meaning remains essentially the same?

Q5: How many of the words in word group 2 could be used in the marked place in sentence 1 so that the meaning remains essentially the same?

For the high-resource language results, we gathered 3 judgements each for 100 sentence pairs. The judges were recruited from an online crowdsourcing platform and they received a monetary reward for participating in the study. The judge recruitment was restricted to countries where majority of people are native speakers of English. For the low-resource language results, 21 judges evaluated 20 sentence pairs. The judges were recruited via student mailing lists of University of Helsinki in Finland and were not compensated monetarily. All but one of the participants in the low-resource evaluation were native speakers of the target language. The final participant self-identified as having a 'working proficiency.'

5 Results

Table 1 presents our results in applying both the insertion and replacement methods to both a high-resource language (English) and a low-resource language (Finnish).

In the high-resource insertion case, the results indicate that inducing variation using the proposed method does not decrease output quality, as both the original sentences' qualities (Q1 mean 5.57) and modified sentences' qualities (Q2 mean 5.76) were similar. As the sentence meaning also remained largely unchanged (Q3 mean 5.54), we interpret this result as a success. The results for Q4 and Q5 indicate that our filtering method based on a threshold language model score can be improved: results for Q4 (mean 3.11 on a 5-point Likert scale) indicate that unsuitable words are left unfiltered, while Q5 (mean 3.03) indicates that some acceptable words are filtered out.

	Range	Statement	Insertion En	Insertion Fi	Replacement En	Replacement Fi
Q1	(1–7 ↑)	'Sentence 1 is a good quality sentence in the target language'	5.57 (1.46)	6.43 (0.88)	5.55 (1.46)	6.67 (0.66)
Q2	(1–7 ↑)	'Sentence 2 is a good quality sentence in the target language'	5.76 (1.41)	5.12 (1.36)	5.60 (1.40)	3.89 (1.43)
Q3	(1–7 ↑)	'Sentences 1 and 2 have essentially the same meaning'	5.54 (1.36)	4.34 (1.61)	5.65 (1.27)	3.39 (1.30)
Q4	(1–5 ↑)	'How many of the words in word group 1 could be used in the marked place in sentence 1 so that the meaning remains essentially the same?'	3.11 (1.49)	2.53 (0.82)	3.39 (1.31)	1.76 (0.78)
Q5	(1–5 ↓)	'How many of the words in word group 2 could be used in the marked place in sentence 1 so that the meaning remains essentially the same?'	3.03 (1.41)	1.46 (0.62)	3.21 (1.27)	1.62 (0.76)

Table 1: Evaluation results for the insertion and replacement approaches. English ('En') examples were generated using the high-resource variations, while the Finnish ('Fi') examples were generated using the low-resource variations. Arrows in the range column indicate whether higher (↑) or lower (↓) values indicate better performance. Values are the mean evaluation result and the standard deviation (in parentheses). In the context of the statements, sentence 1 is the original, unmodified sentence, while sentence 2 is a sentence with added variety.

In the low-resource case insertion, we observe some change in meaning (Q3 mean value 4.34) and a slight loss of quality, but even after variety induction the output quality is acceptable (Q1 mean 6.43 vs. Q2 mean 5.12). Interestingly, in the low-resource setting, we observe that the language model is slightly better at distinguishing between suitable and unsuitable candidates (Q4 and Q5 means 2.53 and 1.46, respectively) than in the high-resource case. We are, at this point, uncertain of the reason behind the difference in the ratios of Q4 and Q5 answers between the high-resource and the low-resource case. Notably, even this 'better' result is far from perfect.

We also conducted POS tag specific analyses for both the high-resource and the low-resource insertion cases. In the high-resource case, no major differences were observed between various POS tags. In the low-resource (Finnish) case, however, we observed that with some POS tags, such as adverbs, the results are similar to those observed with English. Low-resource results for adverbs only are shown in Figure 3. We emphasize that this is the best observed subresult and should be viewed as post-hoc analysis.

In the high-resource replacement case, we observe promising results. Inducing variation did not negatively affect sentence quality (Q1 mean 5.55 vs. Q2 mean 5.60) and concurrently retained meaning (Q3 mean 5.65). Results for Q4 and Q5 (means 3.39 and 3.21, respectively) indicate that, as above, the filtering method still has room for improvement, with poor quality options passing the filter and high-quality options being filtered out.

However, in the low-resource case replacement case, we observe a significant drop in sentence quality after variation induction (Q1 mean 6.67 vs Q2 mean 3.89), as well as significant change in sentence meaning (Q3 mean 3.39). While Q5 results are relatively good (mean 1.62), as in very few if any good candidate words are filtered out, Q4 results (mean 1.76) indicate some fundamental problem in the candidate generation process: as there are few if any good candidates in either group, it seems that most of the proposed words are unsuitable.

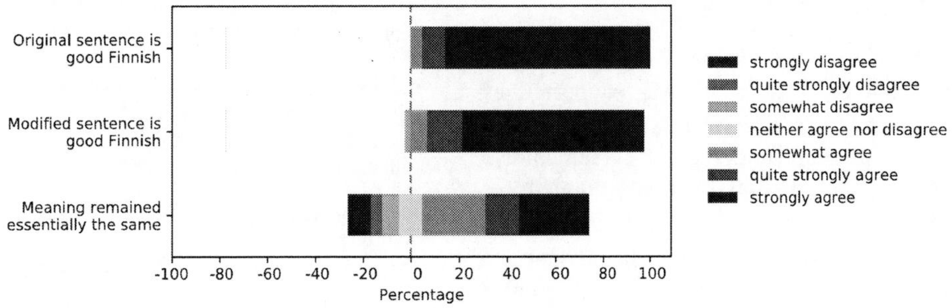

Figure 3: Quality of sentences with low-resource insertion in Finnish with English as the high-resource language, and preservation of sentence meaning. Results shown for adverbs only, representing the best observed performance across the various parts of speech generated. We emphasize that the graph shows only a subset of the complete results (See Table 1), identified as best-performing during post-hoc analysis.

6 Discussion

Our high-resource results indicate that the proposed approach is suitable for inducing some light variation into automatically generated language. The use of synonym dictionaries removes the need to manually construct variants into the templates used in the generation, while the use of language models allows for contextual scoring of the proposed variants so that higher quality results are selected.

We suspect that a major contributor to the low quality of the modified sentences in the low-resource scenarios was the complex morphology of the Finnish language. Especially in the case of Finnish, the process wherein the original word was grammatically analyzed and the replacement word reinflected into the same form would have likely resulted in cases where the resulting word is technically grammatically feasible in isolation, but not grammatical in the context of the rest of the sentence. Our post-hoc investigation also indicates that at least in some cases the resulting reinflected words were outright ungrammatical.

In addition, it seems that the language model employed did not successfully distinguish these failure cases from plausible cases, which led to significant amounts of ungrammatical words populating the proposed set of replacement words. Our post-hoc analysis further indicates that the methods led to better results when use of compound words was avoided in the Finnish templates. We hypothesize that applying the method to a morphologically less complex language might yield significantly better results.

At the same time, in the case of low-resource variation induction using insertion, our results indicate that some success could be found if the method is applied while restrained to certain pre-screened parts of speech, such as adverbs (See Figure 3). This further indicates that the performance of the replacement approach might be improved significantly if the morphology issues were corrected.

Notably, our analysis of the results did not include an in-depth error analysis to determine what parts of the relatively complex procedure fundamentally caused the errors, i.e. were the errors introduced during POS-tagging, language model based scoring, or some other stage. Furthermore, we did not rigorously analyze whether the generation errors were semantic or grammatical in nature.

As a final note, we emphasise that these results were evaluated on local (sentence) rather than on global (full news report) level. We anticipate that, for example, when inserting a word like 'still' in a sentence (see Figure 1), the results might differ when evaluating on a global level.

7 Conclusions

In this work, we proposed two approaches, with variations for both high-resource and low-resource languages, for increasing the variety of language in NLG system output in context of news, and presented empirical results obtained by human evaluation. The evaluation suggests that the high-resource variants of our approaches are promising: using them in the context of a case study did create variety, while preserving quality and meaning. The low-resource variants did not perform as well, but we show that there are some positive glimpses in these initial results, and suggest future improvements.

Acknowledgements

This article is based on the Master's thesis of the first author. The work was supported by the European Union's Horizon 2020 research and innovation program under grant agreement No 825153, project EMBEDDIA (Cross-Lingual Embeddings for Less-Represented Languages in European News Media). We thank Matej Ulčar and Marko Robnik-Šikonja for the VecMap alignment of the FastText embeddings.

References

Mikel Artetxe, Gorka Labaka, and Eneko Agirre. 2018. Generalizing and improving bilingual word embedding mappings with a multi-step framework of linear transformations. In *Thirty-Second AAAI Conference on Artificial Intelligence*.

Yoshua Bengio, Réjean Ducharme, Pascal Vincent, and Christian Janvin. 2003. A neural probabilistic language model. *The journal of machine learning research*, 3:1137–1155.

Steven Bird, Ewan Klein, and Edward Loper. 2009. *Natural Language Processing with Python*, 1st edition. O'Reilly Media, Inc.

Piotr Bojanowski, Edouard Grave, Armand Joulin, and Tomas Mikolov. 2016. Enriching Word Vectors with Subword Information. *CoRR*, abs/1607.04606.

Matt Carlson. 2015. The robotic reporter: Automated journalism and the redefinition of labor, compositional forms, and journalistic authority. *Digital journalism*, 3(3):416–431.

David L Chen and Raymond J Mooney. 2008. Learning to sportscast: a test of grounded language acquisition. In *Proceedings of the 25th international conference on Machine learning*, pages 128–135.

Alexander Fanta. 2017. Putting Europe's robots on the map: Automated journalism in news agencies. *Reuters Institute Fellowship Paper*, 9.

Albert Gatt and Emiel Krahmer. 2017. Survey of the State of the Art in Natural Language Generation: Core tasks, applications and evaluation. *Journal of Artificial Intelligence Research*, 61.

Eli Goldberg, Norbert Driedger, and Richard I Kittredge. 1994. Using natural-language processing to produce weather forecasts. *IEEE Expert*, 9(2):45–53.

Andreas Graefe. 2016. Guide to automated journalism.

Mika Hämäläinen. 2019. UralicNLP: An NLP library for Uralic Languages. *Journal of Open Source Software*, 4(37):1345.

Chris van der Lee, Albert Gatt, Emiel van Miltenburg, Sander Wubben, and Emiel Krahmer. 2019. Best practices for the human evaluation of automatically generated text. In *Proceedings of the 12th International Conference on Natural Language Generation*, pages 355–368, Tokyo, Japan. Association for Computational Linguistics.

Leo Leppänen, Myriam Munezero, Mark Granroth-Wilding, and Hannu Toivonen. 2017. Data-Driven News Generation for Automated Journalism. In *The 10th International Natural Language Generation conference, Proceedings of the Conference*, pages 188–197, United States. The Association for Computational Linguistics.

Carl-Gustav Linden. 2017. Decades of automation in the newsroom: Why are there still so many jobs in journalism? *Digital journalism*, 5(2):123–140.

Tomas Mikolov, Kai Chen, Greg Corrado, and Jeffrey Dean. 2013. Efficient estimation of word representations in vector space. *arXiv preprint arXiv:1301.3781*.

George A Miller. 1995. WordNet: a lexical database for English. *Communications of the ACM*, 38(11):39–41.

Kim Anh Nguyen, Sabine Schulte im Walde, and Ngoc Thang Vu. 2016. Integrating distributional lexical contrast into word embeddings for antonym-synonym distinction. In *Proceedings of the 54th Annual Meeting of the Association for Computational Linguistics (Volume 2: Short Papers)*, pages 454–459.

Vassilis Plachouras, Charese Smiley, Hiroko Bretz, Ola Taylor, Jochen L Leidner, Dezhao Song, and Frank Schilder. 2016. Interacting with financial data using natural language. In *Proceedings of the 39th International ACM SIGIR conference on Research and Development in Information Retrieval*, pages 1121–1124.

Ehud Reiter. 2019. ML is used more if it does not limit control. `https://ehudreiter.com/2019/08/15/ml-limits-control/`. Accessed: 2020-07-25.

Ehud Reiter and Robert Dale. 2000. *Building natural language generation systems*. Cambridge university press.

David E Rumelhart, Geoffrey E Hinton, and Ronald J Williams. 1986. Learning representations by back-propagating errors. *nature*, 323(6088):533–536.

Stefanie Sirén-Heikel, Leo Leppänen, Carl-Gustav Lindén, and Asta Bäck. 2019. Unboxing news automation: Exploring imagined affordances of automation in news journalism. *Nordic Journal of Media Studies*, 1(1):47–66.

Matej Ulčar and Marko Robnik-Šikonja. 2020. FinEst BERT and CroSloEngual BERT: less is more in multilingual models. *arXiv preprint arXiv:2006.07890*.

Aligning Estonian and Russian news industry keywords with the help of subtitle translations and an environmental thesaurus

Andraž Repar
International Postgraduate School / Jamova 39, 1000 Ljubljana, Slovenia
andraz.repar@ijs.si
Andrej Shumakov
Ekspress Meedia / Narva mnt 13, 10151 Tallinn, Estonia

Abstract

This paper presents the implementation of a bilingual term alignment approach developed by Repar et al. (2019) to a dataset of unaligned Estonian and Russian keywords which were manually assigned by journalists to describe the article topic. We started by separating the dataset into Estonian and Russian tags based on whether they are written in the Latin or Cyrillic script. Then we selected the available language-specific resources necessary for the alignment system to work. Despite the domains of the language-specific resources (subtitles and environment) not matching the domain of the dataset (news articles), we were able to achieve respectable results with manual evaluation indicating that almost 3/4 of the aligned keyword pairs are at least partial matches.

1 Introduction and related work

The ability to accurately align concepts between languages can provide significant benefits in many practical applications. For example, in terminology, terms can be aligned between languages to provide bilingual terminological resources, while in the news industry, keywords can be aligned to provide better news clustering or search in another language. Accurate bilingual resources can also serve as seed data for various other NLP tasks, such as multilingual vector space alignment.

In this paper, we describe the experiments on an Estonian-Russian dataset of news tags — labels that were manually assigned to news articles by journalists and editors at Ekspress Meedia, one of the largest news publishers in the Baltic region. The dataset contains both Estonian and Russian tags, but they are not aligned between the two languages. We adapted the machine learning term alignment approach described by Repar et al. (2019) to align the Russian and Estonian tags in the dataset.

The alignment approach in Repar et al. (2019) is a reproduction and adaptation of the approach described by Aker et al. (2013a). Repar et al. (2019) managed to reach a precision of over 0.9 and therefore approach the values presented by Aker et al. (2013a) by tweaking several parameters and developing new machine learning features. They also developed a novel cognate-based approach which could be effective in texts with a high proportion of novel terminology that cannot be detected by relying on dictionary-based features. In this work, we perform the implementation of the proposed method on a novel, Estonian-Russian language pair, and in a novel application of tagset alignment.

Section 1 lists the related work, Section 2 contains a description of the tag dataset used, Section 3 describes the system architecture, Section 4 explains the resources used in this paper, Section 5 contains the results of the experiments and Section 6 provides conclusions and future work.

2 Dataset description

The dataset of Estonian and Russian tags was provided by Ekspress Meedia as a simple list of one tag per line. The total number of tags was 65,830. The tagset consists of keywords that journalists assigne to articles to describe an article's topic, and was cut down recently by the editors from more than 210,000 tags.

The number of Russian tags was 6,198 and they were mixed with the Estonian tags in random order. Since Russian and Estonian use different writing scripts (Cyrillic vs Latin), we were able to separate the tags using a simple regular expression to detect Cyrillic characters. The vast majority of the tags are either unigrams or bigrams (see Table 1 for details).

Proceedings of the EACL Hackashop on News Media Content Analysis and Automated Report Generation, pages 71–75
April 19, 2021 © Association for Computational Linguistics

Grams	Estonian	Russian
1	0.49	0.49
2	0.44	0.41
3	0.05	0.06
4	0.01	0.02
>4	0.01	0.02

Table 1: An analysis of the provided dataset in terms of multi-word units. The values represent the ratio of the total number of tags for the respective language. The total number of Estonian tags was 59,632, and the total number of Russian tags was 6,198. The largest Estonian tag was a 14-gram and the largest Russian tag was an 11-gram, but the vast majority of tags are either unigrams or bigrams.

3 System architecture

The algoritm used in this paper is based on the approach described in Repar et al. (2019) which is itself a replication and an adaptation of Aker et al. (2013b). The original approach designed by (Aker et al., 2013b) was developed to align terminology from comparable (or parallel) corpora using machine-learning techniques. They use terms from the Eurovoc (Steinberger et al., 2002) thesaurus and train an SVM binary classifier (Joachims, 2002) (with a linear kernel and the trade-off between training error and margin parameter c = 10). The task of bilingual alignment is treated as a binary classification - each term from the source language S is paired with each term from the target language T and the classifier then decides whether the aligned pair is correct or incorrect. (Aker et al., 2013b) use two types of features that express correspondences between the words (composing a term) in the target and source language:

- 7 dictionary-based (using Giza++) features which take advantage of dictionaries created from large parallel corpora of which 6 are direction-dependent (source-to-target or target-to-source) and 1 direction-independent - resulting in altogether 13 features, and
- 5 cognate-based (on the basis of (Gaizauskas et al., 2012)) which utilize string-based word similarity between languages.

To match words with morphological differences, they do not perform direct string matching but utilize Levenshtein Distance. Two words were considered equal if the Levenshtein Distance (Levenshtein, 1966) was equal or higher than 0.95. For closed-compounding languages, they check whether the compound source term has an initial prefix that matches the translation of the first target word, provided that translation is at least 5 characters long.

Additional features are also constructed by:

- Using language pair specific transliteration rules to create additional cognate-based features. The purpose of this task was to try to match the cognate terms while taking into account the differences in writing systems between two languages: e.g. Greek and English. Transliteration rules were created for both directions (source-to-target and target-to-source) separately and cognate-based features were constructed for both directions - resulting in additional 10 cognate-based features with transliteration rules.
- Combining the dictionary and cognate-based features in a set of combined features where the term pair alignment is correct if either the dictionary or the cognate-based method returns a positive result. This process resulted in additional 10 combined features[1].

A subset of the features is described below (For a full list of features, see Repar et al. (2019)):

- *isFirstWordTranslated*: A dictionary feature that checks whether the first word of the source term is a translation of the first word in the target term (based on the Giza++ dictionary).
- *longestTranslatedUnitInPercentage*: A dictionary feature representing the ratio of the longest contiguous sequence of source words which has a translation in the target term (compared to the source term length).
- *Longest Common Subsequence Ratio*: A cognate feature measuring the longest common non-consecutive sequence of characters between two strings
- *isFirstWordCovered*: A combined feature indicating whether the first word in the source

[1]For combined features, a word is considered as covered if it can be found in the corresponding set of Giza++ translations or if one of the cognate-based measures (Longest Common Subsequence, Longest Common Substring, Levensthein Distance, Needleman-Wunsch Distance, Dice) is 0.70 or higher (set experimentally by (Aker et al., 2013b))

term has a translation or transliteration in the target term.

- *isFirstWordCognate*: a binary feature which returns True if the longest common consecutive string (LCST) of the first words in the source and target terms divided by the length of the longest of the two words is greater than or equal to a threshold value of 0.7 and both words are longer than 3 characters.

Repar et al. (2019) start by reproducing this approach, but were unable to replicate the results. During the subsequent investigation, they discovered that using the same balance ratio in the training and test sets (i.e. 1:200, which was set by Aker et al. (2013b) to mimic real-world scenarios) have a significant impact on the performance of the algorithm. Furthermore, they filter training set term pairs based on term length and feature values (hence the different training set sizes in Table 2) and develop new cognate-based features.

The system requires several language-specific resources:

- A large parallel corpus to calculate word alignment probability with Giza++. The system in Repar et al. (2019) uses the DGT translation memory (Steinberger et al., 2013).
- A list of aligned terms that serve as training data. The system in Repar et al. (2019) uses the Eurovoc thesaurus (Steinberger et al., 2002). 600 Eurovoc term pairs are used as test data, while the rest is used for training.
- Transliteration rules for the construction of reverse cognate-based features (cognate features are constructed twice: first the target word is transliterated into the source language script, then the source word is transliterated in the target language script).

The constructed features are then used to train the SVM classifier which can be used to predict the alignment of terms between two languages.

4 Resources for the Estonian-Russian experiment

While the DGT translation memory and the Eurovoc thesaurus support all official EU languages, there is no Russian support since Russia is not an EU member state. In order to train the classifier, we therefore had to find alternative resources.

For the parallel corpus, we made experiments with the Estonian Open Parallel corpus[2] and the Estonian-Russian OpenSubtitles corpus from the Opus portal[3]. The OpenSubtitles corpus performed better, most likely due to its much larger size (85,449 parallel Estonian-Russian segments in the Estonian Open Parallel corpus vs. 7.1 million segments in the OpenSubtitles corpus).

While finding parallel Estonian-Russian corpora was trivial due the the list of available corpora on the Opus portal, finding an appropriate bilingual terminological database proved to be more difficult. Ideally, we would want to use a media or news-related Estonian-Russian terminological resource, but to the best of our knowledge, there was none available. Note that the terminological resource needs to have at least several thousand entries: the Eurovoc version used by Repar et al. (2019) contained 7,083 English-Slovene term pairs. We finally settled on the environmental thesaurus Gemet[4], which at the time had 3,721 Estonian-Russian term pairs. For the transliteration rules, we used the Python pip package transliterate [5] to generate the reverse dictionary-based features.

5 Results

Repar et al. (2019) ran a total of 10 parameter configurations. We selected three of those to test on the Estonian-Russian dataset. The first one is the configuration with a positive/negative ratio of 1:200 in the training set, which significantly improved recall compared to the reproduction of Aker et al. (2013b), the second one is the same configuration with additional term filtering, which was overall the best performing configuration in Repar et al. (2019), and the third one is the Cognates approach which should give greater weight to cognate words. As shown in Table 2, the overall results are considerably lower than the results in Repar et al. (2019), in particularly in terms of recall. One reason for this could be that the term filtering heuristics developed in Repar et al. (2019) may not work well for Estonian and Russian as they do for other languages. For example, 1.3 million candidate term pairs were constructed for the English-Slovene lan-

[2]https://doi.org/10.15155/9-00-0000-0000-0000-0002AL

[3]opus.nlpl.eu

[4]https://www.eionet.europa.eu/gemet/en/themes/

[5]https://pypi.org/project/transliterate/

No.	Config ET-RU	Training set size	Pos/Neg ratio	Precision	Recall	F-score
1	Training set 1:200	627,120	1:200	0.3237	0.2050	0.2510
2	Training set filtering 3	30,954	1:200	0.9000	0.0900	0.1636
3	Cognates approach	33,768	1:200	0.7313	0.0817	0.1469

Table 2: Results on the Estonian-Russian language pair. No. 1 presents the results of the configuration with a positive/negative ratio of 1:200 in the training set, no. 2 presents the results of the same configuration with additional term filtering, which was overall the best performing configuration in Repar et al. (2019), and No. 3 presents the results of the Cognates approach which should give greater weight to cognate words.

ET	RU	Evaluation
kontsert	концерт	exact match
kosmos	космос	exact match
majandus	экономика	exact match
juhiluba	водительские права	exact match
lõbustuspark	парк развлечений	exact match
unelmate pulm	свадьба	partial match
eesti mees	мужчина	partial match
indiaani horoskoop	гороскоп	partial match
hiina kapsas	капуста	partial match
hulkuvad koerad	собаки	partial match
eesti autospordi liit	эстонский футбольный союз	no match
Kalevi Kull	орел	no match
honda jazz	джаз	no match
tõnis mägi	гора	no match
linkin park	парк	no match

Table 3: Examples of exact, partial and no match tag pairs produced by the system.

guage pair and around one half of those were filtered out during the term filtering phase. On the other hand, only around 33,000 Estonian-Russian candidate pairs out of the total 627,000 survived the term fitering phase in these experiments. Another reason for the lower performance is likely the content of the language resources used to construct the features. Whereas Repar et al. (2019) use resources with similar content (EU legislation), here we have dictionary-based features constructed from a subtitle corpus and term pairs from an environmental thesaurus.

We then used the best performing configuration to try to align the Estonian and Russian tags from the dataset provided by Ekspress Meedia. The size of the dataset (59,632 Estonian tags and 6,198 Russian tags) and the fact that the system must test each possible pairing of source and target tags meant that the system generated around 370 million tag pair candidates which it then tried to classify as positive or negative. This task took more than two weeks to complete, but at the end it resulted in 4,989 positively classified Estonian-Russian tag pairs. A subset of these (500) were manually evaluated by a person with knowledge of both languages provided by Ekspress Meedia according to the following methodology:

- C: if the tag pair is a complete match
- P: if the tag pair is a partial match, i.e. when a multiword tag in one langauge is paired with a single word tag in the other language (e.g. eesti kontsert — концерт, or *Estonian concert — concert*)
- N: if the tag pair is a no match

Of the 500 positively classified tag pairs that were manually evaluated, 49% percent were deemed to be complete matches, a further 25% were evaluated as partial matches, and 26% were considered to be wrongly classified as positive tag pairs. The evaluator observed that "the most difficult thing was to separate people's names from toponyms, such as a famous local singer called "Tõnis Mägi", a district in Talinn called "Tõnismägi" and a mountain named "Muna Mägi". More examples of exact, partial and no match alignments can be found in Table 3.

6 Conclusions and future work

In this paper, we reused an existing approach to terminology alignment by Repar et al. (2019) to align a set of Estonian and Russian tags provided by the media company Ekspress Meedia. The approach requires several bilingual resources to work and it was difficult to obtain relevant resources for the Estonian-Russian language pair. Given the domain of the tagset, i.e. news and media, the selected resources (subtitle translations and an environmental thesaurus) were less than ideal. Nevertheless, the approach provided respectable results with 74% of the positive tag pairs evaluated to be at least a partial match.

When asssessing the performance of the approach, one has to take into account the fact that the tagset is heavily unbalanced with almost 60,000 Estonian tags compared to a little over 6,000 Russian tags. This means that for many Estonian tags, a true equivalent was simply not available in the tagset.

For future work, we plan to integrate additional features into the algorithm, such as those based on novel neural network embeddings which may uncover additional hidden correlations between expressions in two different languages and may provide an alternative to large parallel corpora which are currently needed for the system for work. In terms of the Estonian and Russian language pair, additional improvements could be provided by taking into account the compound-like structure of many Estonian words. Finally, we will look into techniques that would allow us to pre-filter the initial list of tag pairs to reduce the total processing time.

7 Acknowledgements

The work was supported by European Union's Horizon 2020 research and innovation programme under grant agreement No 825153, project EMBEDDIA (Cross-Lingual Embeddings for Less-Represented Languages in European News Media).

References

Ahmet Aker, Monica Paramita, and Rob Gaizauskas. 2013a. Extracting bilingual terminologies from comparable corpora. In *Proceedings of the 51st Annual Meeting of the Association for Computational Linguistics (Volume 1: Long Papers)*, pages 402–411, Sofia, Bulgaria. Association for Computational Linguistics.

Ahmet Aker, Monica Paramita, and Rob Gaizauskas. 2013b. Extracting bilingual terminologies from comparable corpora. In *Proceedings of the 51st Annual Meeting of the Association for Computational Linguistics (Volume 1: Long Papers)*, volume 1, pages 402–411.

Robert Gaizauskas, Ahmet Aker, and Robert Yang Feng. 2012. Automatic bilingual phrase extraction from comparable corpora. In *24th International Conference on Computational Linguistics*, pages 23–32.

Thorsten Joachims. 2002. *Learning to classify text using support vector machines: Methods, theory and algorithms*. Kluwer Academic Publishers.

V. I. Levenshtein. 1966. Binary Codes Capable of Correcting Deletions, Insertions and Reversals. *Soviet Physics Doklady*, 10:707.

Andraž Repar, Matej Martinc, and Senja Pollak. 2019. Reproduction, replication, analysis and adaptation of a term alignment approach. *Language Resources and Evaluation*, pages 1–34.

Ralf Steinberger, Andreas Eisele, Szymon Klocek, Spyridon Pilos, and Patrick Schlüter. 2013. DGT-TM: A freely available translation memory in 22 languages. In *Proceedings of the 8th international conference on Language Resources and Evaluation (LREC'2012)*.

Ralf Steinberger, Bruno Pouliquen, and Johan Hagman. 2002. Cross-lingual document similarity calculation using the multilingual thesaurus eurovoc. *Computational Linguistics and Intelligent Text Processing*, pages 101–121.

Exploring Neural Language Models via Analysis of Local and Global Self-Attention Spaces

Blaž Škrlj
Jožef Stefan International Postgraduate School
Jožef Stefan Institute, Slovenia
blaz.skrlj@ijs.si

Shane Sheehan
University of Edinburgh, United Kingdom

Nika Eržen
Jožef Stefan Institute, Slovenia

Marko Robnik-Šikonja
University of Ljubljana, Slovenia

Saturnino Luz
University of Edinburgh, United Kingdom

Senja Pollak
Jožef Stefan Institute, Slovenia

Abstract

Large pretrained language models using the transformer neural network architecture are becoming a dominant methodology for many natural language processing tasks, such as question answering, text classification, word sense disambiguation, text completion and machine translation. Commonly comprising hundreds of millions of parameters, these models offer state-of-the-art performance, but at the expense of interpretability. The attention mechanism is the main component of transformer networks. We present AttViz, a method for exploration of self-attention in transformer networks, which can help in explanation and debugging of the trained models by showing associations between text tokens in an input sequence. We show that existing deep learning pipelines can be explored with AttViz, which offers novel visualizations of the attention heads and their aggregations. We implemented the proposed methods in an online toolkit and an offline library. Using examples from news analysis, we demonstrate how AttViz can be used to inspect and potentially better understand what a model has learned.

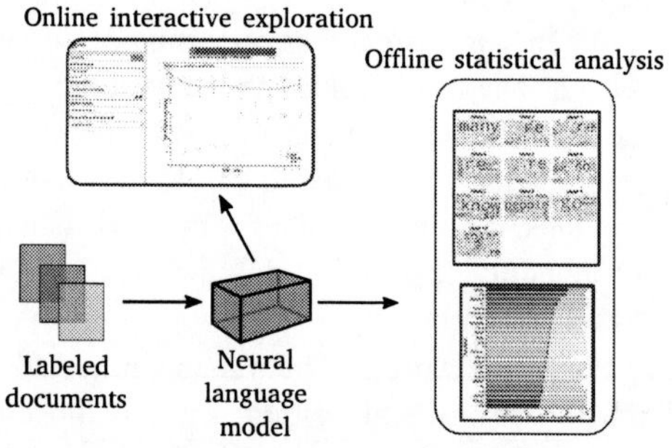

Figure 1: An overview of AttViz suite. The system consists of two main functional modules supporting online and offline visualizations. The online visualization (`http://attviz.ijs.si`; first part of the paper) offers direct exploration of token attention across the space of input documents; its purpose is anomaly detection and general inspection of the attention space (of trained models). The offline part of AttViz (second part of the paper) is a Python library that offers computationally more demanding statistical analyses, ranging from visualization of key tokens for each attention head, comparison of the attention head properties via FUJI integrals, and inspection of the attention distribution per-token basis.

1 Introduction

Currently the most successful machine learning approaches for text-related tasks predominantly use large *language models*. They are implemented with transformer neural network architecture (Vaswani et al., 2017), extensively pretrained on large text corpora to capture context-dependent meanings of individual tokens (Devlin et al., 2019; Liu et al., 2019; Yang et al., 2019). Even though training of such neural networks with hundreds of millions of parameters is long and expensive (Radford et al., 2019), many pre-trained models have been made freely available. This has created an opportunity to explore how, and why these models perform well on many tasks. One of the main problems with neural network models is their lack of *interpretability*. Even though the models learn the given task well, understanding the reasons behind the predictions, and assessing whether the model is

Proceedings of the EACL Hackashop on News Media Content Analysis and Automated Report Generation, pages 76–83
April 19, 2021

susceptible to undue biases or spurious correlations is a non-trivial task.

Approaches to understanding black-box (non-interpretable) models include *post-hoc* perturbation methods, such as IME (Štrumbelj and Kononenko, 2010) and SHAP (Lundberg and Lee, 2017). These methods explain a given decision by assigning a credit to inputs (i.e. attributes or tokens) that contributed to it. These methods are not internal to the model itself and are not well adapted to the sequential nature of text-based inputs. Another way of extracting token relevance is the attention mechanism (Bahdanau et al., 2015; Luong et al., 2015) that learns token pair-value mappings, potentially encoding relations between token pairs. The attention of a token with respect to itself (called self-attention due its position on diagonal of the token attention matrix) offers certain insight into the importance of the token. Typically, a trained transformer network contains several attention heads, each bringing a different focus to the final decision of the network. Exploration of attention can be analytically and numerically cumbersome task, resulting in development of several approaches aimed at attention visualization collection.

As neural networks require numerical input, words are first transformed into a high dimensional numeric vector space, in a process called embedding that aims to preserve similarities and relations between words. Visualizations of embedding spaces is becoming ubiquitous in contemporary natural language processing. For example, Google's online Embedding Projector[1] offers numerous visualizations for technically non-savvy users, by projecting word vectors to low dimensional (human-understandable) spaces. While visualization of embedding spaces is already accessible, visualization of internal workings of complex transformer neural networks (e.g.,their self-attention mechanism) is a challenging task. The works of (Liu et al., 2018) and (Yanagimto et al., 2018) attempt to unveil the workings of black-box attention layers and offer an interface for human researches to learn and inspect their models. Liu et al. (2018) visualize the attention space by coloring it, and Yanagimto et al. (2018) visualize the self-attention with examples from a sentiment analysis.

In this work, we present AttViz, an online system that focuses exclusively on self-attention and introduces two novel ways of visualizing this property. The tool serves as an additional tool in the toolbox of a language model researcher, offering exploration of the learned models with minimal effort. AttViz can interactively aggregate the attention vectors and offers simultaneous exploration of the output probability space, as well as the attention space. A schematic overview of the proposed work is shown in Figure 1, and the main contributions are summarised as follows:

1. We present and describe AttViz, an interactive, online toolkit for visualization of the attention space of trained transformer neural language models.

2. We demonstrate the capabilities of AttViz on three problems: news classification, hate speech detection, and insults detection.

3. AttViz includes a stand-alone python library for offline analysis of the attention space, with the key focus on the relations between *the attention heads*.

The remainder of the paper is structured as follows. In Section 2, we discuss works related to the proposed AttViz approach. In Section 3, we present the key ideas and technical implementation of the online part of the AttViz system, including a use case on news classification. In Section 4, we discuss the capabilities of the AttViz library, available in an offline mode, and showcase its use on additional two datasets. In Section 5 we discuss capabilities and limitations of AttViz, present conclusions, and propose ideas for future work.

2 Background and related work on attention visualization

Neural language models are becoming the prevailing methodology for solving various text-related tasks, from entity recognition to classification. Visualization of the attention mechanism that is the key component of such models has recently emerged as an active research area due to an increased popularity of attention based methods in natural language processing. Recent deep neural network language models such as BERT (Devlin et al., 2019), XLNet (Yang et al., 2019), and RoBERTa (Liu et al., 2019) consist of multiple attention heads—separate weight spaces each associated with the input sequence in *a unique way*. These transformer language models consist of multiple attention matrices, all contributing to the final prediction. Visualising the attention weights

[1] `https://projector.tensorflow.org/`

from each of the attention matrices is an important component in understanding and interpreting these models.

The attention mechanism, which originated in the neural machine translation, lends itself naturally to visualisation. Bahdanau et al. (2015) used *heat maps* to display the attention weights between input and output text. This visualisation technique was first applied in machine translation but found its use in many other tasks. Rush et al. (2015) visualized an input sentence and the output abstractive summary, while Rocktäschel et al. (2016) showed an association between an input document and a textual entailment hypothesis on the output. In these heat map visualisations, a matrix is used to represent the token-token pairs and color intensity illustrates attention weights. This provides a summary of the attention patterns describing how they map the input to the output. For classification tasks, a similar visualisation approach can be used to display the attention weights between the classified document and the predicted label (Yang et al., 2016; Tsaptsinos, 2017). Here, the visualisation of attention often displays the input document with the attention weights superimposed onto individual words. The superimposed attention weights are represented similarly to heat map visualisations, using the color saturation to encode attention value. The neat-vision tool[2] encodes attention weights associated with input text in this manner. Similarly, the Text Attention Heatmap Visualization (TAHV[3]) which is included in the NCRF++ toolkit (Yang and Zhang, 2018) can be used to generate weighted sequences which are visualised using superimposed attention scores.

The purpose of the proposed AttViz is to unveil the attention layer space to human explorers in an intuitive manner. The tool emphasizes *self-attention*, that is, the diagonal of the token-token attention matrix which possibly corresponds to the *relevance* of individual tokens. Using different encoding techniques, attention weights across the layers and attention heads can be explored dynamically to investigate the interactions between the model and the input data. The AttViz tool differs from other tools in that if focuses on self-attention, thus allowing visualization of (attention-annotated) input token sequences to be carried out directly.

[2]https://github.com/cbaziotis/neat-vision

[3]https://github.com/jiesutd/Text-Attention-Heatmap-Visualization

3 AttViz: An online toolkit for visualization of self-attention

AttViz is an online visualization tool that can visualize neural language models from the PyTorch-transformers library[4]—one of the most widely used resources for natural language modeling. The idea behind AttViz is that it is *simple to use* and *lightweight*, therefore it does not offer computationally expensive (online) neural model training, but facilitates the exploration of *trained* models. Along with AttViz, we provide a set of Python scripts that take as an input a trained neural language model and output a JSON file to be used by the AttViz visualisation tool. A common pipeline for using AttViz is outlined in Figure 1. First, a transformer-based trained neural network model is chosen to obtain predictions on a desired set of instances (documents or some other texts). The predictions are converted into the JSON format suitable for use with the AttViz tool, along with the attention space of the language model. The JSON file is loaded into the AttViz tool (on the user's machine, i.e. on the client side), where its visualization and exploration is possible. In Sections 3.1 and 3.3, we present the proposed self-attention visualizations, followed by an example of their use on the news classification task in Section 3.4.

3.1 Visualization of self-attention heads

We discuss the proposed visualization schemes that emphasize different aspects of self-attention. Following the first row that represents the input text, consequent rows correspond to attention values that represent the importance of a given token with respect to a given attention head. As discussed in the empirical part of the paper (Section 3.4), the rationale for this display is that typically only a certain number of attention heads are activated (colored fields). Thus, the visualization has to entail both the whole attention space, as well as emphasize individual heads (and tokens). The initial AttViz view offers sequence-level visualization, where each (byte-pair encoded) token is equipped with a self-attention value based on a given attention head (see Figure 4; central text space). The same document can also be viewed in the "aggregation" mode (Figure 2), where the attention sequence is shown across the token space. The user can interactively explore how the self-attention varies for individ-

[4]https://github.com/huggingface/transformers

ual input tokens, by changing the scale, as well as the type of the aggregation. The visualization can emphasize various aspects of the self-attention space.

The third proposed visualization (Figure 3) is the overall distribution of attention values across the whole token space. For each consequent token, the attention values are plotted separately, resembling a time series. This visualization offers an insight into *self-attention peaks*, i.e. parts of the attention space around certain tokens that potentially impact the performance and decision making process of a given neural network. This view can emphasize different aggregations of the attention vector space for a single token (e.g., mean, entropy, and maximum). The visualization, apart from the mean self-attention (per token), offers the information on maximum and minimum attention values (red dots), as well as the remainder of the self-attention values (gray dots). In this way, a user can explore both the self-attention peaks, as well as the overall spread.

3.2 Comparison with state-of-the-art

In the following section, we discuss similarities and differences between AttViz and other state-of-the-art visualization approaches. Comparisons are summarized in Table 1.

Novel functionality introduced by AttViz include the capability to aggregate the attention vectors with four different aggregation schemes, offering insights both into the average attention but also its dispersion around a given token. The neat-vision project[5] is the closest to AttViz in terms of functionality. However, a few differences should be noted. First, neat-vision is not directly bound to the PyTorch transformers library, requiring additional pre-processing on the user-side. Second, switching between the sequence and aggregate view is faster and more emphasized in AttViz, as it offers a more general overview of the attention space.

3.3 Aggregation of self-attention

The self-attention is captured in the matrix $A \in \mathbb{R}^{h \times t}$, where h is the number of attention vectors and t the number of tokens. Aggregation operators are applied the second dimension of the attention matrix A (index j). We denote with P_{ij} the probability of observing A_{ij} in the j-th column. The m_j corresponds to the number of unique values in that column. The proposed schemes are summarized in Table 2. The attention aggregates are visualized as part of the the aggregate view (see Figure 4). For example, the mean attention is plotted as a line along with the attention space for each token, depicting the *dispersion* around certain parts of the input text.

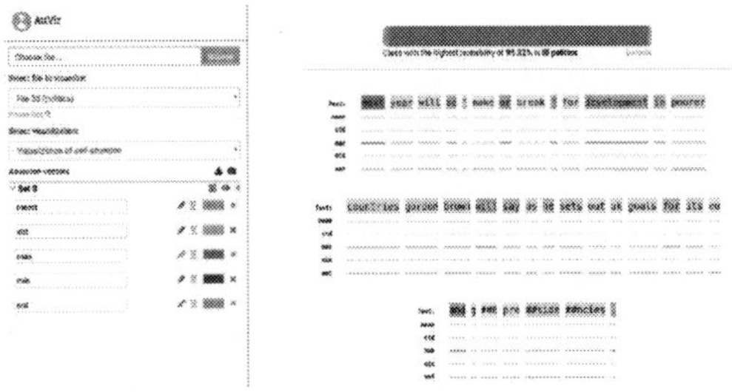

Figure 2: Visualization of aggregations. The document was classified as a politics-related topic; the aggregations emphasize tokens such as "development","uk" and "poorer". The user can highlight desired head information – in this example the maximum attention (purple) is highlighted.

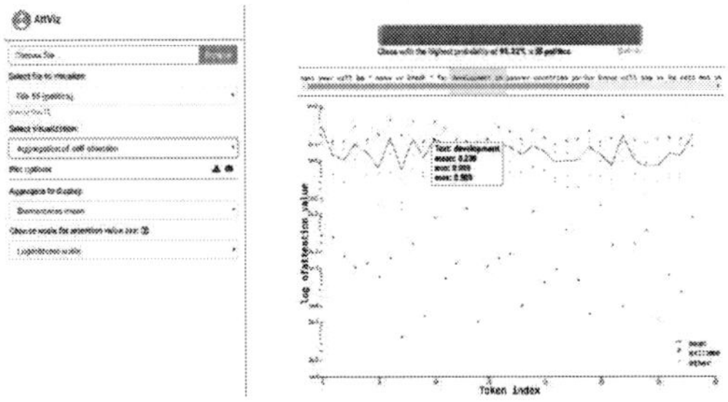

Figure 3: The interactive series view. The user can, by hoovering over the desired part of the sequence, inspect the attention values and their aggregations. The text above the visualization is highlighted automatically.

3.4 Example: News visualization

In this section, we present a step-by-step use of the AttViz system along with potential insights a user can obtain.

The examples are based on the BBC news data set[6] (Greene and Cunningham, 2006) that contains 2,225 news articles on five different topics (business, entertainment, politics, sport, tech). The documents from the dataset were split into short segments. The splits allow easier training (manage-

[5]Available at https://github.com/cbaziotis/neat-vision

[6]https://github.com/suraj-deshmukh/BBC-Dataset-News-Classification/blob/master/dataset/dataset.csv

Approach	AttViz (this work)	BertViz (Vig, 2019)	neat-vision	NCRF++ (Yang and Zhang, 2018)
Visualization types	sequence, aggregates	head, model, neuron	sequence	sequence
Open source	✓	✓	✓	✓
Language	Python + Node.js	Python	Python + Node.js	Python
Accessibility	Online	Jupyter notebooks	Online	script-based
Sequence view	✓	✓	✓	✓
Interactive	✓	✓	✓	✗
Aggregated view	✓	✗	✗	✗
Target probabilities	✓	✗	✓	✗
Compatible with PyTorch Transformers? (Wolf et al., 2020)	✓	✓	✗	✗
token-to-token attention	✗	✓	✗	✓

Table 1: Comparison of different aspects of the attention visualization approaches.

Table 2: Aggregation schemes used in AttViz. The A represents a real valued (attention) matrix.

Aggregate name	Definition
Mean(j) (mean)	$\frac{1}{h}\sum_i A_{ij}$
Entropy(j) (ent)	$-\frac{1}{m_j}\sum_{i=0}^{h} A_{ij}\log A_{ij}$
Standard deviation(j) (std)	$\sqrt{\frac{1}{h-1}\sum_i (A_{ij}-\overline{A_{ij}})^2}$
Elementwise Max(j) (max)	$\max_i(A_{ij})$
Elementwise Min(j) (min)	$\min_i(A_{ij})$

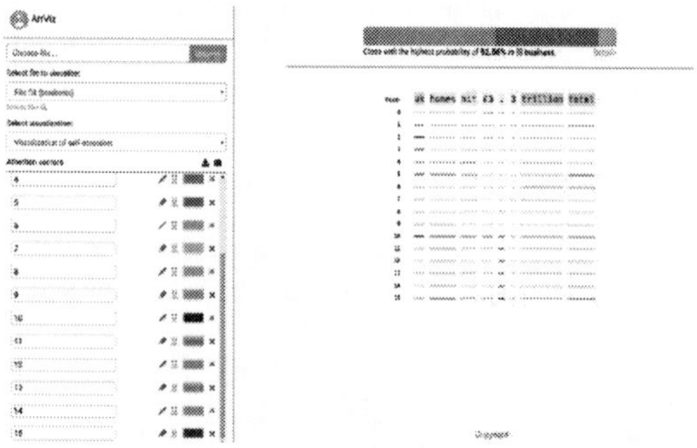

Figure 4: Visualization of all attention heads. The sixth heads's self attention is used to highlight the text. The document was classified as a business-related, which can be linked to high self attention at the "trillion" and "uk" tokens. Compared to the first two examples (Figures 2 and 3), the network is less *certain* – in this example, the business (orange) and politics (red) classes were predicted with similar probabilities (orange and red parts of the bar above visualized text).

able sequence lengths), as well as easier inspection of the models. We split the dataset into 60% of the documents that were used to fine-tune the BERT-base (Devlin et al., 2019) model, 20% for validation and 20% for testing. The Nvidia Tesla V100 GPU processor was used for these experiments. The resulting model classified the whole documents into five categories with 96% accuracy, which is comparable with the state-of-the-art performance (Trieu et al., 2017). For prediction and visualisation, we used only short segments. The fine-tuning of the BERT model follows examples given in the PyTorch-Transformers library (Wolf et al., 2020). The best-performing hyper parameter combination used 3 epochs with the sequence length of 512 (other hyper parameters were left at their default values). While we have used BERT, similar explorations could be made for more recent larger models such as XLNet (Yang et al., 2019) that might could produce better classification accuracy.

The user interface of AttViz is displayed in Figures 2, 3, and 4. In the first example (Figure 3), the user can observe the main view that consists of two parts. The leftmost part shows (by id) individual self-attention vectors, along with visualization, aggregation and file selection options. The file selection indexes all examples contained in the input (JSON) file. Attention vectors can be colored with custom colors, as shown in the central (token-value view). The user can observe that, for example, the violet attention head (no. 5) is active, and emphasizes tokens such as "development", which indicates a politics-related topic (as correctly classified). Here, the token (byte-pair encoded) space is shown along with self-attention values for each token. The attention vectors are shown below the token space and aligned for direct inspection (and correspondence).

In Figure 4, the user can observe the same text segment as an attention series spanning the input token space. Again, note that tokens, such as "trillion" and "uk" correspond to high values in a subset of the attention heads, indicating their potential importance for the obtained classification. However, we observed that only a few attention heads activate with respect to individual tokens, indicating that other attention heads are not focusing on the tokens themselves, but possibly on *relations* between them. This is possible, and the attention matrices contain such information (Vig, 2019). However, as mentioned earlier, the study of token relations is not the focus of this work. As self-attention information can be mapped across token sequences, emphasizing tokens that are of relevance to the classification task at hand, we see AttViz as being the most useful when exploring models used for text classification tasks, such as hate speech detection and sentiment analysis, where individual tokens contain the key information for classification.

The example above shows how different attention heads detect different aspects of the sentence, even at the single token (self-attention) level. The user can observe that the next most probable category for this topic was politics (red color), which is indeed a more sensible classification than, for instance, sports. The example shows how interpretation of the attention can be coupled with the model's output for increased interpretability.

4 AttViz library: statistical analysis of the attention space

In Section 3 we presented how the online version of AttViz can be used for *direct analysis* of model output (in the JSON format). Albeit suitable for quick inspections, the online system has its limitations such as poor support for computationally more intensive types of analysis (in terms of waiting times), and the lack of customized visualization tools accessible in the Python ecosystem. To address these aspects, we developed AttViz library that offers more detailed analysis of a given neural language model's properties. The library operates on the same JSON structures as the online version and is compatible with the initial user input. We demonstrate the analytical capabilities of our visualization tools on three datasets. The BBC news classification was already presented in Section 3.4.

4.1 Dissecting the token space

The first offline functionality is a barplot visualization that offers insight into relevant aspects of the attention distribution at token level. Whilst understanding the attention peaks is relevant for direct inspections (Section 3), the attention space of a given token can be contextualized on the dataset level as well. The AttViz library offers fast visualization of the mean and spread of attention distributions, simultaneously showing the attention peaks for individual tokens. We visualized the distribution for three classification datasets (Figure 5): BBC news (5a), insults[7] (5b), and hate speech comments (5c)[8].

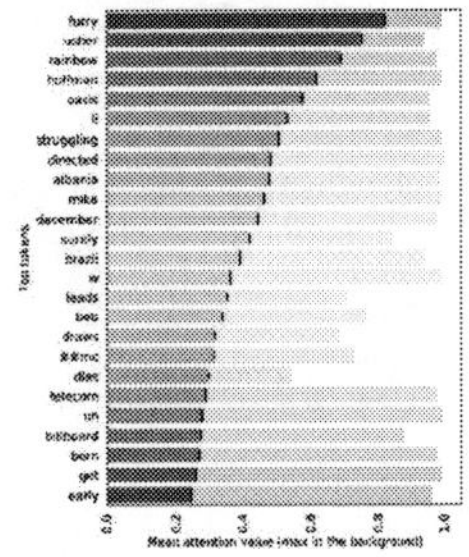

(a) Top 35 tokens in the BBC dataset.

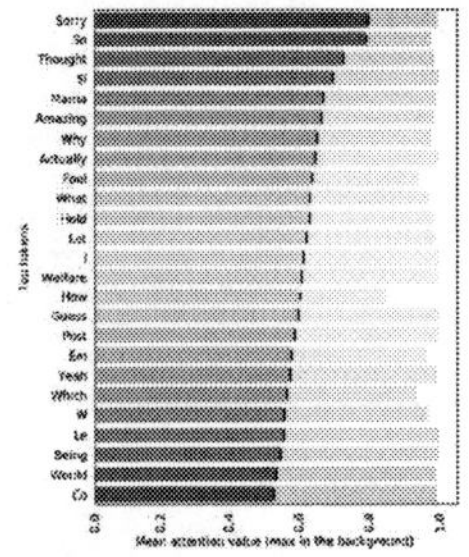

(b) Top 35 tokens in the insults dataset.

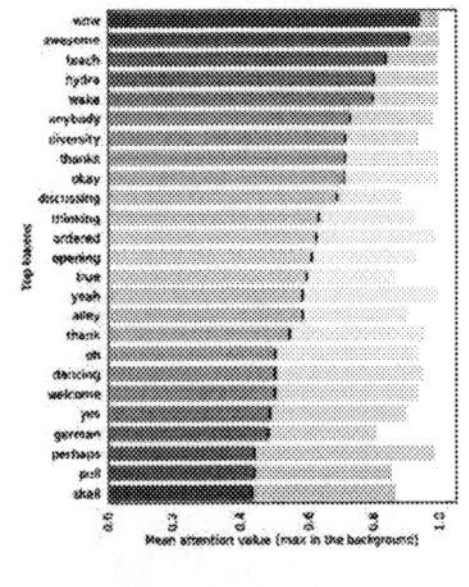

(c) Top 35 tokens in the hate speech dataset.

Figure 5: Visualization of the 35 most attended-to tokens for the three inspected data sets. Interestingly, the attention peaks of tokens (maximum, in the background) all take high values, albeit lower-ranked tokens are on average characterized by lower mean attention values.

The proposed visualizations present top k tokens according to their mean attention throughout the whole dataset. It is interesting to observe, that the insults and hate speech data sets are not completely characterized by swear words or similar single-token-like features. This potentially indicates that the attention tries to detect interactions between the byte-pair encoded tokens, even for data sets where the attention could be focused on single tokens. It is interesting to observe that the terms with the highest attention are not necessarily keywords or other tokens carrying large semantic meaning. Similarly, the high maxima indicate that the emphasis of the tokens is very contextual, and potentially not as informative for global aggregation.

[7]https://www.kaggle.com/c/detecting-insults-in-social-commentary/overview

[8]https://github.com/aitor-garcia-p/hate-speech-dataset

4.2 Visualization of attention head focus

(a) Insults.

(b) Hatespeech.

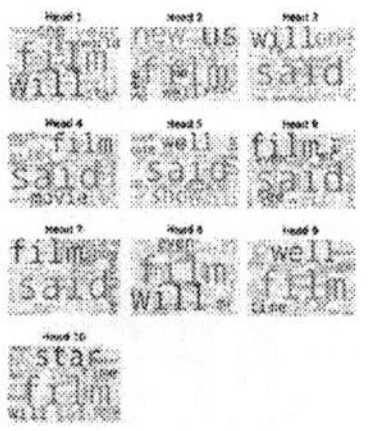

(c) BBC news.

Figure 6: The distribution of tokens over individual attention heads for the three datasets summarised with word clouds.

Contemporary neural language model architectures comprise multiple attention heads. These separate weight spaces capture distinct aspects of the considered learning task. Even though the weight spaces are easily accessible, it is not trivial to convert the large amount of information into a quick-to-inspect visualization. With the proposed visualization, shown in Figure 6, we leverage word clouds (Kaser and Lemire, 2007) to reveal human-understandable patterns captured by separate attention heads and display this information in a compact way.

5 Discussion and conclusions

As AttViz is an online and offline toolkit for attention exploration, we discuss possible concerns regarding its use, namely: privacy, memory and performance overheads, and coverage. Privacy is a potential concern for most web-based systems. As currently AttViz does not employ any anonymization strategy, private processing of the input data is not guaranteed. While we intend to address this issue in furture work, a private installation of the tool can be done to get around this current limitation. AttViz uses the users' computing capabilities, which means that large data sets may cause memory overheads when a large number of instances is loaded (typically several million). Such situations are difficult to address with AttViz and similar web-based tool, but users can filter instances before using them in AttViz and explore a subset of the data (e.g., only (in)correctly predicted instances, or certain time slot of instances). Finally, AttViz is focused on the exploration of *self-attention*. This is not the only important aspect of a transformer neural network, but it is the one, where visualisation techniques have not yet been sufficiently explored. Similarly to the work of (Liu et al., 2018), we plan to further explore potentially interesting *relations* emerging from the attention matrices.

6 Availability

The software is available at `https://github.com/SkBlaz/attviz`.

Acknowledgements

We acknowledge European Union's Horizon 2020 research and innovation programme under grant agreement No 825153, project EMBEDDIA (Cross-Lingual Embeddings). The first author was also funded by Slovenian Research Agency as a young researcher.

References

Dzmitry Bahdanau, Kyunghyun Cho, and Yoshua Bengio. 2015. Neural machine translation by jointly learning to align and translate. In *3rd International Conference on Learning Representations, ICLR 2015, San Diego, CA, USA, May 7-9, 2015, Conference Track Proceedings*.

Jacob Devlin, Ming-Wei Chang, Kenton Lee, and Kristina Toutanova. 2019. BERT: Pre-training of deep bidirectional transformers for language understanding. In *Proceedings of the 2019 Conference of the North American Chapter of the Association for Computational Linguistics: Human Language Technologies, Volume 1 (Long and Short Papers)*, pages 4171–4186, Minneapolis, Minnesota. Association for Computational Linguistics.

Derek Greene and Padraig Cunningham. 2006. Practical solutions to the problem of diagonal dominance in kernel document clustering. In *Machine Learning, Proceedings of the Twenty-Third International Conference (ICML 2006), Pittsburgh, Pennsylvania, USA, June 25-29, 2006*, volume 148 of *ACM International Conference Proceeding Series*, pages 377–384. ACM.

Owen Kaser and Daniel Lemire. 2007. Tag-cloud drawing: Algorithms for cloud visualization. In *Procedings of WWW Workshop on Tagging and Metadata for Social Information Organization*.

Shusen Liu, Tao Li, Zhimin Li, Vivek Srikumar, Valerio Pascucci, and Peer-Timo Bremer. 2018. Visual interrogation of attention-based models for natural language inference and machine comprehension. In *Proceedings of the 2018 Conference on Empirical Methods in Natural Language Processing: System Demonstrations*, pages 36–41, Brussels, Belgium. Association for Computational Linguistics.

Yinhan Liu, Myle Ott, Naman Goyal, Jingfei Du, Mandar Joshi, Danqi Chen, Omer Levy, Mike Lewis, Luke Zettlemoyer, and Veselin Stoyanov. 2019. Roberta: A robustly optimized bert pretraining approach. *arXiv preprint arXiv:1907.11692*.

Scott M. Lundberg and Su-In Lee. 2017. A unified approach to interpreting model predictions. In *Advances in Neural Information Processing Systems 30: Annual Conference on Neural Information Processing Systems 2017, December 4-9, 2017, Long Beach, CA, USA*, pages 4765–4774.

Thang Luong, Hieu Pham, and Christopher D. Manning. 2015. Effective approaches to attention-based neural machine translation. In *Proceedings of the 2015 Conference on Empirical Methods in Natural Language Processing*, pages 1412–1421, Lisbon, Portugal. Association for Computational Linguistics.

Alec Radford, Jeffrey Wu, Rewon Child, David Luan, Dario Amodei, and Ilya Sutskever. 2019. Language models are unsupervised multitask learners. *OpenAI Blog*, 1(8).

Tim Rocktäschel, Edward Grefenstette, Karl Moritz Hermann, Tomás Kociský, and Phil Blunsom. 2016. Reasoning about entailment with neural attention. In *4th International Conference on Learning Representations, ICLR 2016, San Juan, Puerto Rico, May 2-4, 2016, Conference Track Proceedings*.

Alexander M. Rush, Sumit Chopra, and Jason Weston. 2015. A neural attention model for abstractive sentence summarization. In *Proceedings of the 2015 Conference on Empirical Methods in Natural Language Processing*, pages 379–389, Lisbon, Portugal. Association for Computational Linguistics.

Lap Q. Trieu, Huy Q. Tran, and Minh-Triet Tran. 2017. News classification from social media using twitter-based doc2vec model and automatic query expansion. In *Proceedings of the Eighth International Symposium on Information and Communication Technology*, SoICT 2017, pages 460–467.

Alexandros Tsaptsinos. 2017. Lyrics-based music genre classification using a hierarchical attention network. *CoRR*, abs/1707.04678.

Ashish Vaswani, Noam Shazeer, Niki Parmar, Jakob Uszkoreit, Llion Jones, Aidan N. Gomez, Lukasz Kaiser, and Illia Polosukhin. 2017. Attention is all you need. In *Advances in Neural Information Processing Systems 30: Annual Conference on Neural Information Processing Systems 2017, December 4-9, 2017, Long Beach, CA, USA*, pages 5998–6008.

Jesse Vig. 2019. Visualizing attention in transformer-based language representation models. *CoRR*, abs/1904.02679.

Thomas Wolf, Lysandre Debut, Victor Sanh, Julien Chaumond, Clement Delangue, Anthony Moi, Pierric Cistac, Tim Rault, Rémi Louf, Morgan Funtowicz, Joe Davison, Sam Shleifer, Patrick von Platen, Clara Ma, Yacine Jernite, Julien Plu, Canwen Xu, Teven Le Scao, Sylvain Gugger, Mariama Drame, Quentin Lhoest, and Alexander M. Rush. 2020. Transformers: State-of-the-art natural language processing. In *Proceedings of the 2020 Conference on Empirical Methods in Natural Language Processing: System Demonstrations*, pages 38–45, Online. Association for Computational Linguistics.

H. Yanagimto, K. Hashimoto, and M. Okada. 2018. Attention visualization of gated convolutional neural networks with self attention in sentiment analysis. In *2018 International Conference on Machine Learning and Data Engineering (iCMLDE)*, pages 77–82.

Jie Yang and Yue Zhang. 2018. NCRF++: An open-source neural sequence labeling toolkit. In *Proceedings of ACL 2018, System Demonstrations*, pages 74–79, Melbourne, Australia. Association for Computational Linguistics.

Zhilin Yang, Zihang Dai, Yiming Yang, Jaime Carbonell, Russ R Salakhutdinov, and Quoc V Le. 2019. Xlnet: Generalized autoregressive pretraining for language understanding. In *Advances in neural information processing systems*, pages 5754–5764.

Zichao Yang, Diyi Yang, Chris Dyer, Xiaodong He, Alex Smola, and Eduard Hovy. 2016. Hierarchical attention networks for document classification. In *Proceedings of the 2016 Conference of the North American Chapter of the Association for Computational Linguistics: Human Language Technologies*, pages 1480–1489, San Diego, California. Association for Computational Linguistics.

Erik Štrumbelj and Igor Kononenko. 2010. An efficient explanation of individual classifications using game theory. *Journal of Machine Learning Research*, 11:1–18.

Comment Section Personalization: Algorithmic, Interface and Interaction Design

Yixue Wang
Northwestern University
yixue.wang@u.northwestern.edu

Abstract

Comment sections allow users to share their personal experiences, discuss and form different opinions, and build communities out of organic conversations. However, many comment sections present chronological ranking to all users. In this paper, I discuss personalization approaches in comment sections based on different objectives for newsrooms and researchers to consider. I propose algorithmic and interface designs when personalizing the presentation of comments based on different objectives including relevance, diversity, and education/background information. I further explain how transparency, user control, and comment type diversity could help users most benefit from the personalized interacting experience.

1 Introduction

Comment sections provide a public digital space for users to exchange ideas, share personal experiences, and form opinions, which are all key elements of deliberative democracy (Kim et al., 1999). However, many comments ranked highly by comment sections tend to be early comments due to greater visibility and resulting in greater capacity for a high community rating (Hsu et al., 2009), making other good quality and relevant comments less visible, and providing the same reading experience for all users. While comment sections can utilize different moderation strategies to promote high-quality comments (Wang and Diakopoulos, 2021b) and reduce the likelihood of uncivil conversations (Cheng et al., 2017)), they lack the ability to promote diverse, and/or minority opinions and offer background information on the topics (Janssen and Kies, 2005) according to users' needs.

Personalization might help address this issue. News personalization has been defined as "a form of user-to-system interactivity that uses a set of technological features to adapt the content, delivery, and arrangement of a communication to individual users' explicitly registered and/or implicitly determined preferences "(Thurman and Schifferes, 2012). 70 percent of 200 publishers personalize the content they deliver to their visitors (Weiss, 2019). Newsrooms have implemented different personalization approaches, including automatic content tagging and ad-targeting, documenting readers' locations, and reading behaviors (e.g., keywords and phrases in the articles), in order to customize the delivery of news and encourage users' engagement [1] [2].

Though many newsrooms have incorporated different personalization approaches, the personalization of comments is still under-examined. How will comment personalization help the audience better understand the topic and promote deliberative conversations online in the future? And how can researchers, developers, and journalists design comment sections to customize readers' reading experience while maintaining the comment section as a common ground for all users? This short paper seeks to propose different design and algorithmic approaches to support different personalization objectives.

2 Objectives and Design of Personalized Comment Sections

People read news comments for various reasons: to learn about the opinions of others, to be entertained or amused by others' comments, to see how their opinion of the story or topic differs from others' views, to get more information on a story, to get

[1] https://www.nytimes.com/2017/03/18/public-editor/a-community-of-one-the-times-gets-tailored.html

[2] https://www.niemanlab.org/2016/05/the-washington-post-tests-personalized-pop-up-newsletters-to-promote-its-big-stories/

Proceedings of the EACL Hackashop on News Media Content Analysis and Automated Report Generation, pages 84–88
April 19, 2021 © Association for Computational Linguistics

additional reporting/updates on a story, or to gauge the pulse of the community. And people comment on news for various reasons: to express an emotion or opinion, to add information, to correct inaccuracies or misinformation, to take part in the debate, to discuss with others, etc. (Stroud et al., 2016). How can newsrooms better personalize the comment sections according to these reading and commenting needs? This section will introduce several personalization objectives including relevance, diversity, education/background information, and how algorithms could support them.

2.1 Relevance

Relevance is the key driver of news consumption (Schrøder, 2019). People are more likely to like and understand those who are similar to them and their experiences, i.e., language and demographics (McPherson et al., 2001). Therefore, it is important to keep the personalized comments relevant to readers. Relevance could be achieved via different approaches, such as by localization based on self-reported geographic information (i.e., geographic relevance), by collaborative filtering based on previous like history in comments and articles (i.e., topic relevance), or by ranking content and language similarity based on word embeddings' cosine similarities (Kenter and De Rijke, 2015) (i.e., writing language relevance).

With this objective, newsrooms need to collect metrics around users' historical commenting behaviors (e.g., likes and comment content) and users' location information. Then comment sections could rank the comments from high to low relevance based on users' historical comments. This design would be similar to what (Wang and Diakopoulos, 2021a) proposed in their ranking algorithm, in which the algorithm automatically ranks the comments based on language relevance between users' example input query and the sample comments in the system. One potential problem with merely focusing on this objective is that users might fear being trapped in filter bubbles where most comments they interact with are from people who are very similar to them and share similar opinions (Monzer et al., 2020), which leads to the next objective I want to discuss: diversity.

2.2 Diversity

People not only look for similar personal experiences and opinions, but also compare their own opinions to others' views to gauge the community's overall trends (Stroud et al., 2016). Therefore a comment section only focusing on users' relevance might make the user lose the full picture of public interest (Plattner, 2018). Offering a variety of comments could also help users better understand others' views, opinions, and eventually promote online deliberation, and enable "a diverse and in-depth news diet" that readers value (Bodó et al., 2019).

To personalize diversity across comments, newsrooms need to again collect metrics around users' historical commenting behaviors (e.g., likes and comment content), location, etc. Comment sections could be grouped into different groups based on whether or not the content is similar to users' previous comment content (e.g., "comments that you might find familiar" and "comments that you might find not familiar"), or whether the content is from a close location (i.e. rural and urban could be treated as different groups). These comments could be grouped into different tabs for users to interact with, similar to the three-column comment section structure (i.e., "Supporting Legalization", "Questions about Legalization", and "Opposing Legalization") that Peacock et al. (Peacock et al., 2019) proposed. Comments could also be tagged as "similar comments to yours" and "different comments compared to yours" along with the comment content.

2.3 Education/Background Information

Comments not only open a common ground for users to share their expertise, personal stories and opinions for every user to learn from and compare with the stories, but they also hold journalists accountable (Greenwald and Fillion, 2017). To provide such a common ground for all users, comment sections should work as a platform for users to either contribute their knowledge in the comment section to interact with journalists' reporting and/or learn background information while reading comments. When users are experts in a specific topic they are browsing, and/or they find a topic less familiar and they need more information, how can comment sections personalize their reading and commenting experience?

I propose that comment sections could collect users' expertise areas and topics unfamiliar to them, through implicitly inferring users' interests based on users' reading history and users' explicit feedback (e.g., self-report ratings in a survey about

Objective	Algorithm Approach	Interface Design
Relevance	Localization, collaborative filtering, and word embedding similarity	Ranking
Diversity	Word embedding similarity	Tab/tagging
Education/Background Information	Text similarity and keyword extraction/matching	Prompt/links to resources

Table 1: Summary of different objectives, their corresponding algorithmic design and interface design

users' knowledge in different topics) (Thurman and Schifferes, 2012). Comment sections would then match these topics with the current article users interact with via text similarity (e.g. cosine similarity) and/or keyword matching. Comment sections would prompt users to comment in the comment section when an article potentially matches their expertise. If users find a specific topic in a comment unfamiliar and not directly related to the main topic in the article they interact with, and want to explore this unfamiliar topic in depth, the comment section could also aggregate a combination of external Wikipedia links and internal news article links to provide background information.

Note that these three objectives could be pursued by the newsrooms at the same time, which could eventually be helpful to avoid users' concern of filter bubbles and losing the big picture of public interest (Monzer et al., 2020). I summarize the three objectives along with their algorithmic design and data collection methods in Table 1.

3 User Interaction with Personalized Comment Section

I discuss how comment sections could be personalized in different designs based on different objectives in Section 2 and summarize how algorithms could support each objective in Table 1. In this section, I streamline an ideal interaction between users and a personalized comment section in Section 3.1 based on the three objectives in Section 2 and I further discuss how transparency, user control, and diversity of content types could help users have a better interactive experience with a personalized comment section.

3.1 An example interaction between a personalized comment section and users

Imagine you are about to interact with a comment section. You open the personalized comment section, and then it shows the default ranking of all comments (either in chronological order or by popularity) to provide the same reading experience to all users. On top of the comment section, you have the ability to turn the personalization on or off through a drop-down menu. In this drop-down menu, you could select how you want to personalize the comments (i.e., personalized by relevance/diversity, more details in Section 2.1 and 2.2).

Once you select your personalization objective, the comment section will then automatically show the personalized curation and notify you that the comments are personalized based on geographics, previous commenting history, or pre-selected topic interests. You can choose to comment directly in the comment section and/or reply to others' comments in a sub-thread. The system presents the opportunity to interact easily with not just "personal stories" but other content types, such as "opinions" and "questions" from the community, by filtering and selecting content based on their tags. A pop-up window notifies you that this topic is within your area of expertise, and it encourages to share your expertise with other users (see Section 2.3).

When interacting with the comment section, you discover some relevant experiences and opinions, you understand what others are talking about, and you contribute back to the community. And if you are not satisfied with the personalization, there is always a way to go back to the default interface.

This is an ideal interaction experience with a personalized comment section. To better support this interaction with a personalized comment section, I propose two interaction objectives for researchers and newsrooms to consider in the design process: transparency/user control and comment type diversity.

3.1.1 Transparency and User Control

The lack of transparency about the personalization process may lead to a lack of trust in receiving personalized news (Monzer et al., 2020). To gain users' trust, a personalized comment section should notify users whenever the comments are being personalized. Power users (i.e., highly self-motivated learners who have the expertise and interest in adopting new technologies and interface features) prefer having user controls that allow them to determine when to start/stop personalization (Sundar and Marathe, 2010). Therefore, a personalized comment section should allow users to turn personalization on and off by selecting personalization objectives from a dropdown menu. Users should also have the ability to independently change different personalization objectives.

3.1.2 Comment Type Diversity

Apart from diversifying the content based on the similarity between comments and users' previous posts, one way to further diversify and personalize the experience would be to provide a mix of different types of comment content (e.g., personal stories, opinions, threads containing questions, expertise, etc.), which may be detected through clustering algorithms or classification algorithms based on crowd-sourcing tags. Comments could be tagged with multiple types (e.g., personal story and opinions). In a personalized system, users should be able to interact with various types of content (Stray, 2021).

Access to diverse content could further benefit users' personalization experience by allowing them to filter what they want to see based on different tags (i.e., "personal story", "opinions", etc.) attached to different comments. And it may encourage users to learn the topic and the community more deeply if they want to focus on a specific perspective to investigate the topic (e.g., to follow commenters who have specific domain knowledge, to participate in the community debate, and to understand if community members have questions/doubts on a topic). In order to encourage users to read and interact with various kinds of content, a personalized comment section could even extend this interaction by notifying users when they only consume one type of content (e.g., personal story) while ignoring other potential types (e.g., opinions).

To summarize, an ideal comment section should personalize comment content based on different objectives, including relevance, diversity, and education/background information, and also provide a transparent and diversified interaction experience for users. By implementing these design objectives and approaches, comment sections could achieve a personalized yet representative reading experience for all users.

References

Balázs Bodó, Natali Helberger, Sarah Eskens, and Judith Möller. 2019. Interested in diversity: The role of user attitudes, algorithmic feedback loops, and policy in news personalization. *Digital Journalism*, 7(2):206–229.

Justin Cheng, Michael Bernstein, Cristian Danescu-Niculescu-Mizil, and Jure Leskovec. 2017. Anyone can become a troll: Causes of trolling behavior in online discussions. In *Proceedings of the 2017 ACM conference on computer supported cooperative work and social computing*, pages 1217–1230.

Glenn Greenwald and Rubina Madan Fillion. 2017. Comment sections are essential for news sites. we're making changes to improve ours. Accessed: 2021-02-28.

Chiao-Fang Hsu, Elham Khabiri, and James Caverlee. 2009. Ranking comments on the social web. In *2009 International Conference on Computational Science and Engineering*, volume 4, pages 90–97. IEEE.

Davy Janssen and Raphaël Kies. 2005. Online forums and deliberative democracy. *Acta política*, 40(3):317–335.

Tom Kenter and Maarten De Rijke. 2015. Short text similarity with word embeddings. In *Proceedings of the 24th ACM international on conference on information and knowledge management*, pages 1411–1420.

Joohan Kim, Robert O Wyatt, and Elihu Katz. 1999. News, talk, opinion, participation: The part played by conversation in deliberative democracy. *Political communication*, 16(4):361–385.

Miller McPherson, Lynn Smith-Lovin, and James M Cook. 2001. Birds of a feather: Homophily in social networks. *Annual review of sociology*, 27(1):415–444.

Cristina Monzer, Judith Moeller, Natali Helberger, and Sarah Eskens. 2020. User perspectives on the news personalisation process: Agency, trust and utility as building blocks. *Digital Journalism*, 8(9):1142–1162.

Cynthia Peacock, Joshua M Scacco, and Natalie Jomini Stroud. 2019. The deliberative influence of comment section structure. *Journalism*, 20(6):752–771.

Titus Plattner. 2018. Five risks of news personalization. Accessed: 2020-10-07.

Kim Christian Schrøder. 2019. What do news readers really want to read about? how relevance works for news audiences. *Reuters Institute for the Study of Journalism*.

Jonathan Stray. 2021. Beyond engagement: Aligning algorithmic recommendations with prosocial goals. Accessed: 2021-01-30.

Natalie Jomini Stroud, Emily Van Duyn, and Cynthia Peacock. 2016. News commenters and news comment readers. *Engaging News Project*, pages 1–21.

S Shyam Sundar and Sampada S Marathe. 2010. Personalization versus customization: The importance of agency, privacy, and power usage. *Human Communication Research*, 36(3):298–322.

Neil Thurman and Steve Schifferes. 2012. The future of personalization at news websites: Lessons from a longitudinal study. *Journalism Studies*, 13(5-6):775–790.

Yixue Wang and Nicholas Diakopoulos. 2021a. Journalistic source discovery: Supporting the identification of news sources in user generated content. In *Proceedings of the 2021 CHI Conference on Human Factors in Computing Systems*, CHI '21. Association for Computing Machinery.

Yixue Wang and Nicholas Diakopoulos. 2021b. The role of new york times picks in comment quality and engagement. In *Proceedings of the 54th Hawaii International Conference on System Sciences*, page 2924.

Mark Weiss. 2019. Digiday research: 70 percent of publishers say they personalize content. Accessed: 2020-10-07.

Unsupervised Approach to Multilingual User Comments Summarization

Aleš Žagar, Marko Robnik-Šikonja
University of Ljubljana, Faculty of Computer and Information Science
Večna pot 113, 1000 Ljubljana, Slovenia
Ales.Zagar@fri.uni-lj.si Marko.Robnik@fri.uni-lj.si

Abstract

User commenting is a valuable feature of many news outlets, enabling them a contact with readers and enabling readers to express their opinion, provide different viewpoints, and even complementary information. Yet, large volumes of user comments are hard to filter, let alone read and extract relevant information. The research on the summarization of user comments is still in its infancy, and human-created summarization datasets are scarce, especially for less-resourced languages. To address this issue, we propose an unsupervised approach to user comments summarization, which uses a modern multilingual representation of sentences together with standard extractive summarization techniques. Our comparison of different sentence representation approaches coupled with different summarization approaches shows that the most successful combinations are the same in news and comment summarization. The empirical results and presented visualisation show usefulness of the proposed methodology for several languages.

1 Introduction

Readers of news articles are often interested in what others think, what their perspectives are, and whether they can get any additional information from them. User comment sections on news web pages are often a good source for extending, presenting, and challenging their own views. On the other hand, many news providers see user comments sections of their websites as a way to connect to their readers, get relevant feedback, and sometimes even extract complementary information.

Many news articles get a large number of comments in a short time, which is especially true for popular and controversial topics. When dealing with an individual article, users can usually sort comments by relevancy or publishing time. While not ideal, this is satisfactory to get insight into the most popular thread or discussion but lacks in providing an overview of the whole discussion (Llewellyn et al., 2014). This, together with the low amount of time users are willing to spend in reading comments, is one of the reasons to automatically provide comprehensive overviews of discussions.

User comments can be irrelevant, deceiving, and may contain hate speech. Language is often informal with ill-formed sentences full of spelling and grammatical errors that are hard to understand. Because of that, comments are easily dismissed as not worth the attention and time. In addition, non-standard expressed content is difficult to encode into an informative numerical representation as standard embedding techniques are mostly based on more standard language (Gu and Yu, 2020).

The goal of text summarization is to compress original data and present it in a shorter form conveying the essential information (Allahyari et al., 2017). Two main approaches exist, extractive and abstractive. The extractive summarization approach selects essential information and does not modify content; its goal is to copy the most informative non-redundant sentences, phrases, or other units of a text. The abstractive approach is similar to how humans summarise documents. It may use new words and expressions, compress long sentences, combine multiple sentences, replace phrases, etc. Current neural network based abstractive approaches mostly provide useful and fluent summaries for short texts but offer no guarantee concerning text correctness (Dong et al., 2020; Cao et al., 2020).

News article summarization is a well-defined and the most studied task within the field of automatic text summarization with several available datasets suitable for supervised learning (Bommasani and Cardie, 2020). For this task also several unsupervised methods exist, based on graph

Proceedings of the EACL Hackashop on News Media Content Analysis and Automated Report Generation, pages 89–98
April 19, 2021

centrality approaches or clustering. On the other hand, the user comment summarization task is not well-defined and established. In a survey paper on user comments, Potthast et al. (2012) describe it as the extraction of sentences that express an opinion. This proposal categorises it as an information retrieval task, close to comment filtering and comment ranking. We believe that this categorisation is limited as it does not consider many other aspects, such as complementarity of information, coverage of different topics and opinions, impact on public discourse, possibly offensive speech, non-standard language, etc.

Cross-lingual approaches to text processing (Ruder et al., 2019) enable the transfer of trained models from resource-rich languages to low-resource languages. Many multilingual neural sentence representation models were released (Artetxe and Schwenk, 2019; Reimers and Gurevych, 2019; Feng et al., 2020; Yang et al., 2020), which presents an opportunity to improve standard unsupervised extractive approaches (Mihalcea and Tarau, 2004; Erkan and Radev, 2004; Llewellyn et al., 2014) that use sparse representations such as TF-IDF weighted bag-of-words.

In this work, we developed an unsupervised extractive approach to text summarization that combines traditional unsupervised methods (graph and clustering-based) with the above-mentioned state-of-the-art multilingual sentence encoders. We assess these encoders in combination with different extractive summarizers and dimensionality reduction techniques. We used Croatian, English and German datasets containing news articles and user comments.

Our main contributions are:

- To the best of our knowledge, we present the first multilingual unsupervised approach to automatic summarization of user comments using modern neural sentence embeddings.

- We analyse and visualize the performance of state-of-the-art multilingual sentence encoders on both clustering-based and graph-based summarization methods.

- We create a dataset of Croatian news articles appropriate for news summarization task.

The paper consists of six sections. In Section 2, we present the related work. Section 3 contains description of datasets we used. In Section 4, we outline and explain our approach to unsupervised text summarization. Section 5 presents visual and automatic evaluation of the results. In Section 6, we summarize the work done, present limitations of our approach, and ideas for further work.

2 Related work

In this section, we present related research on comment summarization and other related summarization tasks.

User comments can be divided into comments on non-textual resources (photos or videos) and comments on textual resources (news articles, product reviews, etc.) (Ma et al., 2012). Potthast et al. (2012) argue that the most important tasks done on comments are filtering, ranking, and summarization. We focus on the latter two.

Most of the research on user comments summarization uses unsupervised extractive approaches that combine ranking and clustering methods. Khabiri et al. (2011) used LDA for clustering, and ranking algorithms (MEAD, LexRank) to summarize comments on YouTube videos. Ma et al. (2012) developed a topic-driven approach in which they compared clustering methods and ranking methods (Maximal Marginal Relevance, Rating & Length) on comments from Yahoo News. Llewellyn et al. (2014) used standard clustering and ranking methods (K-means, PageRank, etc.) to summarize the comments section of the UK newspaper The Guardian. Hsu et al. (2011) proposed a hierarchical comments-based clustering approach to summarize YouTube user comments. All listed methods use classical text representation approaches, while we propose the use of modern neural sentence embedding methods.

A related task to comment summarization is discussion thread summarization. The distinctive difference is that original posts are very different from news articles. van Oortmerssen et al. (2017) used text mining to analyze cancer forum discussions. In addition to ranking and clustering, Alharbi et al. (2020) use hand-crafted text quality features such as common words between the thread reply and the initial post, a semantic distance between thread reply and thread centroid, etc. The conversation summarization (Murray and Carenini, 2008; Chen and Yang, 2020), email summarization (Kaur and Kaur, 2017), and Twitter Topics summarization (Sharifi et al., 2010) are also relevant related tasks.

3 Datasets

In this section, we first describe the creation of two Croatian summarization datasets used in our research: news articles, and user comments. We also present English and German dataset of user comments.

The CroNews summarization dataset was created from the corpus of approximately 1.8 million news articles from the popular Croatian 24sata news portal[1]. The second dataset (CroComments) is a small evaluation dataset (Milačić, 2020) and contains user comments of 42 articles from Croatian Večernji list website[2], together with their short human-written abstractive summaries[3].

We preprocessed the news articles from the news corpus into a one-sentence-per-line form using the Croatian tokenizer available in the Stanza NLP package (Qi et al., 2020). The user comments in CroComments were already preprocessed in a similar way (Milačić, 2020).

The articles in the original news dataset contained no summaries. We took the first paragraph of an article as a proxy for a summary. In the dataset, this paragraph is named 'lead'. We sampled 5000 (from a total of 17 194) examples that satisfied the next criteria: more than 6 and less than 30 sentences were present in an article (we presupposed that articles with less than 6 sentences are too short for summarization), and the overlap between the abstract (lead) and article text was within 40 and 90 ROUGE-L points. The last criterion was designed to make sure that the first paragraph of an article overlaps with the rest of it in terms of content but we avoided strictly duplicated content. Most of the abstracts have a missing period at the end. We fixed that by appending it at the end of an article. We call the resulting dataset CroNews in the remainder of the paper.

While we focused on the Croatian language, to assess the multilingual potential of the proposed approach, we tested it also on English and German. For English, we used the New York Times Comments corpus[4] with over 2 million comments. For German, we used One Million Posts Corpus (Schabus and Skowron, 2018) with 1 million comments from the Austrian daily broadsheet newspaper DER STANDARD.

[1] https://www.24sata.hr/

[2] https://www.vecernji.hr/

[3] Available upon email request.

[4] https://www.kaggle.com/aashita/nyt-comments

4 Methodology

In this section, we describe our approach to unsupervised (multilingual) summarization which is comprised of two main components:

1. Neural sentence encoders represent the text in a numeric form as described in Section 4.1. This can be done in a cross-lingual manner to project many languages in the same numeric space and makes our approach multilingual.

2. From the numeric representation of sentences in the commentaries below a given article, we select the most representative sentences to be returned as summaries. To achieve that, we use two groups of approaches as described in Section 4.2: clustering-based and graph-based. Clustering approaches group similar sentence vectors and select the representative sentences based on the proximity to the centroid vector. Graph-based methods construct a graph based on the similarity of sentence vectors and then use graph node rankings to rank the sentences. The best-ranked sentences are returned as the summary.

As a further, optional component of our approach, the sentence vectors can be mapped to two-dimensional space with dimensionality reduction techniques (we use PCA or UMAP) and visualized in an interactive graph. To demonstrate these capabilities, we released a Jupyter notebook on Google Colab[5].

4.1 Sentence representation

In order to cluster or rank sentences in user comments, we have to first transform them from a symbolic to numeric form. In our work, we use sentence-level representation, as the extractive summarization techniques we use work on this level. Sentence embeddings aim to map sentences with a similar meaning close to each other in a numerical vector space. Initial approaches to sentence embeddings averaged word embeddings, e.g., GloVe (Pennington et al., 2014) vectors, or created Skip-Thought vectors (Kiros et al., 2015). A successful massively multilingual sentence embeddings approach LASER is built from a large BiLSTM neural network on parallel corpora (Artetxe and Schwenk, 2019).

[5] https://colab.research.google.com/drive/12wUDg64k4oK24rNSd4DRZL9xywNMiPil?usp=sharing

Recently, the Transformer architecture (Vaswani et al., 2017) is the most successful and prevalent neural architecture for the majority of language processing tasks, especially if pretrained on large corpora using masked language model objective, such as the BERT model (Devlin et al., 2019). In sentence embedding, naive solutions, e.g., averaging BERT output layer or using the first CLS token in the BERT architecture, often produced results worse than averaging of word vectors.

We used three competitive transformer-based sentence encoders. Reimers and Gurevych (2019) created siamese and triplet networks to update the weights and enable comparison of sentences. Their model called SBERT adds a pooling operation to the output of BERT to derive a sentence embedding. They trained it on natural language inference (NLI) datasets. Feng et al. (2020) combined masked language model and translation language model to adapt multilingual BERT and produced language-agnostic sentence embeddings for 109 languages. Their model is called LaBSE (Language-agnostic BERT Sentence Embedding). Yang et al. (2020) proposed a novel training method, conditional masked language modeling (CMLM) to learn sentence embeddings on unlabeled corpora. In CMLM, a sentence depends on the encoded sentence level representation of the adjacent sentence.

Our sentence embedding vectors have 768 dimensions. A dimensionality reduction may improve clustering due to noise reduction. To test that hypothesis, we tested two variants of sentence selection approaches (both graph and clustering-based): with and without dimensionality reduction. For the dimensionality reduction down to two dimensions, we tested PCA and UMAP (McInnes et al., 2018) mthods. We set the neighbourhood value of UMAP to 5, the number of components to 2, and the metric to Euclidian.

4.2 Selecting representative sentences

Once the sentences of comments belonging to a certain article are represented as numeric vectors, we have to select sentences for the summary. We use two types of approaches: i) clustering the sentences and returning the most central sentences from each cluster, and ii) representing sentences as nodes in a graph, based on their similarities and selecting the highest-ranked nodes as the summary.

For clustering, we used k-means and Gaussian mixture algorithm. We set the number of clusters to 2 because in our experimental evaluation we decided to extract only the best two sentences. We extracted the best sentences based on their proximity to centroid vectors of the clusters returned by the clustering algorithms. Clustering methods deal well with the redundancy of extracted sentences as the extracted sentences are by construction very different.

Graph-based ranking algorithms score the importance of vertices within a graph. A popular method to determine the importance of a vertex uses the number of other vertices pointing to it and the importance of the pointing vertices. In our case, each vertex in a graph represents a sentence. We used the TextRank (Mihalcea and Tarau, 2004) method, inspired by the PageRank algorithm (Page et al., 1999) that can be intuitively explained with the concept of eigenvector centrality or stationary distribution of random walks. For a similarity measure of sentences, we used the cosine similarity computed on sentence vectors.

We used two baseline summarization methods: i) selecting random $n = 2$ sentences (BaseRand), and ii) selecting the first $n = 2$ sentences (BaseLead).

For both clustering and dimensionality reduction, we used the scikit-learn implementations in python (Pedregosa et al., 2011). For the graph-based approach, we used PageRank from the NetworkX python library (Hagberg et al., 2008).

5 Evaluation

In this section, we first provide visualization of sentence embeddings, followed by the analysis of summarization. The visualization demonstrates the suitability of the proposed cross-lingual sentence representation for unsupervised summarization. In summarization experiments, we first present results of news article summarization, followed by the commentaries.

5.1 Visualization of sentence embeddings

We first visually demonstrate the utility of used sentence embeddings in a multilingual setting. In Figure 1, we show a visual evaluation of the proposed cross-lingual sentence representation for the unsupervised summarization. The dots in the image are sentence vectors of the synthetic sentences (described below). The image was produced using the Gaussian Mixture clustering using the sentence representation produced with the SBERT encoder and PCA dimensionality reduction. Sentences of various lengths corresponding to three topics (school, weather, and music) were written in Slovene and translated into English, Croatian, and German. The three large colored clusters correspond to three topics, which is an indication that the sentence representation captures different contents well. We can observe also small groups of four sentences (an original Slovene sentence and three translations of it) that confirm the accuracy of the multilingual sentence encoder. The translated sentences are close together which is an indication that the representation is semantically adequate even in the multilingual setting. The rectangle on the top contains the sentences: Šolsko leto se je začelo drugače kot ponavadi; The school year started differently than usual; Školska godina započela je drugačije nego inače; Das Schuljahr begann anders als gewöhnlich. The rectangle on the right shows: Vreme bo jutri lepo; The weather will be nice tomorrow; Vrijeme će sutra biti lijepo; Das Wetter wird morgen schön sein. The rectangle on the left consists of: Kitara je zelo popularen glasbeni inštrument; The guitar is a very popular musical instrument; Gitara je vrlo popularan glazbeni instrument; Die Gitarre ist ein sehr beliebtes Musikinstrument.

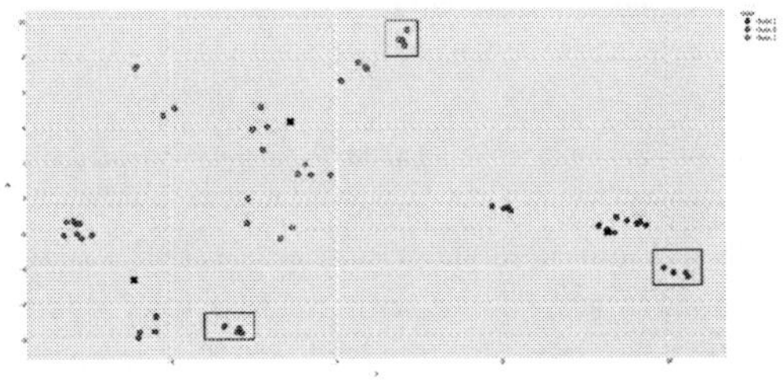

Figure 1: Example of Gaussian Mixture clustering with SBERT encoder and PCA dimensionality reduction of sentences from three topics (school, music, and weather, shown in green, blue, and red, respectively) and four languages. The sentences in the rectangles contain the same text in four languages (Slovene, English, Croatian, and English). The rectangle on the top contains the sentence "The school year started differently than usual.", the right one is "The weather will be nice tomorrow.", and the left one is "The guitar is a very popular musical instrument.".

5.2 News summarization

Due to the shortage of supervised data for automatic evaluation of user comments, we first test our unsupervised approach on the CroNews dataset, constructed as described in Section 3. We expected that the results would give us an insight into the performance of different combinations of methods, described in Section 4.

The results in Table 1 show commonly used ROUGE metric. The best performing experimental setup uses the LaBSE sentence encoder, no scaling, and the TextRank algorithm for sentence selection. The BaseLead baseline is 4.5 points behind the best model and ranked somewhere in the middle of all combinations. This corresponds with the findings of Zhu et al. (2019), who analysed the phenomenon of lead bias in news article summarization task. The BaseRand baseline is near the end of the ranks, as expected.

Enc.	Scaling	Summary	R-1	R-2	R-L
None	None	BaseLead	36.46	24.04	34.52
None	None	BaseRand	35.07	23.69	33.47
CMLM	None	GaussMix	35.29	22.77	33.52
CMLM	None	K-means	34.33	21.87	32.58
CMLM	None	TextRank	39.37	26.95	37.65
CMLM	PCA	GaussMix	35.71	23.90	34.17
CMLM	PCA	K-means	35.69	23.93	34.12
CMLM	PCA	TextRank	39.58	27.61	37.98
CMLM	UMAP	GaussMix	36.99	25.14	35.35
CMLM	UMAP	K-means	37.05	25.15	35.42
CMLM	UMAP	TextRank	38.65	26.94	37.06
LaBSE	None	GaussMix	38.81	26.41	37.04
LaBSE	None	K-means	37.70	25.18	35.92
LaBSE	None	TextRank	40.07	28.42	39.00
LaBSE	PCA	GaussMix	36.04	24.06	34.41
LaBSE	PCA	K-means	35.95	23.85	34.30
LaBSE	PCA	TextRank	38.69	26.80	37.10
LaBSE	UMAP	GaussMix	36.84	24.92	35.28
LaBSE	UMAP	K-means	37.22	25.31	35.63
LaBSE	UMAP	TextRank	37.90	25.86	36.29
SBERT	None	GaussMix	37.36	25.09	35.64
SBERT	None	K-means	37.05	24.65	35.26
SBERT	None	TextRank	38.63	26.55	36.99
SBERT	PCA	GaussMix	36.34	24.34	34.71
SBERT	PCA	K-means	36.42	24.48	34.81
SBERT	PCA	TextRank	37.86	26.11	36.31
SBERT	UMAP	GaussMix	36.94	25.14	35.38
SBERT	UMAP	K-means	36.92	25.06	35.38
SBERT	UMAP	TextRank	36.38	24.48	34.83

Table 1: Results expressed as ROUGE scores on the CroNews dataset. Colors correspond to ranks, darker hues correspond to better scores.

Statistics of different parameters in Table 2 show that LaBSE achieved on average 0.6 more ROUGE-L points than SBERT and CMLM, which are close in terms of performance. UMAP scaling preserved information better than PCA for 0.3 points but achieved 0.4 points less compared to no scaling. TextRank ranking method is superior to clustering for more than 2 points.

MatchSum (Zhong et al., 2020) is currently the

Group	Mean	Std	Min	Max	95%CI	Size
Encoder						
LaBSE	36.11	1.47	34.30	39.01	(34.98, 37.25)	9
SBERT	35.49	0.75	34.71	36.99	(34.91, 36.06)	9
CMLM	35.32	1.91	32.58	37.99	(33.86, 36.79)	9
Scaling						
None	35.96	2.01	32.58	39.01	(34.42, 37.50)	9
UMAP	35.63	0.66	34.84	37.06	(35.12, 36.14)	9
PCA	35.33	1.44	34.12	37.99	(34.22, 36.43)	9
Summarizer						
TextRank	37.03	1.18	34.84	39.01	(36.13, 37.93)	9
Clustering	34.94	1.00	32.58	37.04	(34.45, 35.44)	18

Table 2: ROUGE-L scores grouped by sentence encoder, scaling, and type of summarizer.

best extractive summarization model. It was trained on the large CNN/Daily Mail dataset and achieved 44.41 ROUGE-1 and 40.55 ROUGE-L scores. As we can observe from Table 1, our best scores for the Croatian news lag approximately 4.3 ROUGE-1 and 2.5 ROUGE-L points behind these scores which is a relevant difference in performance. However, we have to take into account that we use leads as an approximation for the summaries.

5.3 User commentaries summarization

We used the same experimental setup, as reported in Table 1, to summarize the CroComments dataset. The results of both datasets are very similar if we rank the models, with the best models being identical. TextRank with CMLM or LaBSE encoder is superior to clustering. Surprisingly, SBERT shows significantly lower performance with both clustering and ranking (with ranking worse than clustering).

We identified a few reasons that explain the lower scores of comment summarization compared to news summarization. For comments, the sentence encoders face a more challenging task of encoding the informal language; for the same reason, the accuracy of a sentence tokenizer is also significantly lower, as our inspection revealed. A single CroComment document (containing all comments related to one news article) is usually comprised of texts by several authors, of variable length, and written in different styles. CroComment documents are longer and exhibit a greater length variability. The average length of a document is 19.81 sentences with the standard deviation of 13.16 in comparison to CroNews dataset which contains 7.85 sentences with the standard deviation of 1.42. These differences make the comment summarization task difficult for a model trained on standard language in much shorter news articles.

Enc.	Scaling	Summary	R-1	R-2	R-L
CMLM	None	K-means	24.44	11.50	23.18
CMLM	None	TextRank	33.08	17.24	31.09
CMLM	PCA	GaussMix	19.71	08.53	18.79
CMLM	PCA	K-means	22.30	10.66	20.64
CMLM	PCA	TextRank	26.01	12.50	24.60
CMLM	UMAP	GaussMix	24.83	12.18	23.28
CMLM	UMAP	K-means	23.88	10.44	22.37
CMLM	UMAP	TextRank	23.02	11.78	22.31
LaBSE	None	GaussMix	26.77	13.39	25.77
LaBSE	None	K-means	26.59	12.89	25.01
LaBSE	None	TextRank	34.35	18.50	32.28
LaBSE	PCA	GaussMix	24.15	11.61	22.90
LaBSE	PCA	K-means	25.32	14.17	24.63
LaBSE	PCA	TextRank	28.53	15.60	26.95
LaBSE	UMAP	GaussMix	26.39	12.99	24.28
LaBSE	UMAP	K-means	27.36	14.45	26.04
LaBSE	UMAP	TextRank	24.99	12.50	23.80
SBERT	None	GaussMix	25.34	12.43	23.82
SBERT	None	K-means	26.13	12.84	24.67
SBERT	None	TextRank	25.20	11.71	23.25
SBERT	PCA	GaussMix	21.78	09.98	20.51
SBERT	PCA	K-means	23.96	11.46	22.47
SBERT	PCA	TextRank	25.44	11.40	23.76
SBERT	UMAP	GaussMix	25.29	13.00	24.16
SBERT	UMAP	K-means	24.94	12.04	23.62
SBERT	UMAP	TextRank	24.44	10.92	22.98

Table 3: Results expressed with ROUGE scores on the CroComments evaluation dataset with human-written summaries of comments. Colors correspond to ranks, darker hues correspond to better scores.

As an example, Table 4 shows comments belonging to one selected article. We tokenized comments, encoded them with the LaBSE sentence encoder, and scored with the TextRank algorithm. The sentences with the highest score in each user comment are typeset with red, and two highest scored sentences are shown in green. The value 'ref' in the column 'Id' indicates the human-written abstractive summary of the listed comments; the value 'lead' means the first paragraph of the article. Notice that the human-written summary and the high-scored sentences strongly overlap.

Comment no. 54412 demonstrates how the tokenizer and encoder face a difficult task. It is evident that the comment should have been split into several sentences to improve readability, has missing punctuation, and does not contain letters with the caron. Comment no. 54299 shows the limitation of extractive approaches since it cannot be understood properly without the context. The comment with the lowest score (no. 56141) does not add much to the conversation.

Table 5 shows an example from New York Times

Id	Croatian text	English translation
lead	Svaki gost koji je došao u Hrvatsku 2009. godine nije poklonjen, morali smo se za njega izborili. Ovakav učinak, uz ostalo, rezultat je mjera koje smo poduzeli, uz lijepo, sunčano vrijeme. Sunce je ove godine sjalo i u Turskoj, Francuskoj, Španjolskoj, ali očito nešto bolje u Hrvatskoj, slikovit je bio ministar Bajs.	Every guest who came to Croatia in 2009 was not given away, we had to fight for him. This effect, among other things, is the result of the measures we have taken, with nice, sunny weather. This year, the sun was shining in Turkey, France, Spain, but obviously somewhat better in Croatia, Minister Bajs was picturesque.
54279 score: 0.0552	Hrvatski turizam je u plusu za 0,2 Bravo,bravo,bravo . Pravi turizam ce poceti u Hrvatskoj tek tada kad nebude vise nitko od vas smdljivaca u vladi . Otvorite ovi ljudi , pa austrija napravi vise novaca od turizma nego Hrvatska . Svaku godinu smo u plusu a love nigdje pa naravno kad od 10-15% ostane samo 0.2 % . Koji su to muljat3ori i od kuda imate taj podatak . Revolucija je jedini spas , skidam kapu Rumunjima , oni su to fino rijesili . Bog i Hrvati	Croatian tourism is in the plus by 0.2 Bravo, bravo, bravo. Real tourism will start in Croatia only when there are no more of you smugglers in the government. Open these people, and Austria will make more money from tourism than Croatia. Every year we are in the red and the money is nowhere to be found, so of course when only 0.2 % of 10-15 % remains. What are these scammers and where do you get that information from. Revolution is the only salvation, I take my hat off to the Romanians, they solved it fine. God and Croats
54299 score: 0.0587	To vam je tako : 1999 godine Amerikanci su sredili stanje na Kosovu i cijela Europa a i druge države dale su zeleno svjetlo svojim građanima da mogu na ljetovanja u hrvatsku i ostali dio Balkana.2000 godine dolazi za ministricu turizma gospođa Župan - Rusković . Ta godina pokazuje se za turizam dobra i to se pripisuje SDP -u i gospođi ministarki . Ove godine sunce jaće i duđe sije pa eto to se pripisuje ministru Bajsu . Ja ču im samo poručiti . Ne bacajte pare na \" promocije \" jer svijet zna za nas , radije te novce ulažite u izobrazbu turističkoga i ugostiteljskoga osoblja . To bi bio naš največi uspjeh .	This is how it is for you: in 1999, the Americans settled the situation in Kosovo and the whole of Europe, and other countries gave the green light to their citizens to go on vacation to Croatia and the rest of the Balkans. In 2000, Ms. Župan - Rusković came to be Minister of Tourism. That year proves to be a good thing for tourism and it is attributed to the SDP and the Minister. This year the sun is shining stronger and longer, so that is attributed to Minister Bajs. I'll just tell them. Don't waste money on \"promotions \" because the world knows about us, rather invest that money in the training of tourism and catering staff. That would be our greatest success.
54311 0.0448	Sezona je ove godine bila iznad prosjeka i normalno da je Bajs ponosan	This season has been above average and it's normal for Bajs to be proud
54412 score: 0.0534	slazem se sa Somelier , a po izjavama i komentarima sto daje ministar Bajs vidi se nema veze s turizmom , HR je konkurentna samo u o dredjenim vrstama turizma (nauticki turizam) i trebalo bi se fokusirati upravo na njih koji usput najvise i trose , a ne slusati ove gluposti Bajsa da je sezona uspjesna zato sto je dozvolio onim krsevima od aviona da slijecu ili zato sto je dao 20 miliona € za reklamu na googlu i eurosportu	I agree with Somelier, and according to the statements and comments given by Minister Bajs, there is nothing to do with tourism. HR is competitive only in o dredged types of tourism (nautical tourism) and we should focus on those who spend the most, and not listen to this nonsense of Bajs that the season was successful because he allowed those breaches of planes to land or because he gave 20 million € for advertising on google and eurosport
54413 score: 0.0582	Bajs , kaj nas briga kak su turistički tržili u Austriji , Italiji , Francuskoj ili Grčkoj ? Raci ti nama zakaj je u Hrvatskoj bilo manje turistof neg lani iako ti tvrdiš da mi imamo kakti prednost kao auto destinacija ? Zakaj i u onom jednom jadnom mesecu kad je bilo više turistof nek lani ima manje lovice ? Zakaj se inšpekcije i dalje zezaju sa boravišnim taksama vikendaša dok ugostitelji premlaćuju goste , ne izdaju račune i jasno , ne plačaju poreze , uključujući i PDV ?	Bajs, do we care how they marketed tourism in Austria, Italy, France or Greece? Tell us why there were fewer tourists in Croatia than last year, even though you claim that we have some advantage as a car destination? Why, even in that poor month when there were more tourists, let there be less money last year? Why do the inspections continue to mess with the weekend taxes of the weekenders while the caterers beat the guests, do not issue invoices and clearly do not pay taxes, including VAT?
56141 0.0376	Nakon ove kostatacije sa zadovoljstvom mogu kostatirati da je Bajs napredovao sa jedne na dvije litre dnevno.	After this casting, I am pleased to say that Bajs has progressed from one to two liters a day.
ref.	Hrvatski turizam u porastu , uspješna sezona . Vlada je problem i ne ostaje dovoljno novca . Ne bacajt pare ne promocije već ulažite u izobrazbu turističkoga i ugostiteljskoga osoblja . Baj ponosan na sezonu iznad prosjeka . HR je konkurentna samo u određenim vrstama turizma i trebalo bi se fokusirati na njih . Zakaj je manje turista nego lani i nanje novca . Inspekcije se zezaju sa boravišnim taksama a ugostitelji premlaćuju goste , ne izdaju račune i ne plaćaju poreze .	Croatian tourism on the rise, successful season. The government is a problem and there is not enough money left. Don't waste money on promotions, but invest in the training of tourism and catering staff. Bajs proud of the above average season. HR is competitive only in certain types of tourism and should focus on them. Why are there fewer tourists than last year and money for them. Inspections mess with sojourn taxes and caterers beat guests, do not issue invoices and do not pay taxes.

Table 4: Visualization of the most important sentences in each user comment (in red). The original comments are on the left-hand side and their machine translations on the right-hand side. The reference score is at the bottom. Two sentences with the highest score are shown in green.

Comments, which was preprocessed and evaluated in the same manner as the example from Table 4. The selected sentences capture both prevalent themes (artistic freedom and racial questions) but exhibit the problem of redundancy. More examples from English, along with German, can be found on our source code repository[6].

6 Conclusion

We developed a multilingual unsupervised approach to user commentary summarization and tested it on a less-resourced Croatian language. Our models are based on cross-lingual neural sentence encoders, which make them easily applicable to many languages with little or no preprocessing. We tested several sentence representations and assessed the effect of dimensionality reduction. We used clustering and graph-based ranking algorithms to select sentences that form the final summaries. The results were promising both on the news articles dataset and the user comments evaluation dataset. The source code of our approach is freely available under the open-source licence.

The presented approach has several limitations. It only works within extractive summarization approaches, which do not allow sentence modification. With abstraction techniques, e.g., sentence compression, we could further distill the important information. We only tested sentence representation methods, while paragraph or document embeddings would also be sensible. We also did not exploit the information contained in the threading structure of the commentaries and possible relation of comments with the text of an original article.

In further work, we intend to exploit additional information in comments which was not used in the present study. The number of likes that a comment received could be used to weight sentences. Instead of working on a sentence-level, we could take a comment as a whole and embed it as a document. We plan to extend the work on visualization since it showed promising results, especially in the interactive exploration mode, inaccessible in the paper format.

Acknowledgments

The work was partially supported by the Slovenian Research Agency (ARRS) core research programme P6-0411 and the Ministry of Culture of Slovenia through project RSDO (Development of Slovene in a Digital Environment – Language Resources and Technologies). This paper is supported by European Union's Horizon 2020 research and innovation programme under grant agreement No 825153, project EMBEDDIA (Cross-Lingual Embeddings for Less-Represented Languages in European News Media).

[6]`https://github.com/azagsam/xl-user-comments`

References

Abdullah Alharbi, Qaiser Shah, Hashem Alyami, Muhammad Adnan Gul, M Irfan Uddin, Atif Khan, and Fasee Ullah. 2020. Sentence embedding based semantic clustering approach for discussion thread summarization. *Complexity*, 2020:1–11.

Mehdi Allahyari, Seyedamin Pouriyeh, Mehdi Assefi, Saeid Safaei, Elizabeth D Trippe, Juan B Gutierrez, and Krys Kochut. 2017. Text summarization techniques: a brief survey. *arXiv preprint arXiv:1707.02268*.

Mikel Artetxe and Holger Schwenk. 2019. Massively multilingual sentence embeddings for zero-shot cross-lingual transfer and beyond. *Transactions of the Association for Computational Linguistics*, 7:597–610.

Rishi Bommasani and Claire Cardie. 2020. Intrinsic evaluation of summarization datasets. In *Proceedings of the 2020 Conference on Empirical Methods in Natural Language Processing (EMNLP)*, pages 8075–8096.

Meng Cao, Yue Dong, Jiapeng Wu, and Jackie Chi Kit Cheung. 2020. Factual error correction for abstractive summarization models. In *Proceedings of the 2020 Conference on Empirical Methods in Natural Language Processing (EMNLP)*, pages 6251–6258.

Jiaao Chen and Diyi Yang. 2020. Multi-view sequence-to-sequence models with conversational structure for abstractive dialogue summarization. In *Proceedings of the 2020 Conference on Empirical Methods in Natural Language Processing (EMNLP)*, pages 4106–4118.

Jacob Devlin, Ming-Wei Chang, Kenton Lee, and Kristina Toutanova. 2019. BERT: Pre-training of deep bidirectional transformers for language understanding. In *Proceedings of the 2019 Conference of the North American Chapter of the Association for Computational Linguistics: Human Language Technologies, Volume 1 (Long and Short Papers)*, pages 4171–4186.

Yue Dong, Shuohang Wang, Zhe Gan, Yu Cheng, Jackie Chi Kit Cheung, and Jingjing Liu. 2020. Multi-fact correction in abstractive text summarization. In *Proceedings of the 2020 Conference on Empirical Methods in Natural Language Processing (EMNLP)*, pages 9320–9331.

Id	Text
24107006 score: 0.0282	This art is all about perception . It is about the point the artist is trying to make and how the viewer sees it . This art should not be limited because it is attached to an emotion these moments being recorded through art of a society that claims to be post racial opens the eyes of those who do not want to see and forces them to . This illustration does that and in my opinion that makes it so much more valuable because it does not just sit in silence it sends a message .
23235619 score: 0.0283	Artists should n't be limited or restricted in what they can do as an artist . Everyone should have a voice or take on a matter no matter how unpopular or offensive the opinion is . Censoring art defeats the creativity and free expression in art . Censorship perverts the message the artist try 's to convey .
22099108 score: 0.0273	I believe that all subjects should be fair game for an artist . It should n't matter if they are depicting a murder , or even if it 's " black subject matter " , every artist has a voice that deserves to be heard . As Smith writes " We all encounter art we do n't like , that upsets and infuriates us . " (1) I understand that some topics are difficult to talk about and that some art is can cause anger but I think that it is irrational to make topics off - limits because people do n't agree with it .
22098876 score: 0.0264	I personally believe that artists should be able to write about anything they want , drive to the studio , then turn those words into beautiful music . Music is an art and in art there are no limits so honestly whatever they feel is relevant to write about , they should have the freedom to do so . Regardless of peoples personal opinions artist should be comfortable to talk about what they want to talk about . " We all encounter art we do n't like , that upsets and infuriates us . " (Gilpin , 1) I understand that some subjects are very sensitive , but most of the things people do n't like to hear are usually cold hard facts about the dark side of society . A few examples would be , hate crimes against all races , racism in america , people killing other people . It s just the sad truth that a lot of people hate to hear . Music is a powerful - subject that can really impact a person .
22075721 0.0258	nothing should be in limited to artist . they should have the freedom to do what they pleased .
22054073 0.0252	I believe there is n't a problem when a white artist draws a topic that is related to discrimination against the Blacks . This artist may want to show that killing black people is wrong . It does n't matter if she 's white or black .
22041906 score: 0.0280	I do n't think that any topic is out of bounds to an artist . That is the idea of an artist , is n't it ? To talk about subjects that they think should be talked about , or that they feel motivated to bring attention to . I do n't think it is right to throw blame and anger towards one group because they are creating art about a different group . I understand why there is anger , but demanding that a work be destroyed is just absurd to me . Could the artist have done something differently ? Possibly , but demanding empathy and understanding from a group different than your own , and then saying their act of trying to do so is inappropriate just does n't make sense . I do n't think any one group " owns " history . History is a human experience . People as a collective own the histories that shaped the world they live in . That is the point of the exhibition . The exhibition description on the Whitney site says , " Throughout the exhibition , artists challenge us to consider how these realities affect our senses of self and community . " Instead of focusing on the color of the artists skin , we should be focusing on the point of the show .. how the painting makes us feel about ourselves and our communities , because I am sure that everyone could say that there is room for improvement when it comes to both .
22031632 score: 0.0219	The question of whether or not any group " owns " a portion of history is not the issue . It is about how that imagery is used , if it is used intelligently , and that it mimics an aspect of white racism : the historic practice of whites displaying the mutilated corpses of black people . To make the issue about censorship is to miss the point . Instead students should be asked to consider how a white person might have better handled her desire to show empathy .

Table 5: Visualization of the most important sentences in each user comment for a sample from the New York Times Comments dataset. Since the conversation is very long, we show here only a part of it. The green color stresses the best two sentences.

Günes Erkan and Dragomir R Radev. 2004. LexRank: Graph-based lexical centrality as salience in text summarization. *Journal of artificial intelligence research*, 22:457–479.

Fangxiaoyu Feng, Yinfei Yang, Daniel Cer, Naveen Arivazhagan, and Wei Wang. 2020. Language-agnostic BERT sentence embedding. *arXiv preprint arXiv:2007.01852*.

Jing Gu and Zhou Yu. 2020. Data Annealing for Informal Language Understanding Tasks. In *Findings of the Association for Computational Linguistics: EMNLP 2020*, pages 3153–3159.

Aric A. Hagberg, Daniel A. Schult, and Pieter J. Swart. 2008. Exploring network structure, dynamics, and function using networkx. In *Proceedings of the 7th Python in Science Conference*, pages 11 – 15.

Chiao-Fang Hsu, James Caverlee, and Elham Khabiri. 2011. Hierarchical comments-based clustering. In *Proceedings of the 2011 ACM Symposium on Applied Computing*, pages 1130–1137.

Kuldeep Kaur and Anantdeep Kaur. 2017. A survey on email summarisation techniques and its challenges. *Asian Journal of Computer Science And Information Technology*, pages 40–43.

Elham Khabiri, James Caverlee, and Chiao-Fang Hsu. 2011. Summarizing user-contributed comments. In *Proceedings of the International AAAI Conference on Web and Social Media*, volume 5, pages 534–537.

Ryan Kiros, Yukun Zhu, Ruslan Salakhutdinov, Richard S. Zemel, Raquel Urtasun, Antonio Torralba, and Sanja Fidler. 2015. Skip-thought vectors.

In *Advances in Neural Information Processing Systems*, pages 3294–3302.

Clare Llewellyn, Claire Grover, and Jon Oberlander. 2014. Summarizing newspaper comments. In *Proceedings of the International AAAI Conference on Web and Social Media*, volume 8, pages 599–602.

Zongyang Ma, Aixin Sun, Quan Yuan, and Gao Cong. 2012. Topic-driven reader comments summarization. In *21st ACM International Conference on Information and Knowledge Management*, pages 265–274.

Leland McInnes, John Healy, Nathaniel Saul, and Lukas Großberger. 2018. UMAP: Uniform manifold approximation and projection. *Journal of Open Source Software*, 3(29):861.

Rada Mihalcea and Paul Tarau. 2004. TextRank: Bringing order into text. In *Proceedings of the Empirical Methods in Natural Language Processing*, pages 404–411.

Katarina Milačić. 2020. Summarization of web comments. Master's thesis, University of Ljubljana, Faculty of Computer and Information Science.

Gabriel Murray and Giuseppe Carenini. 2008. Summarizing spoken and written conversations. In *Proceedings of the Empirical Methods in Natural Language Processing*, pages 773–782.

Gerard van Oortmerssen, Stephan Raaijmakers, Maya Sappelli, Erik Boertjes, Suzan Verberne, Nicole Walasek, and Wessel Kraaij. 2017. Analyzing cancer forum discussions with text mining. *Knowledge Representation for Health Care Process-Oriented Information Systems in Health Care Extraction & Processing of Rich Semantics from Medical Texts*, pages 127–131.

Lawrence Page, Sergey Brin, Rajeev Motwani, and Terry Winograd. 1999. The pagerank citation ranking: Bringing order to the web. Technical report, Stanford InfoLab.

F. Pedregosa, G. Varoquaux, A. Gramfort, V. Michel, B. Thirion, O. Grisel, M. Blondel, P. Prettenhofer, R. Weiss, V. Dubourg, J. Vanderplas, A. Passos, D. Cournapeau, M. Brucher, M. Perrot, and E. Duchesnay. 2011. Scikit-learn: Machine learning in Python. *Journal of Machine Learning Research*, 12:2825–2830.

Jeffrey Pennington, Richard Socher, and Christopher Manning. 2014. GloVe: Global vectors for word representation. In *Proceedings of Empirical Methods in Natural Language Processing (EMNLP)*, pages 1532–1543.

Martin Potthast, Benno Stein, Fabian Loose, and Steffen Becker. 2012. Information retrieval in the commentsphere. *ACM Transactions on Intelligent Systems and Technology (TIST)*, 3(4):1–21.

Peng Qi, Yuhao Zhang, Yuhui Zhang, Jason Bolton, and Christopher D. Manning. 2020. Stanza: A Python natural language processing toolkit for many human languages. In *Proceedings of the 58th Annual Meeting of the Association for Computational Linguistics: System Demonstrations*, pages 101–108.

Nils Reimers and Iryna Gurevych. 2019. Sentence-BERT: Sentence embeddings using Siamese BERT-networks. In *Proceedings of Empirical Methods in Natural Language Processing and International Joint Conference on Natural Language Processing (EMNLP-IJCNLP)*, pages 3982–3992.

Sebastian Ruder, Ivan Vulić, and Anders Søgaard. 2019. A survey of cross-lingual word embedding models. *J. Artif. Int. Res.*, 65(1):569–630.

Dietmar Schabus and Marcin Skowron. 2018. Academic-industrial perspective on the development and deployment of a moderation system for a newspaper website. In *Proceedings of the 11th International Conference on Language Resources and Evaluation (LREC)*, pages 1602–1605, Miyazaki, Japan.

Beaux Sharifi, Mark-anthony Hutton, and Jugal Kalita. 2010. Automatic summarization of Twitter topics. In *Proceedings of National Workshop on Design and Analysis of Algorithm*.

Ashish Vaswani, Noam Shazeer, Niki Parmar, Jakob Uszkoreit, Llion Jones, Aidan N. Gomez, Lukasz Kaiser, and Illia Polosukhin. 2017. Attention is all you need. In *Advances in Neural Information Processing Systems*, pages 5998–6008.

Ziyi Yang, Yinfei Yang, Daniel Cer, Jax Law, and Eric Darve. 2020. Universal sentence representation learning with conditional masked language model. *arXiv preprint arXiv:2012.14388*.

Ming Zhong, Pengfei Liu, Yiran Chen, Danqing Wang, Xipeng Qiu, and Xuan-Jing Huang. 2020. Extractive summarization as text matching. In *Proceedings of the 58th Annual Meeting of the Association for Computational Linguistics*, pages 6197–6208.

Chenguang Zhu, Ziyi Yang, Robert Gmyr, Michael Zeng, and Xuedong Huang. 2019. Make lead bias in your favor: Zero-shot abstractive news summarization. *arXiv preprint arXiv:1912.11602*.

EMBEDDIA Tools, Datasets and Challenges: Resources and Hackathon Contributions

Senja Pollak
Jožef Stefan Institute
senja.pollak@ijs.si

Marko Robnik Šikonja
University of Ljubljana

Matthew Purver
Queen Mary University of London
Jožef Stefan Institute

Michele Boggia
University of Helsinki

Ravi Shekhar
Queen Mary University of London

Marko Pranjić
Trikoder d.o.o.

Salla Salmela
Suomen Tietotoimisto STT

Ivar Krustok
Tarmo Paju
Ekspress Meedia

Carl-Gustav Linden
University of Bergen

Leo Leppänen
Elaine Zosa
University of Helsinki

Matej Ulčar
University of Ljubljana

Linda Freienthal
Silver Traat
TEXTA OÜ

Luis Adrián Cabrera-Diego
University of La Rochelle, L3i

Matej Martinc
Nada Lavrač
Blaž Škrlj
Jožef Stefan Institute

Martin Žnidaršič
Andraž Pelicon
Boshko Koloski
Jožef Stefan Institute

Vid Podpečan
Janez Kranjc
Jožef Stefan Institute

Shane Sheehan
Usher Institute
University of Edinburgh

Emanuela Boros
University of La Rochelle, L3i

Jose G. Moreno
University of Toulouse, IRIT

Antoine Doucet
University of La Rochelle, L3i

Hannu Toivonen
University of Helsinki
hannu.toivonen@helsinki.fi

Abstract

This paper presents tools and data sources collected and released by the EMBEDDIA project, supported by the European Union's Horizon 2020 research and innovation program. The collected resources were offered to participants of a hackathon organized as part of the EACL Hackashop on News Media Content Analysis and Automated Report Generation in February 2021. The hackathon had six participating teams who addressed different challenges, either from the list of proposed challenges or their own news-industry-related tasks. This paper goes beyond the scope of the hackathon, as it brings together in a coherent and compact form most of the resources developed, collected and released by the EMBEDDIA project. Moreover, it constitutes a handy source for news media industry and researchers in the fields of Natural Language Processing and Social Science.

1 Introduction

News media industry is the primary provider of information for society and individuals. Since the first newspaper was published, the propagation of information has continuously changed as new technologies are adopted by the news media, and the advent of the internet has made this change faster than ever (Pentina and Tarafdar, 2014). Internet-based media (e.g., social media, forums and blogs) have made news more accessible, and dissemination more affordable, resulting in drastically increased media coverage. Social media can also help provide source information for newsrooms, as shown in e.g., disaster response tasks (Alam et al., 2018).

Suitable Natural Language Processing techniques are needed to analyze news archives and gain insight about the evolution of our society, while dealing with the constant flow of information. Relevant datasets are equally important in

Proceedings of the EACL Hackashop on News Media Content Analysis and Automated Report Generation, pages 99–109
April 19, 2021 © Association for Computational Linguistics

order to train data-driven approaches. To encourage the development and uptake of such techniques and datasets, and take on the challenges presented by the introduction of new technologies in the news media industry, the EMBEDDIA project[1] organized, in conjunction with EACL 2021, a hackathon[2] as part of the EACL Hackashop on News Media Content Analysis and Automated Report Generation[3].

For this event, held virtually in February 2021, the datasets and tools curated and implemented by the EMBEDDIA project were publicly released and made available to the participants. We also provided examples of realistic challenges faced by today's newsrooms, and offered technical support and consultancy sessions with a news media expert throughout the entire duration of the hackathon.

The contributions of this paper are structured as follows. Section 2 presents the tools released for the event. The newly gathered, publicly released EMBEDDIA datasets are reported in Section 3. Section 4 presents sample news media challenges. Section 5 outlines the projects undertaken by the teams who completed the hackathon. The hackathon outcomes are summarized in Section 6.

2 Tools

The EMBEDDIA tools and models released for the hackathon include general text processing tools like language processing frameworks and text representation models (Section 2.1), news article analysis (Section 2.2), news comment analysis (Section 2.3), and news article and headline generation (Section 2.4) tools.

These tools require different levels of technical proficiency. Language processing tools and frameworks require little to no programming skills. On the other hand, for some tasks, we provide fully functional systems that can be used out of the box but require a certain level of technical knowledge in order to be fully utilized. Moreover, some tools and text representation models require programming skills and can be employed to improve existing systems, implement new analytic tools, or to be adapted to new uses.

[1] http://embeddia.eu

[2] http://embeddia.eu/hackashop2021-call-for-hackathon-participation/

[3] http://embeddia.eu/hackashop2021/

2.1 General Text Analytics

We first present two general frameworks, requiring no programming skills: the EMBEDDIA Media Assistant, incorporating the TEXTA Toolkit that is focused exclusively on text, and the ClowdFlows toolbox, which is a general data science framework incorporating numerous NLP components. Finally, we describe BERT embeddings, a general text representation framework that includes variants of multilingual BERT models, which are typically part of programming solutions.

2.1.1 TEXTA Toolkit and EMBEDDIA Media Assistant

The TEXTA Toolkit (TTK) is an open-source software for building RESTful text analytics applications.[4] TTK can be used for:

- searching and aggregating data (using e.g. regular expressions),
- training embeddings,
- building machine learning classifiers,
- building topic-related lexicons using embeddings,
- clustering and visualizing data, and
- extracting and creating training data.

The TEXTA Toolkit is the principal ingredient of the EMBEDDIA Media Assistant (EMA), which includes the TEXTA Toolkit GUI and API, an API Wrapper with a number of APIs for news analysis, and a Demonstrator for demonstrating the APIs.

2.1.2 ClowdFlows

ClowdFlows[5] is an open-source online platform for developing and sharing data mining and machine learning workflows (Kranjc et al., 2012). It works online in modern Web browsers, without client-side installation. The user interface allows combining software components (called widgets) into functional workflows, which can be executed, stored, and shared in the cloud. The main aim of ClowdFlows is to foster sharing of workflow solutions in order to simplify the replication and adaptation of shared work. It is suitable for prototyping, demonstrating new approaches, and exposing solutions to potential users who are not proficient in programming but would like to experiment with their own datasets and different tool parameter settings.

[4] https://docs.texta.ee/

[5] https://cf3.ijs.si/

2.1.3 BERT Embeddings

CroSloEngual[6] BERT and FinEst[7] BERT (Ulčar and Robnik-Šikonja, 2020) are trilingual models, based on the BERT architecture (Devlin et al., 2019), created in the EMBEDDIA project to facilitate easy cross-lingual transfer. Both models are trained on three languages: one of them being English as a resource-rich language, CroSloEngual BERT was trained on Croatian, Slovenian, and English data, while FinEst BERT was trained on Finnish, Estonian, and English data.

The advantage of multi-lingual models over monolingual models is that they can be used for cross-lingual knowledge transfer, e.g., a model for a task for which very little data is available in a target language such as Croatian or Estonian can be trained on English (with more data available) and transferred to a less-resourced language. While massive multilingual BERT-like models are available that cover more than 100 languages (Devlin et al., 2019), a model trained on only a few languages performs significantly better on these (Ulčar and Robnik-Šikonja, 2020). The two trilingual BERT models here are effective for the languages they cover and for the cross-lingual transfer of models between these languages. The models represent words/tokens with contextually dependent vectors (word embeddings). These can be used for training many NLP tasks, e.g., fine-tuning the model for any text classification task.

2.2 News Article Analysis Tools

The majority of provided tools cover different aspects of news article analysis, processing, and generation. We present keyword extraction tools TNT-KID and RaKUn, named entity recognition approaches, tools for diachronic analysis of words, tools for topic analysis and visualization, and tools for sentiment analysis.

2.2.1 Keyword Extraction

Two tools are available for keyword extraction: TNT-KID and RaKUn.

TNT-KID[8] (Transformer-based Neural Tagger for Keyword Identification, Martinc et al., 2020) is a supervised tool for extracting keywords from news articles in several languages (English, Estonian, Croatian, and Russian). It relies on the modified Transformer architecture (Vaswani et al., 2017) and leverages language model pretraining on a domain-specific corpus. This gives competitive and robust performance while requiring only a fraction of the manually labeled data needed by the best performing supervised systems. This makes TNT-KID especially appropriate for less-resourced languages where large manually labeled datasets are scarce.

RaKUn[9] (Škrlj et al., 2019) offers unsupervised detection and exploration of keyphrases. It transforms a document collection into a network, which is pruned to keep only the most relevant nodes. The nodes are ranked, prioritizing nodes corresponding to individual keywords and paths (keyphrases comprised of multiple words). Being unsupervised, RaKUn is well suited for less-resourced languages where expensive pre-training is not possible.

2.2.2 Named Entity Recognition[10]

The Named Entity Recognition (NER) system is based on the architecture proposed by Boros et al. (2020). It consists of fine-tuned BERT with two additional Transformer blocks (Vaswani et al., 2017). We provided models capable of predicting three types of named entities (Location, Organisation and Person) for eight European languages: Croatian, Estonian, Finnish, Latvian, Lithuanian, Russian, Slovene and Swedish. These models were trained using the WikiANN corpus (Pan et al., 2017), specifically using the training, development and testing partitions provided by Rahimi et al. (2019). Regarding BERT, for Croatian and Slovene we used *CroSloEngual BERT* (Ulčar and Robnik-Šikonja, 2020); for Finnish and Estonian *FinEst BERT* (Ulčar and Robnik-Šikonja, 2020); for Russian *RuBERT* (Kuratov and Arkhipov, 2019); for Swedish *Swedish BERT* (Malmsten et al., 2020); for Latvian and Lithuanian *Multilingual BERT* (Devlin et al., 2019).

2.2.3 Diachronic News Analysis[11]

The tool for diachronic semantic shift detection (Martinc et al., 2019a) leverages the BERT contextual embeddings (Devlin et al., 2019) for generat-

[6] https://huggingface.co/EMBEDDIA/crosloengual-bert

[7] https://huggingface.co/EMBEDDIA/finest-bert

[8] https://github.com/EMBEDDIA/tnt_kid

[9] https://github.com/EMBEDDIA/RaKUn

[10] https://github.com/EMBEDDIA/stacked-ner

[11] https://github.com/EMBEDDIA/semantic_shift_detection

ing time-specific word representations. It checks whether a specific word (or phrase) in the corpus has changed across time by measuring the rate of change for time-specific relations to semantically similar words in distinct time periods. Besides measuring long-term semantic changes, the method can also be successfully used for the detection of short-term yearly semantic shifts and has even been employed in the multilingual setting.

2.2.4 Topic Analysis

We present three tools dealing with news topics: PTM, PDTM and TeMoCo. The first two use topics to link articles across languages, and the third one visualizes distributions of topics over time.

PTM[12] (Polylingual Topic Model, Mimno et al., 2009) can be used to train cross-lingual topic models and obtain cross-lingual topic vectors for news articles. These vectors can be used to link news articles across languages. An ensemble of cross-lingual topic vectors and document embeddings can outperform stand-alone methods for cross-lingual news linking (Zosa et al., 2020).[13]

PDTM[14] (Polylingual Dynamic Topic Model, Zosa and Granroth-Wilding, 2019) is an extension of the Dynamic Topic Model (Blei and Lafferty, 2006) for multiple languages. This model can track the evolution of topics over time aligned across multiple languages.

TeMoCo[15] (Temporal Topic Visualisation, Sheehan et al., 2019, 2020) visualizes changes in topic distribution and associated keywords in a document or collection of articles. The tool can investigate a single document or a corpus which has been temporally annotated (e.g., a transcript or corpus of dated articles). The user can examine an overview of a dataset, processed into time and topic segments. The changes in topic size and keywords describe patterns in the data. Clicking on the segments brings up the related news articles with keyword highlighting.

2.2.5 News Sentiment Analysis[16]

Sentiment analysis is likely the most popular NLP application in industry. Our multilingual model for news sentiment classification is based on multilingual BERT. The model was trained on the Slovenian news sentiment dataset (Bučar et al., 2018) using a two-step training approach with document and paragraph level sentiment labels (Pelicon et al., 2020). The model was tested on the document-level labels of the Croatian news sentiment dataset (Section 3.2.2) in a zero-shot setting. The model maps the input document into one of the three predefined classes: positive, negative, and neutral.

2.3 News Comment Analysis Tools

Several of the tools in the sections above can also be applied to comments. We describe the following comment-specific tools: comment moderation, bot and gender detection, and sentiment analysis tools.

2.3.1 Comment Moderation[17]

Our comment moderation tool flags inappropriate comments that should be blocked from appearing on news sites (Pelicon et al., 2021a,b). It uses multilingual BERT (Devlin et al., 2019) and the trilingual EMBEDDIA BERT models (Section 2.1.3). The models were trained on combinations of five datasets: Croatian and Estonian (see Section 3.3 and details in Shekhar et al. (2020)), Slovenian (Ljubešić et al., 2019), English (Zampieri et al., 2019), and German (Wiegand et al., 2018). For Croatian, we also provide a model to predict which rule is violated, based on the moderation policy of 24 sata, the biggest Croatian news publisher (see Section 3.3.3).

2.3.2 Bot and Gender Detection[18]

An author profiling tool for gender classification and bot detection in Spanish and English, trained on Twitter data (Martinc et al., 2019b), was developed for the PAN 2019 author profiling shared task (Rangel and Rosso, 2019). It uses a two-step approach: in the first step distinguishing between bots and humans, and in the second step determining the gender of human authors. It relies on a Logistic Regression classifier and employs a number of different word and character n-gram features.

---

[12] https://github.com/EMBEDDIA/cross-lingual-linking

[13] https://github.com/EMBEDDIA/cross-lingual-linking

[14] https://github.com/EMBEDDIA/multilingual_dtm

[15] https://github.com/EMBEDDIA/TeMoCo

[16] https://github.com/EMBEDDIA/crosslingual_news_sentiment

[17] https://github.com/EMBEDDIA/hackashop2021_comment_filtering

[18] https://github.com/EMBEDDIA/PAN2019

2.3.3 Sentiment Analysis[19]

The code for sentiment analysis allows training a model that classifies text into one of three sentiment categories: positive, neutral, or negative. The classifier is trained on the Twitter datasets[20] provided by Mozetič et al. (2016). The models and datasets support cross-lingual knowledge transfer from resource-rich language(s) to less-resourced languages.

2.4 News Article and Headline Generation

Two of our tools are for generating text, either news for specific topics, or creative language.

Template-Based NLG System for Automated Journalism The rule-based natural language generation system—similar in concept to Leppänen et al. (2017)—produces news texts in Finnish and English from statistical data obtained from EuroStat. The system provides the text inputs used in the NLG challenges, described in Section 4.3. Access to the tool is provided through an API.[21]

Creative Language Generation We provide a framework[22] to help in generation of creative language using an evolutionary algorithm (Alnajjar and Toivonen, 2020).

3 Datasets

For the purposes of the hackashop, the EMBEDDIA media partners released their news archives, the majority of which are now being made publicly available for use after the project.

3.1 General EMBEDDIA News Datasets

Four publicly available datasets released by the EMBEDDIA project are described below.

3.1.1 Ekspress Meedia News Archive (in Estonian and Russian)

Ekspress Meedia belongs to the Ekspress Meedia Group, one of the largest media groups in the Baltics. The dataset is an archive of articles from the Ekspress Meedia news site from 2009–2019, containing over 1.4M articles, mostly in the Estonian (1,115,120 articles) with some in the Russian language (325,952 articles). Keywords (tags) are included for articles after 2015. The dataset is publicly available in the CLARIN repository.[23]

3.1.2 Latvian Delfi Article Archive (in Latvian and Russian)

Latvian Delfi belongs to Ekspress Meedia Group. This dataset is an archive of articles from the Delfi news site from 2015-2019, containing over 180,000 articles (c. 50% in Latvian and 50% in Russian language). Keywords (tags) for articles are included. The dataset is publicly available in CLARIN.[24]

3.1.3 24sata News Archive (in Croatian)

24sata is the biggest Croatian news publisher, owned by the Styria Media Group. The 24sata news portal consists of a daily news portal and several smaller portals covering news on specific topics, such as automotive news, health, culinary content, and lifestyle advice. The dataset contains over 650,000 articles in Croatian between 2007–2019, as well as assigned tags. The dataset is publicly available in CLARIN.[25]

3.1.4 STT News Archive (in Finnish)

The Finnish corpus (STT, 2019) contains newswire articles in Finnish sent to media outlets by the Finnish News Agency (STT) between 1992–2018. The corpus includes about 2.8 million items in total. The news articles are categorized by department (domestic, foreign, economy, politics, culture, entertainment and sports), as well as by metadata (IPTC subject categories or keywords and location data). The dataset is publicly available via CLARIN,[26] as is a parsed version of the corpus in CoNLL-U format (STT et al., 2020).[27]

3.2 Task-specific News Datasets

For the purposes of the hackashop, a set of task-specific datasets were also gathered.

3.2.1 Keyword Extraction Datasplits

For the keyword extraction challenge, we created train and test data splits, given as article IDs from datasets in Section 3.1. The number of articles for Estonian, Latvian, Russian and Croatian (see Koloski et al. (2021a) for details) are:

[19]https://github.com/EMBEDDIA/cross-lingual-classification-of-tweet-sentiment

[20]http://hdl.handle.net/11356/1054

[21]http://newseye-wp5.cs.helsinki.fi:4220/documentation/

[22]https://github.com/EMBEDDIA/evolutionary-algorithm-for-NLG

[23]http://hdl.handle.net/11356/1408

[24]http://hdl.handle.net/11356/1409

[25]http://hdl.handle.net/11356/1410

[26]http://urn.fi/urn:nbn:fi:lb-2019041501

[27]http://urn.fi/urn:nbn:fi:lb-2020031201

- Croatian: 32,223 train, 3,582 test;
- Estonian: 10,750 train, 7,747 test;
- Russian: 13,831 train, 11,475 test;
- Latvian: 13,133 train, 11,641 test.

The data is publicly available in CLARIN.[28]

3.2.2 News Sentiment Annotated Dataset

We selected a subset of 2,025 news articles from the Croatian 24sata dataset (see Section 3.1.3 and Pelicon et al., 2020). Several annotators annotated the articles on a five-point Likert-scale from 1 (most negative sentiment) to 5 (most positive). The final sentiment label of an article was then based on the average of the scores given by the different annotators: negative if average was less than or equal to 2.4, neutral if between 2.4 and 3.6, or positive if greater than or equal to 3.6. The dataset is publicly available in CLARIN.[29]

3.2.3 Estonian-Latvian Interesting News Pairs

For the purposes of the challenge on finding interesting news from neighbouring countries (see Section 4.1.2 and Koloski et al., 2021b) an Estonian journalist gathered 21 news articles from Latvia that would be of interest for Estonians, paired with 21 corresponding Estonian articles.[30]

3.2.4 Corpus of Computer-Generated Statistical News Texts

This corpus, consisting of a total 188 news texts produced by the rule-based natural language generation system described in Section 2.4, is provided to allow for easier offline development of solutions to the NLG challenges. The corpus contains news texts in both Finnish and English,[31] discussing consumer prices as well as health care spending and funding on the national level within the EU.

3.3 News Comments Datasets

Three news comment datasets have been made publicly available. To ensure privacy, user IDs in all news comment datasets in this section have been obfuscated, so they no longer correspond to the original IDs on the publishers' systems. User IDs for moderated comments have been removed.

3.3.1 Ekspress Meedia Comment Archive (in Estonian and Russian)

This dataset is an archive of reader comments on the Ekspress Meedia news site from 2009–2019, containing approximately 31M comments, mostly in Estonian language, with some in Russian. The dataset is publicly available in CLARIN.[32]

3.3.2 Latvian Delfi Comment Archive (in Latvian and Russian)

The dataset of Latvian Delfi, which belongs to Ekspress Meedia Group, is an archive of reader comments from the Delfi news site from 2014–2019, containing approximately 12M comments, mostly in Latvian language, with some in Russian. The dataset is publicly available in CLARIN.[33]

3.3.3 24sata Comment Archive (in Croatian)

In this archive, there are over 20M user comments from 2007–2019, written mostly in Croatian. All comments were gathered from 24sata, the biggest Croatian news publisher, owned by Styria Media Group. Each comment is given with the ID of the news article where it was posted and with multi-label moderation information corresponding to the rules of 24sata's moderation policy (see Shekhar et al., 2020). The dataset is publicly available in CLARIN.[34]

3.4 Other News Datasets

EventRegistry (Leban et al., 2014), which is a news intelligence platform aiming to empower organizations to keep track of world events and analyze their impact, provided free access to their data for hackathon participants.

Datasets relevant to the hackathon have also been made available for academic use by the Finnish broadcasting company Yle in Finnish[35] and in Swedish[36].

4 Challenges

Sample news media challenge addressed in the EMBEDDIA project come from three different areas: news analysis, news comments analysis, and article and headline generation.

[28] http://hdl.handle.net/11356/1403

[29] http://hdl.handle.net/11356/1342

[30] https://github.com/EMBEDDIA/interesting-cross-border-news-discovery

[31] https://github.com/EMBEDDIA/embeddia-nlg-output-corpus

[32] http://hdl.handle.net/11356/1401

[33] http://hdl.handle.net/11356/1407

[34] http://hdl.handle.net/11356/1399

[35] https://korp.csc.fi/download/YLE/fi/2011-2018-src/

[36] https://korp.csc.fi/download/YLE/sv/2012-2018-src/

4.1 News Analysis Challenges

4.1.1 Keyword Extraction

The EMBEDDIA datasets from Ekspress Meedia, Latvian Delfi and 24sata contain articles together with keywords assigned by journalists (see Section 3.2.1). The project has produced several state-of-the-art approaches for automatic keyword extraction on these datasets (see Section 2.2.1). The challenge consists of providing alternative methods to achieve the most accurate keyword extraction and compare with our results.

4.1.2 Identifying Interesting News from Neighbouring Countries

Journalists are very interested in identifying stories from cross-border countries, that attract a large number of readers and are "special". A journalist at Ekspress Meedia in Estonia gave the example of selecting news from Latvia that would be of interest to Estonian readers. Example topics include: drunk Estonians in Latvia, a person in Latvia living in a boat, stories from Latvia about topics that also interest Estonians (for example, alcohol taxes, newsworthy actions that take place near the border, certain public figures). At the moment it is easy to detect all the news from Latvia with the mentions of words "Estonia" or "Estonians", but the challenge is to identify a larger number of topics, e.g. scandals, deaths, gossip that might be somehow connected to Estonia, and news and stories that Estonians relate to (for example, when similar things have happened in Estonia or similar news has been popular there). Given the collection of news from two different countries (e.g. Estonia, Latvia, see Section 3.1), the task is to identify these special interesting news stories; 21 manually identified examples were provided (see Section 3.2.3).

4.1.3 Diachronic News Article Analysis

Media houses with large news articles collections are interested in analysing the reporting on certain topics to investigate changes over time. This can not only help them understand their reporting, but also help journalists to discover specific aspects related to these concepts.

An example from a news media professional from Estonia is as follows: "the doping affairs in sports regularly appear and for example for one of our skiers, a few years ago, we have already reported on a potential doping affair, but did not analyse it in depth. Few years later it has turned out that the sportsman was indeed involved in a doping affair. Having a better overview of doping related persons and topics over time, would be interesting for us." An even more straightforward application is the monitoring of politicians and parties; controversial topics are also of interest, as they can show general changes in society towards them.

Each of the media partners provided some people/parties/concepts of their interest. Examples are reported in Appendix A.

4.2 News Comments Analysis

4.2.1 Comment Moderation

The EMBEDDIA datasets from Ekspress Meedia and 24sata contain comments with metadata showing the ones blocked by the moderators (see Section 3.3). In the case of the 24sata dataset, specific moderation policies exist with a list of reasons for blocking, and the metadata also shows which of the reasons applied. The policies are applied by humans, though, and therefore the metadata will reflect the way moderators actually behave, including making mistakes and showing biases. During the EMBEDDIA project, we have developed and evaluated multiple automatic filtering approaches on these datasets, which can be used off-the-shelf or can be re-trained or modified (see Section 2.3.1). The hackathon participants were invited to propose alternative comment filtering methods, to improve over the existing approaches, or apply them to other datasets; to use them to investigate how human moderators actually behave; and/or to investigate how to analyse, understand or use the outputs.

4.2.2 Comment Summarization

Each of the comment datasets available contains about 10 years of data. The EMEBDDIA project has developed and evaluated a range of classifiers that can detect useful information in comments and comment-like text (including sentiment, topic, author information etc; see Section 2.3). The participants were invited to use these and other methods to extract meaningful information from comment threads and develop new ways of presenting this information in a way that could be useful to a journalist or analyst. Example approaches given were summarizing topics, views and opinions; and detecting and summarizing constructive or positive comments, as an antidote to the negative comments so often focused on in NLP.

4.3 Natural Language Generation

4.3.1 Improving the Fluency of Automatically Generated Articles

Despite recent strides in neural natural language generation (NLG) methods, neural NLG methods are still prone to producing text that is not grounded in the input data. As such errors are catastrophic in news industry applications, most news generation systems continue to employ rule-based NLG methods. Such methods, however, lack to adequately handle the variety and fluency of expression. One potential solution would be to combine neural post-processing with a rule-based NLG system. In this challenge, participants are provided with black box access to a rule-based NLG system that produces statistical news articles. A corpus of the produced news articles is also provided.[37] The challenge is to use automated post-processing methods to improve the fluency and grammaticality of the system's output without changing the meaning of the text.

The system is multilingual (English and Finnish), and optimally the proposed solutions should be language-independent, taking advantage of e.g., multilingual word embeddings. At the same time, we also welcome monolingual solutions.

4.3.2 Headline Generation

Headlines play an important role in news text, not only summarizing the most important information in the underlying news text, but also presenting it in a light that is likely to entice the reader to engage with the larger text. In this challenge, the participants are invited to create headlines for automatically generated articles (see Section 4.3.1).

5 Hackathon Contributions

Six teams with 24 members in total participated in the hackathon during 1–19 February 2021. The challenges described in Section 4 were offered to the teams as examples of interesting problems in the area of news media analysis and generation. The teams had, however, the freedom to choose and formulate their own aims for the hackathon. Likewise, they were offered the data, tools and models described above.

The hackathon was organized online, with three joint events to kick off the activities, to meet and talk about the ongoing work halfway, and to wrap up the work at the end. Ample support on tools, models, data and challenges was provided by the EMBEDDIA experts via several channels.

The six teams all picked up different challenges and set themselves specific goals. Reports from five teams are included in these proceedings.

Three teams worked on news content analysis:

- One team developed a COVID-19 news dashboard to visualise sentiment in pandemic-related news. The dashboard uses a multilingual BERT model to analyze news headlines in different languages across Europe (Robertson et al., 2021).
- Methods for cross-border news discovery were developed by another team using multilingual topic models. Their tool discovers Latvian news that could interest Estonian readers (Koloski et al., 2021b).
- A third team used sentiment and viewpoint analysis to study attitudes related to LGBTIQ+ in Slovenian news. Their results suggest that political affiliation of media outlets can affect sentiment towards and framing of LGBTIQ+-specific topics (Martinc et al., 2021).

Two teams looked at different challenges related to comment analysis:

- One team automated news comment moderation. They compiled and labeled a dataset of English news and social posts, and experimented with cross-lingual transfer of comment labels from English and subsequent supervised machine learning on Croatian and Estonian news comments (Korenčić et al., 2021).
- Another team looked at the diversity of news comment recommendations, motivated by democratic debate. They implemented a novel metric based on theories of democracy and used it to compare recommendation strategies of New York Times comments in English (Reuver and Mattis, 2021).

Finally, one team worked on a generation task:

- The team experimented with several methods for generating headlines, given the contents of a news story. They found that headlines formulated as questions about the story's content tend to be both informative and enticing.

[37] https://github.com/EMBEDDIA/embeddia-nlg-output-corpus

6 Conclusions

This paper presents the contributions of the EMBEDDIA project, including a large variety of tools, new datasets of news articles and comments from the media partners, as well as challenges that were proposed to the participants of the EACL 2021 Hackathon on News Media Content Analysis and Automated Report Generation. The hackathon had six participating teams who addressed different challenges, either from the list of proposed challenges or their own news-industry-related tasks. In the future, the tools and resources described can be used for a large variety of new experiments, and we hope that the proposed challenges will be addressed by the wider NLP research community.

Acknowledgements

This work has been supported by the European Union's Horizon 2020 research and innovation program under grant 825153 (EMBEDDIA).

We would like to thank EventRegistry for providing free access to their data for hackathon participants.

References

Firoj Alam, Ferda Ofli, Muhammad Imran, and Michael Aupetit. 2018. A Twitter tale of three hurricanes: Harvey, Irma, and Maria. *Proc. of ISCRAM, Rochester, USA*.

Khalid Alnajjar and Hannu Toivonen. 2020. Computational generation of slogans. *Natural Language Engineering*, First View:1–33.

David M Blei and John D Lafferty. 2006. Dynamic topic models. In *Proceedings of the 23rd international conference on Machine learning*, pages 113–120.

Emanuela Boros, Ahmed Hamdi, Elvys Linhares Pontes, Luis Adrián Cabrera-Diego, Jose G. Moreno, Nicolas Sidere, and Antoine Doucet. 2020. Alleviating digitization errors in named entity recognition for historical documents. In *Proceedings of the 24th Conference on Computational Natural Language Learning*, pages 431–441, Online. Association for Computational Linguistics.

Joze Bučar, Martin Žnidarsic, and Janez Povh. 2018. Annotated news corpora and a lexicon for sentiment analysis in Slovene. *Language Resources and Evaluation*, 52:895–919.

Jacob Devlin, Ming-Wei Chang, Kenton Lee, and Kristina Toutanova. 2019. BERT: Pre-training of deep bidirectional transformers for language understanding. In *Proceedings of the 2019 Conference of the North American Chapter of the Association for Computational Linguistics: Human Language Technologies, Volume 1 (Long and Short Papers)*, pages 4171–4186.

Boshko Koloski, Senja Pollak, Blaž Škrlj, and Matej Martinc. 2021a. Extending neural keyword extraction with TF-IDF tagset matching. In *Proceedings of the EACL Hackashop on News Media Content Analysis and Automated Report Generation*. Association for Computational Linguistics.

Boshko Koloski, Elaine Zosa, Timen Stepišnik-Perdih, Blaž Škrlj, Tarmo Paju, and Senja Pollak. 2021b. Interesting cross-border news discovery using cross-lingual article linking and document similarity. In *Proceedings of the EACL Hackashop on News Media Content Analysis and Automated Report Generation*. Association for Computational Linguistics.

Damir Korenčić, Ipek Baris, Eugenia Fernandez, Katarina Leuschel, and Eva Sánchez Salido. 2021. To block or not to block: Experiments with machine learning for news comment moderation. In *Proceedings of the EACL Hackashop on News Media Content Analysis and Automated Report Generation*. Association for Computational Linguistics.

Janez Kranjc, Vid Podpečan, and Nada Lavrač. 2012. ClowdFlows: A cloud based scientific workflow platform. In Peter A. Flach, Tijl Bie, and Nello Cristianini, editors, *Machine Learning and Knowledge Discovery in Databases*, volume 7524 of *Lecture Notes in Computer Science*, pages 816–819. Springer Berlin Heidelberg.

Yuri Kuratov and Mikhail Arkhipov. 2019. Adaptation of Deep Bidirectional Multilingual Transformers for Russian Language. *arXiv cs.CL*. Preprint: 1905.07213.

Gregor Leban, Blaz Fortuna, Janez Brank, and Marko Grobelnik. 2014. Event registry: learning about world events from news. In *Proceedings of the 23rd International Conference on World Wide Web*, pages 107–110.

Leo Leppänen, Myriam Munezero, Mark Granroth-Wilding, and Hannu Toivonen. 2017. Data-driven news generation for automated journalism. In *Proceedings of the 10th International Conference on Natural Language Generation*, pages 188–197.

Nikola Ljubešić, Darja Fišer, and Tomaž Erjavec. 2019. The FRENK Datasets of Socially Unacceptable Discourse in Slovene and English. In *International Conference on Text, Speech, and Dialogue*, pages 103–114. Springer.

Martin Malmsten, Love Börjeson, and Chris Haffenden. 2020. Playing with Words at the National Library of Sweden – Making a Swedish BERT. *arXiv cs.CL*. Preprint: 2007.01658.

Matej Martinc, Petra Kralj Novak, and Senja Pollak. 2019a. Leveraging contextual embeddings for detecting diachronic semantic shift. *arXiv preprint arXiv:1912.01072*.

Matej Martinc, Nina Perger, Andraž Pelicon, Matej Ulčar, Andreja Vezovnik, and Senja Pollak. 2021. EMBEDDIA hackathon report: Automatic sentiment and viewpoint analysis of Slovenian news corpus on the topic of LGBTIQ+. In *Proceedings of the EACL Hackashop on News Media Content Analysis and Automated Report Generation*. Association for Computational Linguistics.

Matej Martinc, Blaz Skrlj, and Senja Pollak. 2019b. Fake or not: Distinguishing between bots, males and females. In *CLEF (Working Notes)*.

Matej Martinc, Blaž Škrlj, and Senja Pollak. 2020. Tnt-kid: Transformer-based neural tagger for keyword identification. *arXiv preprint arXiv:2003.09166*.

David Mimno, Hanna Wallach, Jason Naradowsky, David A Smith, and Andrew McCallum. 2009. Polylingual topic models. In *Proceedings of the 2009 conference on Empirical Methods in Natural Language Processing*, pages 880–889.

Igor Mozetič, Miha Grčar, and Jasmina Smailović. 2016. Multilingual twitter sentiment classification: The role of human annotators. *PLOS ONE*, 11(5):1–26.

Xiaoman Pan, Boliang Zhang, Jonathan May, Joel Nothman, Kevin Knight, and Heng Ji. 2017. Cross-lingual Name Tagging and Linking for 282 Languages. In *Proceedings of the 55th Annual Meeting of the Association for Computational Linguistics (Volume 1: Long Papers)*, pages 1946–1958, Vancouver, Canada. Association for Computational Linguistics.

Andraž Pelicon, Marko Pranjić, Dragana Miljković, Blaž Škrlj, and Senja Pollak. 2020. Zero-shot learning for cross-lingual news sentiment classification. *Applied Sciences*, 10(17):5993.

Andraž Pelicon, Ravi Shekhar, Matej Martinc, Blaž Škrlj, Matthew Purver, and Senja Pollak. 2021a. Zero-shot cross-lingual content filtering: Offensive language and hate speech detection. In *Proceedings of the EACL Hackashop on News Media Content Analysis and Automated Report Generation*.

Andraž Pelicon, Ravi Shekhar, Blaž Škrlj, Matthew Purver, and Senja Pollak. 2021b. Investigating cross-lingual training for offensive language detection. *Submitted, to appear.*

Iryna Pentina and M. Tarafdar. 2014. From "information" to "knowing": Exploring the role of social media in contemporary news consumption. *Comput. Hum. Behav.*, 35:211–223.

Afshin Rahimi, Yuan Li, and Trevor Cohn. 2019. Massively Multilingual Transfer for NER. In *Proceedings of the 57th Annual Meeting of the Association for Computational Linguistics*, pages 151–164, Florence, Italy. Association for Computational Linguistics.

Francisco Rangel and Paolo Rosso. 2019. Overview of the 7th author profiling task at pan 2019: bots and gender profiling in Twitter. In *Working Notes Papers of the CLEF 2019 Evaluation Labs Volume 2380 of CEUR Workshop*.

Myrthe Reuver and Nicolas Mattis. 2021. Implementing evaluation metrics based on theories of democracy in news comment recommendation (Hackathon report). In *Proceedings of the EACL Hackashop on News Media Content Analysis and Automated Report Generation*. Association for Computational Linguistics.

Frankie Robertson, Jarkko Lagus, and Kaisla Kajava. 2021. A COVID-19 news coverage mood map of Europe. In *Proceedings of the EACL Hackashop on News Media Content Analysis and Automated Report Generation*. Association for Computational Linguistics.

Shane Sheehan, Pierre Albert, Masood Masoodian, and Saturnino Luz. 2019. TeMoCo: A visualization tool for temporal analysis of multi-party dialogues in clinical settings. In *2019 IEEE 32nd International Symposium on Computer-Based Medical Systems (CBMS)*, pages 690–695. IEEE.

Shane Sheehan, Saturnino Luz, Pierre Albert, and Masood Masoodian. 2020. TeMoCo-Doc: A visualization for supporting temporal and contextual analysis of dialogues and associated documents. In *Proceedings of the International Conference on Advanced Visual Interfaces*, AVI '20, New York, NY, USA. Association for Computing Machinery.

Ravi Shekhar, Marko Pranjić, Senja Pollak, Andraž Pelicon, and Matthew Purver. 2020. Automating News Comment Moderation with Limited Resources: Benchmarking in Croatian and Estonian. *Journal for Language Technology and Computational Linguistics (JLCL)*, 34(1).

Blaž Škrlj, Andraž Repar, and Senja Pollak. 2019. Rakun: Rank-based keyword extraction via unsupervised learning and meta vertex aggregation. In *Statistical Language and Speech Processing*, pages 311–323, Cham. Springer International Publishing.

STT. 2019. Finnish news agency archive 1992-2018, source (http://urn.fi/urn:nbn:fi:lb-2019041501).

STT, Helsingin yliopisto, and Khalid Alnajjar. 2020. Finnish News Agency Archive 1992-2018, CoNLL-U, source (http://urn.fi/urn:nbn:fi:lb-2020031201).

Matej Ulčar and Marko Robnik-Šikonja. 2020. FinEst BERT and CroSloEngual BERT. In *International*

Conference on Text, Speech, and Dialogue, pages 104–111. Springer.

Ashish Vaswani, Noam Shazeer, Niki Parmar, Jakob Uszkoreit, Llion Jones, Aidan N Gomez, Lukasz Kaiser, and Illia Polosukhin. 2017. Attention is all you need. *arXiv preprint arXiv:1706.03762*.

Michael Wiegand, Melanie Siegel, and Josef Ruppenhofer. 2018. Overview of the GermEval 2018 shared task on the identification of offensive language. In *Proceedings of the GermEval 2018 Workshop (GermEval)*.

Marcos Zampieri, Shervin Malmasi, Preslav Nakov, Sara Rosenthal, Noura Farra, and Ritesh Kumar. 2019. Predicting the Type and Target of Offensive Posts in Social Media. In *Proceedings of NAACL*, pages 1415–1420.

Elaine Zosa and Mark Granroth-Wilding. 2019. Multilingual dynamic topic model. In *Proceedings of the International Conference on Recent Advances in Natural Language Processing (RANLP 2019)*, pages 1388–1396, Varna, Bulgaria. INCOMA Ltd.

Elaine Zosa, Mark Granroth-Wilding, and Lidia Pivovarova. 2020. A comparison of unsupervised methods for ad hoc cross-lingual document retrieval. In *Proceedings of the LREC 2020 Workshop on Cross-Language Search and Summarization of Text and Speech*. European Language Resources Association (ELRA).

A Entities of Interest for Diachronic News Article Analysis Challenge

For the challenge described in Section 4.1.3, each of the media partners provided some people/parties/concepts of their interest. These include the following.

Political parties:

- Estonian (Eskpress meedia): Reformierakond, EKRE, Keskerakond
- Finnish (STT)[38]: Suomen Sosialidemokraattinen Puolue, demarit, SDP, (sd.); Kokoomus, (kok.); Keskusta, (kesk.); Perussuomalaiset, (ps.); Kristillisdemokraatit, KD, (kd.)
- Croatian: Hrvatska demokratska zajednica (HDZ), Socijaldemokratska partija Hrvatske (SDP), Hrvatska narodna stranka (HNS), Most nezavisnih lista (MOST)

Popular people:

- Estonian: Jüri Ratas, Kersti Kaljulaid, Kaja Kallas, Martin Helme
- Croatian: Andrej Plenković (the prime minister), Zoran Milanović (the president), Kolinda Grabar-Kitarović (previous president), Milan Bandić (mayor of Zagreb)

Interesting topics were selected for all three languages to allow also cross-lingual comparisons:

- **corona crisis, pandemics**: Estonian: Koroonakriis, pandeemia; Finnish: korona, koronakriisi, pandemia, koronapandemia; Croatian: korona, koronavirus, korona kriza, pandemija, korona pandemija
- **same sex rights, registered partnership act, marriage referendum**: Estonian:samasooliste õigused, kooseluseadus, abielureferendum; Finnish: tasa-arvoinen avioliitto, rekisteröity parisuhde; Croatian: referendum o braku, životno partnerstvo, civilno partnerstvo
- **financial knowledge, savings, investing, pension:** Estonian: rahatarkus, säästmine, investeerimine, pension; Finnish: sijoittaminen, piensijoittaja, säästäminen, eläke, eläkkeet; Croatian: ulaganje, investiranje, mali ulagači, dionice, ušteđevina, mirovina, penzija
- **doping:** same word in Estonian/Finnish/Croatian.

[38]The names without brackets are names the parties use and the abbreviation inside brackets is the way to mark a mp's / other person's political party within a text. For example Jussi Halla-aho (ps.) said that-

A COVID-19 news coverage mood map of Europe

Frankie Robertson
University of Jyväskylä
frankie@robertson.name

Jarkko Lagus
University of Helsinki
jalagus@cs.helsinki.fi

Kaisla Kajava
University of Helsinki
kaisla.kajava@helsinki.fi

Abstract

We present a COVID-19 news dashboard which visualizes sentiment in pandemic news coverage in different languages across Europe. The dashboard shows analyses for positive/neutral/negative sentiment and moral sentiment for news articles across countries and languages. First we extract news articles from news-crawl. Then we use a pre-trained multilingual BERT model for sentiment analysis of news article headlines and a dictionary and word vectors -based method for moral sentiment analysis of news articles. The resulting dashboard gives a unified overview of news events on COVID-19 news overall sentiment, and the region and language of publication from the period starting from the beginning of January 2020 to the end of January 2021.

1 Introduction

The response to the COVID-19 pandemic and its news coverage worldwide has been marked by tension between state-level actions, and those of regional organisations such as the European Union, and the essentially borderless nature of the virus itself. This paper presents the COVID-19 news coverage mood map of Europe which visualizes sentiment in news coverage in different European languages. Within the European context, with its many small languages, this multi-lingual approach is vital for working beyond the state-level.

In order to evaluate the possibilities of automatic sentiment analysis models in this context, we first created a multilingual COVID-19 news corpus from the websites of state broadcasters. We then applied two types of automatic sentiment analysis to the articles. Finally, we created a dashboard containing a number of interactive plots based on the analysed corpus[1]. This report details work undertaken at the EMBEDDIA Hackashop.

[1]http://covidmoodmap.rahtiapp.fi/

European languages	av az ba be bg bs ca ce cs cv cy da de el en es et eu fi fo fr fy ga gl gv hr hu is it kl kv la lb lt lv mk mt nb nl nn no oc os pl pt rm ro ru sk sl sq sr sv tr tt uk yi
Langdetect	bg ca cs cy da de el en es et fi fr hr hu it lt lv mk nl no pl pt ro ru sk sl sq sv tr uk
mBERT	bg ca cs cy da de el en es et fi fr hr hu it lt lv mk nl no pl pt ro ru sk sl sq sv tr uk
MUSE	bg ca cs da de el en es et fi fr hr hu it mk nl no pl pt ro ru sk sl sv tr uk
>20 items	bg ca cs cy de el en es et fi fr it lt mk nl pl pt ro ru sv tr uk

Table 1: Pictogram with ISO 639-1 language codes summarising language coverage of multilingual techniques along with our COVID-19 news corpus. Rows are subsetted from the row above the previous rule.

2 Corpus extraction

We used the news-please extractor (Hamborg et al., 2017) on news-crawl dumps to obtain a multilingual corpus of European COVID-19 news. News-crawl is a web crawl provided by the Common Crawl organisation which is updated more frequently and contains only data from news websites[2]. In order to keep the size of the corpus manageable and the extraction time reasonable, a list of internet domain names of European state broadcasters was first obtained from Wikidata, since filtering at the domain level allows for faster processing of Common Crawl dumps. Articles without a language detected by the langdetect language detector[3] were discarded. COVID-19 keyword filtering was also applied, detailed in Section 3.1. Table 1 includes a summary of the considered European languages, their support by langdetect, and the set

[2]https://commoncrawl.org/2016/10/news-dataset-available/

[3]https://github.com/Mimino666/langdetect

Proceedings of the EACL Hackashop on News Media Content Analysis and Automated Report Generation, pages 110–115
April 19, 2021 © Association for Computational Linguistics

for which 20 or more items were ultimately extracted.

The resulting corpus contains 468 thousand articles. It is thus just over a quarter of the size of the comparable AYLIEN Coronavirus News Dataset[4] corpus which has 1 673 thousand news articles. Our corpus contains news from a longer period of just over a year versus AYLIEN's, which contains just over a half a year. Most importantly, our corpus has at least 20 items in 22 languages, versus AYLIEN's corpus which is English only.

The full corpus does not include news from all European countries. Table 2 gives a coverage of the countries included in the corpus, while Table 1 gives the coverage of languages in the corpus. There are two possible reasons for the missing countries. The first is that news-crawl uses a fixed set of seeds, so one possibility is that the the websites of the state broadcaster for these countries was not on the seed list. Another possibility is that the article extraction of news-please was not able to deal with these countries. The recall of news-please is estimated at 71%. Possible future work here would be to obtain and audit the seed list from news-crawl and try other article extraction software such as Trafilatura (Barbaresi, 2019) which has an estimated recall of 88% with higher precision.

Covered	AT BE BG CZ DE EE ES FI FR GB GR IE IT LT MD NL PT RO SE SM VA
Missed	AD AL AX BA BY CH CY DK FO GG GI HR HU IM IS JE LI LU LV MC ME MK MT NO PL RS RU SI SJ SK UA

Table 2: Pictogram with ISO 3166-1 alpha-2 country codes summarising European countries covered (>20 items extracted) and missed in our corpus.

3 Analyses

All analyses were multilingual, and their coverage of different languages is compared in Table 1. During development, the full list of tools and resources given by Pollak et al. (2021) was considered.

3.1 Keyword matching

In order to detect keywords from fixed lists across languages, including those with inflectional endings which cause changes to the citation form itself, either lemmatisation or stemming must be performed. Since keyword search is also performed as a filtering step for creating the corpus, it should be fast. To achieve this goal, we applied a simple high-recall stemming-like scheme based on BPE. First we obtained the pretrained BPE (Sennrich et al., 2016) model from XLM-RoBERTa-large (Conneau et al., 2019)[5]. As a next step, all BPE tokens with length $>= 5$ are discarded from the BPE model. The full XLM tokenisation pipeline is then run as normal. The hope is that this segments the word into commonly repeating units, which are likely to include common inflectional endings. The decision to discard longer BPE tokens was made so that common longer words would still be segmented and to bound the maximum number of characters removed from the word, since removing too many is more likely to cause false positives. In cases where at least 3 BPE segments were generated, the last one is discarded. In all cases, the resulting stem or full token is at least 2 BPE characters and 5 characters, a wildcard appended to the end of the token. Matching was performed case-insensitively using the fast *pyre2*[6] library, which uses deterministic automata for matching.

While this scheme is certainly likely have lower precision than using a high quality lemmatiser, it is not language dependent beyond its central assumption: that sounds changes – if they occur – are limited towards the end of the word. The exact same procedure is applied to all languages. For comparison the Snowball stemmer[7] supports 15 languages, leaving 16 of those supported by langdetect unhandled. On the other hand, a state-of-the-art mulitlingual lemmatisers such as the Universal Lemmatiser of Kanerva et al. (2020), which supports over 50 langauges is likely to be slower. Additionally, due to Universal Lemmatiser's architecture being adapted to batch scenarios, this implies adding and extra stage to the pipeline. That said, performing keyword matching based upon Universal Lemmatiser would be a good next step for the keyword matching, and the current scheme could be kept only for the few languages not supported by Universal Lemmatiser.

Keyword lists for both COVID-19 keywords and names of European countries in all considered languages were obtained from Wikidata. For matching the topic of COVID-19, labels from the entities `Q84263196` (the COVID-19 disease), `Q82069695` (the SARS-CoV-2 virus), and

[4] `https://aylien.com/blog/free-coronavirus-news-dataset`

[5] `https://huggingface.co/xlm-roberta-large`

[6] `https://github.com/andreasvc/pyre2`

[7] As described at `https://snowballstem.org/`

Q89469904 (the hypernym of SARS-CoV-2; all corona viruses) were used. For non-English languages, the set of keywords was extended with the English keywords in case they have been used as loans, especially for example in the early stages of the epidemic. In addition, the commonly occurring trans-lingual patterns: corona⋆, korona⋆, covid⋆ and корона⋆ were added to all lists. The lists of country names were used as-is.

3.2 Multilingual sentiment analysis of news headlines

In recent years, deep pre-trained language models have produced state-of-the-art results in various natural language processing tasks. BERT models use self-attention layers from the transformer model (Vaswani et al., 2017), which makes them useful for detecting contextual information in text: this BERT does by looking at the neighboring words on both sides of each word in the text.

We used a multilingual BERT model (Devlin et al., 2018) fine-tuned by Pelicon et al. (2020) to classify news article headlines into the polar sentiment categories *positive*, *neutral*, and *negative*. The model was trained on a Slovenian news dataset and evaluated for zero-shot cross-lingual tasks on Croatian news. As the model was originally developed for classification of full news article texts, it is mostly trained on slices of these using the whole of BERT's maximum sequence length of 512. Here we are typically supplying much shorter sequences from the related, but distinct distribution of news headlines, which is likely to affect performance.

The results of our experiments show a near-consistent peak in news coverage of the COVID-19 pandemic in the spring of 2020 across news sources, with the exception of some languages which are less represented in our overall news dataset. Similarly, the results show a peak in news coverage in the fall of 2020, which coincides with the second wave of the pandemic. *Negative* sentiment is most prevalent in spring 2020. Overall, *negative* was the most commonly predicted label, with *neutral* as the next common, and *positive* the least common. Table 3 shows the five countries with the most news article headlines classified as *negative*. News articles from the national broadcasters of those countries also constitute a significant portion of the overall data.

Country	*Positive*	%	*Neutral*	%	*Negative*	%
Spain	22033	19	40100	36	50092	45
France	17484	17	32717	33	49836	50
U.K.	10233	17	21746	35	29261	48
Germany	9375	15	25256	40	27941	45
Belgium	5626	19	10531	35	14030	46

Table 3: Five countries with the highest absolute number of news headlines predicted as *negative*.

3.3 Multilingual moral sentiment analysis of news articles

Research shows (Kalimeri et al., 2019a; Curry et al., 2019; Mooijman et al., 2018) that accounting for moral sentiment in addition to other personality traits in natural language can give insights into many different societal phenomena. Methods based on moral sentiment have been previously used, for example, to predict street riots based on Twitter data (Mooijman et al., 2018) and analyze moral narratives in social media conversation about vaccination (Kalimeri et al., 2019b).

The basis for moral sentiment analysis is the *moral foundations theory* by Graham et al. (2013) and especially in this case the moral foundations dictionary (MFD) 2.0[8]. MFD is a word list that contains words categorized into five different sentiments: care, fairness, loyalty, authority, and sanctity.

The method we apply here follows the idea described by Kozlowski et al. (2019) in order to extract cultural dimensions from word embeddings. First, we extract antonym pairs using WordNet (Fellbaum, 1998) per sentiment by searching synsets word-by-word and fetching the list of antonyms. This list of antonyms is then filtered based on the list containing words of opposite sentiment polarity. As an example, we search antonyms for word the "peace" from the list of positive polarity words related to care sentiment. We acquire the antonym "war" based on the WordNet synset search. As this word is also found from the negative polarity list of care dimension, we add this pair to the list of antonym pairs for the care sentiment.

These pairs we use to compute vectors representing moral sentiment dimension. This is done via encoding the words as word embeddings, doing simple subtraction of these antonym pairs, and computing the mean of these vectors per sentiment. This gives us one vector per sentiment, onto which

[8] https://osf.io/ezn37/

we can then project any other word to measure the strength of that specific sentiment. As large number of words do not have antonyms that are found from the opposite polarity list, this leads to a noisy estimate of the dimension.

To compute the sentiment of a document, each word of a document is first encoded into word embedding and then projected onto each moral sentiment vector. This gives a list of scores for each word that we can then just sum to obtain the final score for the document.

This way of summing everything up creates an effect where longer documents will have stronger sentiment scores if most words are towards the same polarity per sentiment. This is a somewhat desirable effect since we do not wish to have one-sentence articles to have the same weight as a full article.

Multilinguality creates issues since the original MFD is only officially available in English. The issue is solved by using aligned word embeddings and doing approximate translation via distance-based search in the aligned word embedding space. For this, we use embeddings by Conneau et al. (2017). An alternative option would be to translate the words exactly, but since all languages might have very culture-specific semantics that do not directly translate, it might remove or even change the moral sentiment of the word. Doing approximate translation directly in word embedding space does not suffer from this, as we only search for the word embedding with the closest meaning. This should also preserve the sentiment information.

The distance-based search method does not guarantee a good translation, but should in most cases work better than exact translation. If the exact translation is good and the embedding is close to the actual meaning, the distance-based method will approximately retrieve the same embedding. If the exact translation is good, but because of cultural differences the semantic meaning has shifted, the distance-based method should retrieve an embedding that is closer to original semantics, even though the exact word might be different from the exact translation. So in both of these cases, the distance-based method should yield better results.

The results show that the strongest sentiment in the positive direction was sanctity and in the negative direction loyalty, both being clearly distinct from the other three sentiments in magnitude. Different sentiments showed fluctuation over time and countries, but overall the sentiment seemed to stay in the same polarity, suggesting no drastic changes in the way COVID-19 was covered in the news over time from the moral sentiment point of view.

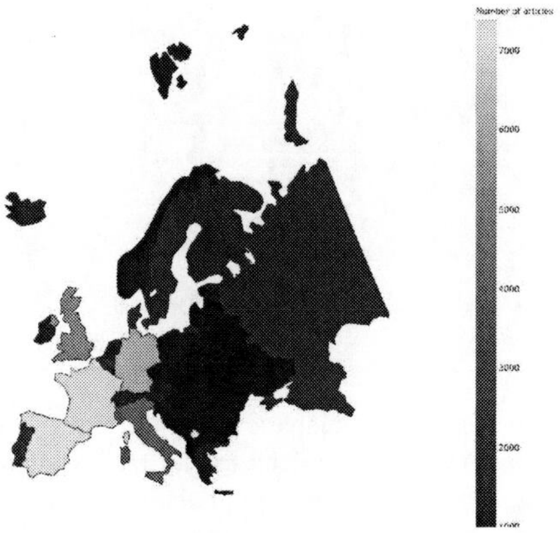

Figure 1: An example choropleth map showing the positive sentiment distribution over countries mentioned. Note that the purple color at the lower end of the spectrum does not indicate a high amount of negative news, but just the lack of positive news.

4 Visualisation

In order to visualise the results of the analyses, we created a dashboard using the Dash framework[9]. The resulting application makes heavy use of analytical queries which tend to feature range selections and grouping based on dates as well as numerical aggregates such as value summations and counts. To run these queries efficiently across the whole data set of 468 thousand articles, we used the DuckDB column database (Raasveldt and Mühleisen, 2019).

The chief dimensions visualised as independent grouping variables in space were date and either the country of production or the country mentioned in articles. For plots in which these variables could not be shown spatially, the user was given the option of filtering using them. The language used in the articles and type of sentiment were also available as filters. The main dependent variables were are either raw article counts or lumped measures. For visualising only time as a visual grouping, a bar chart was used, while for visualising only country, a choropleth map, an example of which is given in Figure 1. Finally, an animated choropleth map showing consecutive time slices corresponding to weeks taken Monday to Sunday groups by both

[9] https://plotly.com/dash/

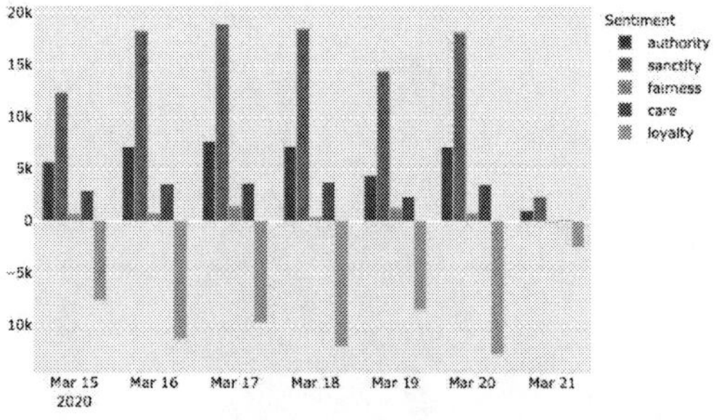

Figure 2: An example bar chart of one week of moral sentiment scores. Height indicates the strength of the sentiment component and polarity tells if it is positive or negative sentiment along that dimension.

time and country.

The lumped measure used for polar sentiment is a simple ratio, with the *neutral* class included to pull the measure towards zero:

$$\frac{\text{positive} + \frac{1}{2}\text{neutral}}{\text{positive} + \text{neutral} + \text{negative}}$$

For moral sentiments, we have already obtained a measure for each document and each moral sentiment. These are simply summed to create a single aggregate bipolar measure of sentiment strength per moral sentiment (see Figure 2 for an example). The sentiment estimate is rather noisy, so looking at the absolute values is not recommended. A better way to look at these numbers, is to look at them in relation to other countries or time spans. This tells how different countries differ in the way they represent this information and how is the overall trend progressing over time.

5 Conclusion

We have presented a COVID-19 news dashboard for exploration of reporting across time and from and about different countries during the COVID-19 epidemic. The dashboard demonstrates the potential of automated multilingual text analysis for understanding reporting on complex phenomena such as the COVID-19 crisis beyond the state-level. This type of tool could be integrated into a system used by news agencies to track news trends. Beyond COVID-19, it could be used to plan coverage of other national or global news events such as elections, international summits, or sports events.

The visualizations in the dashboard do seem to line up with the authors' preconceived ideas about sentiments during COVID-19 and their evolution. However, all analyses in the dashboard were produced automatically and have not undergone evaluation within this context. Since the analyses themselves may not be entirely accurate, the resulting plots may be misleading, and thus should not be used as a basis for decision making. Evaluation of the underlying techniques is a clear next step for this work.

Acknowledgements

The authors wish to thank the organisers of the EMBEDDIA Hackashop 2021 for organising the event and CSC – IT Center for Science, Finland, for computational resources.

References

Adrien Barbaresi. 2019. Generic web content extraction with open-source software. In *KONVENS 2019*, pages 267–268. GSCL.

Alexis Conneau, Kartikay Khandelwal, Naman Goyal, Vishrav Chaudhary, Guillaume Wenzek, Francisco Guzmán, Edouard Grave, Myle Ott, Luke Zettlemoyer, and Veselin Stoyanov. 2019. Unsupervised cross-lingual representation learning at scale. *arXiv preprint arXiv:1911.02116*.

Alexis Conneau, Guillaume Lample, Marc'Aurelio Ranzato, Ludovic Denoyer, and Hervé Jégou. 2017. Word translation without parallel data. *arXiv preprint arXiv:1710.04087*.

O Curry, H Whitehouse, and D Mullins. 2019. Is it good to cooperate? testing the theory of morality-as-cooperation in 60 societies. *Current Anthropology*, 60(1).

Jacob Devlin, Ming-Wei Chang, Kenton Lee, and Kristina Toutanova. 2018. Bert: Pre-training of deep bidirectional transformers for language understanding. *arXiv preprint arXiv:1810.04805*.

Christiane Fellbaum. 1998. *WordNet: An Electronic Lexical Database*. Bradford Books.

Jesse Graham, Jonathan Haidt, Sena Koleva, Matt Motyl, Ravi Iyer, Sean P. Wojcik, and Peter H. Ditto. 2013. Chapter two - moral foundations theory: The pragmatic validity of moral pluralism. volume 47 of *Advances in Experimental Social Psychology*, pages 55–130. Academic Press.

Felix Hamborg, Norman Meuschke, Corinna Breitinger, and Bela Gipp. 2017. news-please: A generic news crawler and extractor. In *Proceedings of the 15th International Symposium of Information Science*, pages 218–223.

Kyriaki Kalimeri, Mariano G Beiró, Matteo Delfino, Robert Raleigh, and Ciro Cattuto. 2019a. Predicting demographics, moral foundations, and human values from digital behaviours. *Computers in Human Behavior*, 92:428–445.

Kyriaki Kalimeri, Mariano G. Beiró, Alessandra Urbinati, Andrea Bonanomi, Alessandro Rosina, and Ciro Cattuto. 2019b. Human values and attitudes towards vaccination in social media. In *Companion Proceedings of The 2019 World Wide Web Conference*, pages 248–254.

Jenna Kanerva, Filip Ginter, and Tapio Salakoski. 2020. Universal lemmatizer: A sequence to sequence model for lemmatizing universal dependencies treebanks. *Natural Language Engineering*, pages 1–30.

Austin C Kozlowski, Matt Taddy, and James A Evans. 2019. The geometry of culture: Analyzing the meanings of class through word embeddings. *American Sociological Review*, 84(5):905–949.

Marlon Mooijman, Joe Hoover, Ying Lin, Heng Ji, and Morteza Dehghani. 2018. Moralization in social networks and the emergence of violence during protests. *Nature human behaviour*, 2(6):389–396.

Andraž Pelicon, Marko Pranji'c, Dragana Miljkovi'c, Blaž Škrlj, and Senja Pollak. 2020. Zero-shot learning for cross-lingual news sentiment classification. *Applied Sciences*, 10(17):5993.

Senja Pollak, Marko Robnik Šikonja, Matthew Purver, Michele Boggia, Ravi Shekhar, Marko Pranjić, Salla Salmela, Ivar Krustok, Tarmo Paju, Carl-Gustav Linden, Leo Leppänen, Elaine Zosa, Matej Ulčar, Linda Freienthal, Silver Traat, Luis Adrián Cabrera-Diego, Matej Martinc, Nada Lavrač, Blaž Škrlj, Martin Žnidaršič, Andraž Pelicon, Boshko Koloski, Vid Podpečan, Janez Kranjc, Shane Sheehan, Emanuela Boros, Jose Moreno, Antoine Doucet, and Hannu Toivonen. 2021. EMBEDDIA tools, datasets and challenges: Resources and hackathon contributions. In *Proceedings of the EACL Hackashop on News Media Content Analysis and Automated Report Generation*. Association for Computational Linguistics.

Mark Raasveldt and Hannes Mühleisen. 2019. Duckdb: an embeddable analytical database. In *Proceedings of the 2019 International Conference on Management of Data*, pages 1981–1984.

Rico Sennrich, B. Haddow, and Alexandra Birch. 2016. Neural machine translation of rare words with subword units. *ArXiv*, abs/1508.07909.

Ashish Vaswani, Noam Shazeer, Niki Parmar, Jakob Uszkoreit, Llion Jones, Aidan N Gomez, Łukasz Kaiser, and Illia Polosukhin. 2017. Attention is all you need. In *Advances in neural information processing systems*, pages 5998–6008.

Interesting cross-border news discovery using cross-lingual article linking and document similarity

Boshko Koloski
Jožef Stefan Institute
Jožef Stefan IPS
Jamova 39, Ljubljana
boshko.koloski@ijs.si

Elaine Zosa
University of Helsinki
Pietari Kalmin katu 5, Helsinki
elaine.zosa@helsinki.fi

Timen Stepišnik-Perdih
Jožef Stefan Institute
Jamova 39, Ljubljana

Blaž Škrlj
Jožef Stefan Institute
Jamova 39, Ljubljana
blaz.skrlj@ijs.si

Tarmo Paju
Ekspress Meedia, Estonia
Narva mnt 13, Tallinn
tarmo.paju@delfi.ee

Senja Pollak
Jožef Stefan Institute
Jamova 39, Ljubljana
senja.pollak@ijs.si

Abstract

Contemporary news media face increasing amounts of available data that can be of use when prioritizing, selecting and discovering new news. In this work we propose a methodology for retrieving interesting articles in a cross-border news discovery setting. More specifically, we explore how a set of seed documents in Estonian can be projected in Latvian document space and serve as a basis for discovery of novel interesting pieces of Latvian news that would interest Estonian readers. The proposed methodology was evaluated by Estonian journalist who confirmed that in the best setting, from top 10 retrieved Latvian documents, half of them represent news that are potentially interesting to be taken by the Estonian media house and presented to Estonian readers.

1 Introduction

This paper presents our results of the participation in the hackaton, which was organised as part of the EACL 2021 Hackashop on news media content analysis and automated report generation. We are addressing the EMBEDDIA hackathon challenge on Identifying Interesting News from Neighbouring Countries (Pollak et al., 2021) in Estonian and Latvian context, which is a fully novel document retrieval task performed on recently released EMBEDDIA news datasets. Estonian journalists are very interested in identifying stories from Latvia, which will attract a large number of readers and are "special". While performing keyword-based search for Latvian news, where Estonians are mentioned is a simple task, this challenge on the contrary aims to identify a small set of documents from a larger number of topics, e.g. scandals, deaths and gossip that might be somehow connected to Estonia: not only by mentioning Estonians but by identifying news and stories that Estonians relate to (for example, when similar things have happened in Estonia or when similar news have been popular in Estonia).

In our approach, we first automatically create a collection of interesting articles using a string-based search and cross-lingual document linking, and then rank the query documents based on the proportion of interesting documents in their neighbourhood (where the neighbourhood is defined by a document similarity) by the newly introduced *Seed news of interest score (SNIR)*.

The article first presents the datasets (Section 2), introduces the methodology (Section 3), and presents our experimental results (Section 4). The code and the data are made publicly available (see Section 5). Finally, Section 6 concludes the paper and presents the ideas for further work.

2 Datasets

In this study, we used the following resources.

- Archives of Estonian news articles from Ekspress Meedia. Ekspress Meedia belongs to Ekspress Meedia Group, one of the largest media groups in the Baltics. From the entire collection of Ekspress Meedia articles (Pollak et al., 2021), we selected the articles from the years 2018 and 2019 (i.e. 64,651 articles in total).

- Dataset of archives of Latvian news articles (Pollak et al., 2021) come from Latvian Delfi that also belongs to Ekspress Meedia Group. We considered only the articles from the years 2018 and 2019 (i.e. 60,802 articles in total).

Proceedings of the EACL Hackashop on News Media Content Analysis and Automated Report Generation, pages 116–120
April 19, 2021 © Association for Computational Linguistics

- Manually identified interesting news for Estonian readers in Latvian (and their Estonian counterparts). These were manually identified as examples of interesting news by Estonian journalist from Ekspress Meedia. Note that the Estonian articles are not their direct translations, as the articles can be slightly adapted to Estonian audience.

3 Methodology

Our methodology consists of two steps. First, we automatically construct the datasets of interesting Latvian articles and next propose a method to retrieve interesting articles by ranking a given query document based on the the proportion of interesting articles in its neighbourhood.

3.1 Automated selection of Latvian example articles

The aim of this step is to automatically construct *Latvian seed news of interest*, which are considered as good examples of interesting Latvian articles. As there are only 21 manually identified examples, which we keep for the evaluation purposes and parameter setting, this step was automatised.

In our approach, we first extract Estonian articles, that specifically mention the source of Latvian Delfi (*Läti Delfi*), which leads to 100 identified Estonian articles which are considered as automatically constructed Estonian example data. Then we follow the methodology of Zosa et al. (2020). More specifically, we use Sentence-BERT (Reimers and Gurevych, 2019) to obtain cross-lingual encodings of the articles from both languages. For each Estonian article, we extract best *k* Latvian candidates (where *k* is a parameter) by taking the cosine similarities between the query Estonian article and all the candidate Latvian articles and finally rank the Latvian articles based on this similarity measure.

Note that also recent work (Litschko et al., 2021) has shown that specialized sentence encoders trained for semantic similarity across languages obtain better results in document retrieval than static cross-lingual word embeddings or averaged contextualized embeddings.

3.2 Retrieval of interesting news articles

In this step, we assign the "interestingness score" to each query article. First, we identify the local neighbourhood of a query article by document similarity. We use the same sentence-embeddings method as in the previous step, with the difference that here the articles similarity is computed in monolingual setting. The number of articles surrounding the query is a parameter m.

We introduce a custom metric called SNIR (*Seed news of interest ratio*), where we compute the ratio of automatically identified interesting news compared to all the articles in the neighbourhood. The hypothesis is that the articles of interest will have more articles from the automatically identified interesting news articles in their surrounding than the articles, which are not relevant for the Estonian readers.

The result of our method is a ranked list of articles for a given time period (e.g. a day, week, month) where a journalist can then decide to manually check top x articles. In addition, in future also a SNIR threshold could be set which would allow interested journalists to be informed about potentially interesting articles in real-time.

The SNIR score is defined as follows. Let $\text{NeighborhoodDocuments}_m$ represent the set of m nearest documents in the final embedding space. Let Interesting_m represent the set of m *interesting* seed documents obtained via the cross-lingual mapping discussed in the previous sections. We can define the SNIR at m as:

$$\text{SNIR}(m) = \frac{|\text{Interesting}_m|}{|\text{NeighborhoodDocuments}_m|}.$$

We report SNIR values for different neighborhood (m) sizes. The goal of SNIR is to score interesting query articles higher than query articles which are not of special interest for Estonian readers.

4 Experiments and results

4.1 Automated analysis

For our experiments, we used the following settings. We test the parameter setting for *k* in cross-lingual article linking to 20 and 100, and the setting of parameter *m* to 10, 20 and 100 for determining the neighbourhood in computing the SNIR score.

First, we evaluated the cross-lingual article linking on the 21 manually linked article pairs. For these article pairs, We obtained an MRR (Mean Reciprocal Rank) score of 64.93%, which shows that for an article in a source language, the correct article is usually proposed as the first or second candidate.

Next, we performed qualitative analysis by visualising the document space. In Figure 1 (using parameter k=20), we can see that automatically defined Latvian seed news of interest (red) are not evenly distributed and support the hypothesis, that random article's neighbourhood will differ in this respect. The figure also presents the manually identified interesting news (orange), where at least some of the documents seem to be positioned together.

Next, we compare the SNIR scores of 21 manually identified interesting articles compared to random Latvian articles. The results of SNIR score for parameter *k*=100 at different *m* can be found in Figure 2. This also suggests that there is some evidence that a threshold could in future be determined, but more extensive experiments should be performed in future work.

4.2 Manual analysis

For final evaluation, we selected the last month of the Latvian collection (1408 articles in total), and ranked the articles according to the SNIR score. These were provided to the Estonian journalist of Ekspress Meedia who evaluated top 10 results for each of the settings.

We prepared four different pairs of $k \in 10, 100$ retrieved documents and $m \in 10, 20, 100$ documents in the neighbourhood which were evaluated by the media expert. The media house expert analyzed the retrieved documents and labeled them with three different labels based on the acceptance:

- No - the article was of *not relevant* significance to the media house.
- Maybe - the article contained news about events that *are potentially relevant* to the Estonian readers.
- Yes - the article contained news about events that *are relevant* to the Estonian readers or contained extraordinarily news.

The evaluation of the top 10 articles retrieved for each k, m pair is listed in Table 1.

From the evaluation we can see that when we have a relatively small number of retrieved documents and a smaller neighbourhood we can benefit from the SNIR metric. As the best performing parameter pairs were the $k = 20$ and $m = 10$ retrieving 50% articles as relevant or of close relevance to the Estonian news house. When larger neighbourhood is introduced the space becomes sparser and the method tends to retrieve more false positives.

k	m	Yes	Maybe	Not
20	10	2	3	5
20	100	1	3	6
100	20	1	3	6
100	100	0	3	7

Table 1: Evaluation of the top-10 retrieved articles by the SNIR ranking for various k interesting Latvian seeds documents and m neighbourhood sizes.

The journalist also explained why a selected news example from positive category is very relevant. The news talks about a scooter accident in court proceedings, which is *extraordinary*, as well as *relevant to Estonians* as the debate around scooters at the streets is also very active in Estonia. Some examples from negative category contain articles about foreign news (terror attack, for example) and these are not the type of news that the Estonian journalists would pick from Latvian media.

5 Availability

The code and data of the experiments is made available on the GitHub: `https://github.com/bkolosk1/Interesting-cross-border-news-discovery`

6 Conclusion and future work

In this work we tackled the problem of retrieving interesting news from one country for the context of another neighbouring country. We focused on finding interesting news in Latvian news space that would be engaging for the Estonian public. We used Latvian and Estonian EMBEDDIA datasets to construct the document space. First we used a string matching approach to identify a subset of news in Estonian media that originated from Latvian news. Next, we utilized the methods for *ad hoc* Cross Lingual document retrieval to find corresponding articles in the Latvian news space. After automatically retrieving this set of Latvian news articles of interest, we used this information in a novel metric defined as SNIR, that analyses a news article's neighbourhood in order to measure it's relevance (interestingness). The assumption of the metric is that if the surrounding documents of a query point are relevant, this new point might be of relevance. The SNIR scores of randomly selected 20 documents and 20 documents identified as examples of interesting news by an Estonian journalist showed that their value differ, which is

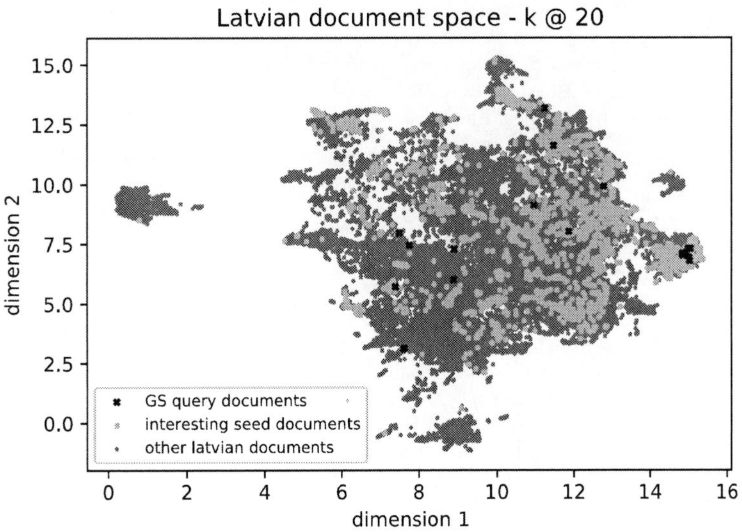

Figure 1: MAP 2D projection of the Latvian data, where black crosses mark query docs (GS) represent gold standard, i.e. manually identified Latvian news of interest to Estonian readers, gray dots represent automatically identified Latvian seeds (identified by string-based search in Estonian and cross-lingual linking to Latvian) and dark-gray dots represent all other Latvian documents.

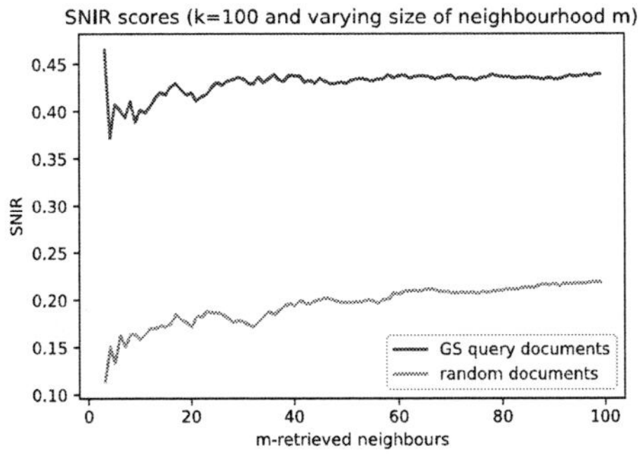

Figure 2: Evaluation of the SNIR metric for the 21 gold standard queries (manually identified news of interest) and 21 random query points. The results indicate that a random documents' neighbourhood is structured differently compared to the one of relevant interesting documents.

promising. Finally, we prepared a test set of news from one month and sent them to manual evaluation by a journalist. Results of top 10 candidates of each setting suggest that the proposed metric works well if the parameters of interesting articles and neighborhood were adjusted right, with the best performing parameter tuple yielding 50% hit-ratio.

For the further work we propose exploring the keywords appearing in the clusters of interesting news and exploiting their named entity tags in order to achieve even better performance. We also want to include background knowledge from knowledge graphs to improve the document similarity evaluation. Special attention will also be paid to setting a threshold for SNIR which would allow for real-time investigation of best candidates in a real journalistic practice.

7 Acknowledgements

The work was supported by European Union's Horizon 2020 research and innovation programme under grant agreement No 825153, project EMBEDDIA (Cross-Lingual Embeddings for Less-Represented Languages in European News Media). The work was also supported by the Slovenian Research Agency (ARRS) through core research programme *Knowledge Technologies* (P2-0103) and the work by B.Š. through the ARRS young researcher grant.

References

Robert Litschko, Ivan Vulić, Simone Paolo Ponzetto, and Goran Glavaš. 2021. Evaluating multilingual text encoders for unsupervised cross-lingual retrieval. In *Proceedings of ECIR*.

Senja Pollak, Marko Robnik Šikonja, Matthew Purver, Michele Boggia, Ravi Shekhar, Marko Pranjić, Salla

Salmela, Ivar Krustok, Tarmo Paju, Carl-Gustav Linden, Leo Leppänen, Elaine Zosa, Matej Ulčar, Linda Freienthal, Silver Traat, Luis Adrián Cabrera-Diego, Matej Martinc, Nada Lavrač, Blaž Škrlj, Martin Žnidaršič, Andraž Pelicon, Boshko Koloski, Vid Podpečan, Janez Kranjc, Shane Sheehan, Emanuela Boros, Jose Moreno, Antoine Doucet, and Hannu Toivonen. 2021. EMBEDDIA tools, datasets and challenges: Resources and hackathon contributions. In *Proceedings of the EACL Hackashop on News Media Content Analysis and Automated Report Generation*. Association for Computational Linguistics.

Nils Reimers and Iryna Gurevych. 2019. Sentence-BERT: Sentence embeddings using Siamese BERT-networks. In *Proceedings of the 2019 Conference on Empirical Methods in Natural Language Processing and the 9th International Joint Conference on Natural Language Processing (EMNLP-IJCNLP)*, pages 3982–3992, Hong Kong, China. Association for Computational Linguistics.

Elaine Zosa, Mark Granroth-Wilding, and Lidia Pivovarova. 2020. A comparison of unsupervised methods for ad hoc cross-lingual document retrieval. In *Proceedings of the workshop on Cross-Language Search and Summarization of Text and Speech (CLSSTS2020)*, pages 32–37, Marseille, France. European Language Resources Association.

EMBEDDIA hackathon report: Automatic sentiment and viewpoint analysis of Slovenian news corpus on the topic of LGBTIQ+

Matej Martinc
Jožef Stefan Institute
Jamova 39, Ljubljana
matej.martinc@ijs.si

Nina Perger
Faculty of Social Sciences
Kardeljeva ploščad 5, Ljubljana
nina.perger@fdv.uni-lj.si

Andraž Pelicon
Jožef Stefan Institute
Jamova 39, Ljubljana
andraz.pelicon@@ijs.si

Matej Ulčar
Faculty of Computer Science
Večna pot 113, Ljubljana
matej.ulcar@fri.uni-lj.si

Andreja Vezovnik
Faculty of Social Sciences
Kardeljeva ploščad 5, Ljubljana
andreja.vezovnik@fdv.uni-lj.si

Senja Pollak
Jožef Stefan Institute
Jamova 39, Ljubljana
senja.pollak@ijs.si

Abstract

We conduct automatic sentiment and viewpoint analysis of the newly created Slovenian news corpus containing articles related to the topic of LGBTIQ+ by employing the state-of-the-art news sentiment classifier and a system for semantic change detection. The focus is on the differences in reporting between quality news media with long tradition and news media with financial and political connections to SDS, a Slovene right-wing political party. The results suggest that political affiliation of the media can affect the sentiment distribution of articles and the framing of specific LGBTIQ+ specific topics, such as same-sex marriage.

1 Introduction

Quantitative content analysis of news related to LGBTIQ+ in general, and specifically, to marriage equality debates show that distinctions can be drawn between those media articles that express positive, neutral or negative stance towards same-sex marriage. Those media articles that express positive stance are grounded in human rights/civil equality discourses and access to benefits (Zheng and Chan, 2020; Colistra and Johnson, 2019; Paterson and Coffey-Glover, 2018), and frame marriage equality as an inevitable path towards equality, as a civil right issue that would reduce existing prejudices and discrimination, and protect threatened LGBTIQ+ minority (Zheng and Chan, 2020).

For media articles that express negative stance towards marriage equality, distinctive discursive elements are present, such as "equal, but separate" (marriage equality should be implemented, but differentiating labels should be kept in the name of protecting the institute of marriage) (Kania, 2020; Zheng and Chan, 2020; Paterson and Coffey-Glover, 2018), and reference procreation/welfare of children (Kania, 2020; Zheng and Chan, 2020), public objection (Kania, 2020) and church – state opposition (Paterson and Coffey-Glover, 2018).

The related work also shows that the differences between "liberal" and "conservative" arguments are not emphasised, mostly because both sides refer to each other's arguments, if only to negate them; yet, political orientation can be identified through the tone of the article (Zheng and Chan, 2020).

When it comes to methods employed for automatic analysis of the LGBTIQ+ topic, most recent approaches rely on embeddings. Hamilton et al. (2016) employed embeddings to research how words (among them also word *gay*) change meaning through time. They built static embedding models for each time slice of the corpus and then make these representations comparable by employing *vector space alignment* by optimising a geometric transformation. This research was recently expanded by (Shi and Lei, 2020), who employed embeddings to explore semantic shifts of six descriptive LGBTIQ+ words from the 1860s to the 2000s: *homosexual, lesbian, gay, bisexual, transgender*, and *queer*.

There are also several general news analysis techniques that can be employed for the task at hand. Azarbonyad et al. (2017) developed a system for semantic shift detection for viewpoint analysis of political and media discourse. A recent study by Spinde et al. (2021) tried to identify biased terms in news articles by comparing news media outlet specific word embeddings. On the other hand, Pelicon et al. (2020) developed a system for analysing the sentiment of news media articles.

While the above described analyses in a large majority of cases covered news in English speaking countries, in this research, we expand the quantitative analysis to Slovenian news, in order to determine whether attitudes towards LGBTIQ+ differs in different cultural environments. We created a corpus of LGBTIQ+ related news and conducted an

Proceedings of the EACL Hackashop on News Media Content Analysis and Automated Report Generation, pages 121–126
April 19, 2021 © Association for Computational Linguistics

automatic analysis of its content covering several aspects:

- Sentiment of news reporting, where we focused on the differences in reporting between well established media with long tradition of news reporting and more recently established media characterised by their financial and political connections to the Slovene conservative political party SDS.

- Usage of words, where we tried to identify the words that are used differently in different news sources and would indicate the difference in the prevailing discourse on the topic of LGBTIQ+ in the specific liberal and conservative media.

The research was performed in the scope of the EMBEDDIA Hackashop (Hackaton track) at EACL 2021 and employs several of the proposed resources and tools (Pollak et al., 2021).

2 Methodology

For **sentiment analysis** we used a multilingual news sentiment analysis tool. The tool was trained using a two-step approach, described in Pelicon et al. (2020). For training, a corpus of sentiment-labeled news articles in Slovenian was used (Bucar et al., 2018) with news covering predominantly the financial and political domains. This model was subsequently applied to the LGBTIQ+ corpus where each news article was labeled with one of the sentiment labels, namely negative, neutral or positive. This allowed us to generate a sentiment distribution of articles for each media source in the corpus.

For **word usage viewpoints analysis**, we applied a system originally employed for diachronic shift detection (Martinc et al., 2020b). Our word usage detection pipeline follows the procedure proposed in the previous work (Martinc et al., 2020a,b; Giulianelli et al., 2020): the created LGBTIQ+ corpus is split into two slices containing news from different news source according to procedure described in Section 3. Next, the corpus is lemmatized, using the Stanza library (Qi et al., 2020), and lowercased. For each lemma that appears more than 100 times in each slice and is not considered a stopword, we generate a slice specific set of contextual embeddings using BERT (Devlin et al., 2019) pretrained on the Slovenian, Croatian and English texts (Ulčar and Robnik-Šikonja, 2020). These representations are clustered using k-means and the derived cluster distributions are compared across slices by employing Wasserstein distance (Solomon, 2018). It is assumed that the ranking resembles a relative degree of usage change, therefore words are ranked according to the distance.

Once the most changed words are identified, the next step is to understand how their usage differs in the distinct corpus slices. The hypothesis is that specific clusters of BERT embeddings resemble specific word usages of a specific word. The problem is that these clusters may consist of several hundreds or even thousands of word usages, i.e. sentences, therefore manual inspection of these usages would be time-consuming. For this reason, we extract the most discriminating unigrams, bigrams, trigrams and fourgrams for each cluster using the following procedure: we compute the term frequency - inverse document frequency (tf-idf) score of each n-gram and the n-grams appearing in more than 80% of the clusters are excluded to ensure that the selected keywords are the most discriminant. This gives us a ranked list of keywords for each cluster and the top-ranked keywords (according to tf-idf) are used for the interpretation of the cluster.

3 Experiments

3.1 Dataset

The corpus was collected from the Event registry (Leban et al., 2014) dataset by searching for Slovenian articles from 2014 to (including) 2020, containing any of the manually defined 125 keywords (83 unigrams and 42 bigrams) and their inflected forms connected to the subject of LGBTIQ+. The resulting corpus contains news articles on the LGBTIQ+ topic from 23 media sources. The corpus statistics are described in Table 1. Out of this corpus, we extracted a subcorpus appropriate for the viewpoint analysis. The subcorpus we used included the following online news media: Delo, Večer, Dnevnik, Nova24TV, Tednik Demokracija and PortalPolitikis. The sources were divided into two groups. The first group, namely Delo, Večer and Dnevnik represent the category of daily quality news media that are published online and in print with a long tradition in the Slovene media landscape. These three media are relatively highly trusted by readers and have the highest readership amongst Slovene dailies. The second group of news media - namely, Nova24TV, Ted-

Source	Num. articles	Num. words
MMC RTV Slovenija	1790	1,555,977
Delo	1194	1,064,615
Nova24TV	844	683,336
Večer	667	552,195
24ur.com	661	313,794
Dnevnik	592	262,482
Siol.net Novice	549	460,561
Slovenske novice	501	236,516
Svet24	430	286,429
Mladina	394	275,506
Tednik Demokracija	361	350,742
Domovina	327	283,478
Primorske novice	255	183,624
Druzina.si	253	149,761
Vestnik	242	263,737
Časnik.si - Spletni magazin z mero	239	280,339
Žurnal24	172	79,953
PortalPolitikis	157	111,683
Revija Reporter	102	62,429
Gorenjski Glas	97	92,751
Onaplus	79	104,343
Športni Dnevnik Ekipa	67	33,936
Cosmopolitan Slovenija	57	71,538

Table 1: LGBTIQ+ corpus statistics.

nik Demokracija and PortalPolitikis have been established more recently and are characterised by their financial and political connections to the Slovene right-wing/conservative political party SDS (Slovenska demokratska stranka) and the Roman Catholic Church.

3.2 Sentiment Analysis

Figure 1 presents sentiment distribution across articles for each specific news media, arranged from left to right according to the share of articles with negative sentiment. Note that all three media houses selected for the viewpoint analysis (Nova24TV, Tednik, Demokracija and PortalPolitikis) because of their financial and political connections to the Slovene right-wing/conservative political party SDS produce more news articles with negative sentiment on the topic of LGBTIQ+ than the mainstream media with the long tradition (Delo, Dnevnik, Večer). The source with the most negative content about LGBTIQ+ is Revija Reporter, which is in most media analyses positioned in the right-wing ideological spectrum[1] (Milosavljević, 2016; Milosavljević and Biljak Gerjevič, 2020). On the other side the source with the smallest share of negative news is Primorske novice, a politically independent daily regional quality news media published online and in print with a long tradition in the regional media landscape. Nevertheless, not all conservative media are characterized by a more negative reporting about the LGBTIQ+ topic. For example, the source with the second lowest share of negative news is Druzina.si, which is strongly connected to Roman Catholic Church.

[1] `https://podcrto.si/mediji-martina-odlazka-1-del-nepregledna-mreza-radiev-tiskovin-televizije/`

3.3 Viewpoint Analysis

The viewpoint analysis was conducted by finding words, whose usage varies the most in the two groups of media sources selected for the analysis (i.e. Delo, Dnevnik, Večer vs. Nova24TV, Tednik Demokracija and PortalPolitiks). The 10 most changed words are presented in Table 2. The word that changed the most was globok (deep), for which our system for interpretation of the change revealed that it was selected due to frequent mentions of *deep state* in the media with connections to political right. The context of *deep state* is interesting, since it is a very frequently used interpretative frame by this group of media sources, regardless of the specific topic. Here it indicates the framing of the LGBTIQ+ questions as part of a political agenda driven by the left-wing politics. The second word roman (novel) was selected because it appears in two contexts: as a novel and also as a constituent word in a name of the Slovenian LGBTIQ+ activist, Roman Kuhar. While the third word, *video*, is a corpus artefact that offers little insight into the attitude towards LGBTIQ+, the fourth word, *razmerje* (relationship), has a direct connection to some of the most dividing LGBTIQ+ topics, such as gay marriage, therefore for this word we provide a more detailed analysis. Figure 2 presents cluster distributions per two media groups and top 5 (translated) keywords for each cluster for word *razmerje(relationship)*. The main difference between the two distributions can be observed when it comes to mention of relationship in the context of family and marriage (see the red cluster), which present a large cluster of usages in the mainstream media but a rather small cluster in the right-wing

1	globok(deep)	6	napaka(mistake)
2	roman(novel)	7	nadaljevanje(continuation)
3	video	8	lanski(last year)
4	razmerje(relationship)	9	kriza(crisis)
5	teorija(theory)	10	pogledat(look)

Table 2: Top 10 most changed words (and their English translations) in the corpus according to Wasserstein distance between k-means ($k = 5$) cluster distributions in distinct chunks of the corpus.

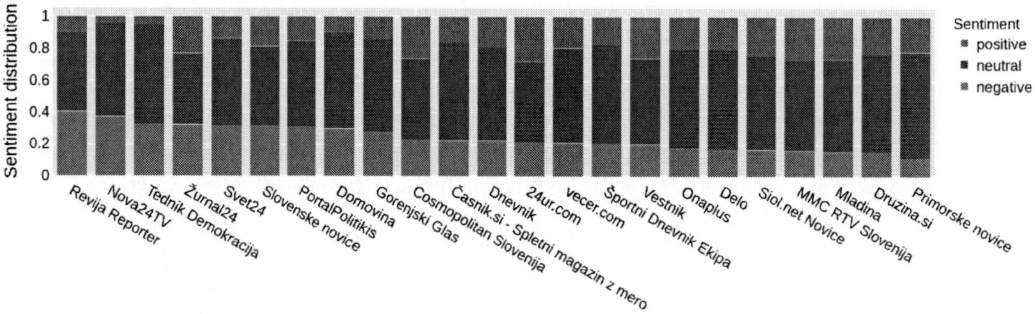

Figure 1: Sentiment distribution for each source in the LGBTIQ+ corpus.

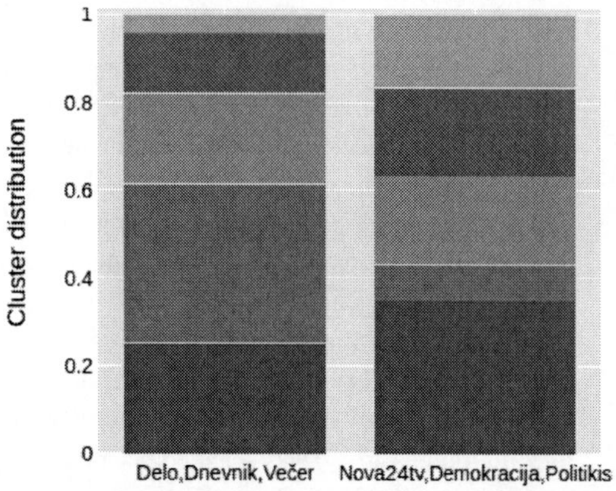

#	Keywords
■	partnership, homosexual relationship, polygamous relationship, intimate relationship, problem
■	family relationship, end work relationship, woman, field, less
■	power in the relationship, relationship between people, percentage, man and woman, story
■	family relationship, marriage, children, Ljubljana, coalition for children
■	woman, love relationship, work relationship, film, meet

Figure 2: Cluster distributions per two media groups and top 5 translated keywords for each cluster for word *razmerje(relationship)*.

media. On the other hand, relationship is in these media mentioned a lot more in the context of partnership, homosexuality and polygamy (see the orange cluster). The other three clusters (i.e., usages) have a rather strong presence in both media groups.

4 Conclusions

We conducted a content analysis of the Slovenian news corpus containing articles related to the topic of LGBTIQ+. The sentiment analysis study shows that there are some differences in the sentiment of reporting about LGBTIQ+ between two distinct groups of media and that the three media houses connected to political right tend to cover the subject in a more negative manner. This supports the thesis by Zheng and Chan (2020), who suggested that political orientation can be identified through the tone of the article. Nevertheless, the obtained results should be interpreted with the grain of caution, since the sentiment classifier we employed cannot distinguish whether it is the stance expressed towards the LGBTIQ+ community, or is it rather the event on which the article is reporting, that is positive or negative (e.g., an attack on the LGBTIQ+ activist). The distinction between these two "types" of sentiment will be analysed in the future work.

The viewpoint analysis suggests that the usage of some specific words has been adapted in order to express specific ideological point of view of the media. For example, the analysis of the word *relationship* suggests that the more conservative media more likely frame LGBTIQ+ relationships as a *partnership* of two homosexual (or even polygamous) partners. On the other hand, they rarely consider LGBTIQ+ relationships as family or talk about marriage.

In the future we plan to conduct topic analysis of the corpus in order to identify the most common LGBTIQ+ related topics covered by the news media. We will also employ embeddings to research relations between LGBTIQ+ specific words.

Acknowledgments

This work was supported by the Slovenian Research Agency (ARRS) grants for the core programme Knowledge technologies (P2-0103), the project Computer-assisted multilingual news discourse analysis with contextual embeddings (CANDAS, J6-2581), as well as the European Union's Horizon 2020 research and innovation programme under grant agreement No 825153, project EMBEDDIA (Cross-Lingual Embeddings for Less-Represented Languages in European News Media).

References

Hosein Azarbonyad, Mostafa Dehghani, Kaspar Beelen, Alexandra Arkut, Maarten Marx, and Jaap Kamps. 2017. Words are malleable: Computing semantic shifts in political and media discourse. In *Proceedings of the 2017 ACM on Conference on Information and Knowledge Management*, pages 1509–1518.

Joze Bucar, M. Znidarsic, and J. Povh. 2018. Annotated news corpora and a lexicon for sentiment analysis in slovene. *Language Resources and Evaluation*, 52:895–919.

Rita Colistra and Chelsea Betts Johnson. 2019. Framing the legalization of marriage for same-sex couples: An examination of news coverage surrounding the us supreme court's landmark decision. *Journal of homosexuality*.

Jacob Devlin, Ming-Wei Chang, Kenton Lee, and Kristina Toutanova. 2019. BERT: Pre-training of deep bidirectional transformers for language understanding. pages 4171–4186.

Mario Giulianelli, Marco Del Tredici, and Raquel Fernández. 2020. Analysing lexical semantic change with contextualised word representations. In *Proceedings of the 58th Annual Meeting of the Association for Computational Linguistics*, pages 3960–3973, Online. Association for Computational Linguistics.

William L. Hamilton, Jure Leskovec, and Dan Jurafsky. 2016. Diachronic word embeddings reveal statistical laws of semantic change. In *Proceedings of the 54th Annual Meeting of the Association for Computational Linguistics*, pages 1489–1501.

Ursula Kania. 2020. Marriage for all ('ehe fuer alle')?! a corpus-assisted discourse analysis of the marriage equality debate in germany. *Critical Discourse Studies*, 17(2):138–155.

Gregor Leban, Blaz Fortuna, Janez Brank, and Marko Grobelnik. 2014. Event registry: learning about world events from news. In *Proceedings of the 23rd International Conference on World Wide Web*, pages 107–110.

Matej Martinc, Syrielle Montariol, Elaine Zosa, and Lidia Pivovarova. 2020a. Capturing evolution in word usage: Just add more clusters? In *Companion Proceedings of the Web Conference 2020*, WWW '20, page 343–349, New York, NY, USA. Association for Computing Machinery.

Matej Martinc, Syrielle Montariol, Elaine Zosa, and Lidia Pivovarova. 2020b. Discovery team at semeval-2020 task 1: Context-sensitive embeddings not always better than static for semantic change detection. In *Proceedings of the Fourteenth Workshop on Semantic Evaluation*, pages 67–73.

Marko Milosavljević. 2016. Media pluralism monitor 2016 monitoring risks for media pluralism in the EU and beyond - country report: Slovenia.

Marko Milosavljević and Romana Biljak Gerjevič. 2020. Monitoring media pluralism in the digital era: Application of the media pluralism monitor in the European Union, Albania and Turkey in the years 2018-2019 - country report: Slovenia.

Laura L Paterson and Laura Coffey-Glover. 2018. Discourses of marriage in same-sex marriage debates in the uk press 2011–2014. *Journal of Language and Sexuality*, 7(2):175–204.

Andraž Pelicon, Marko Pranjić, Dragana Miljković, Blaž Škrlj, and Senja Pollak. 2020. Zero-shot learning for cross-lingual news sentiment classification. *Applied Sciences*, 10(17):5993.

Senja Pollak, Marko Robnik Šikonja, Matthew Purver, Michele Boggia, Ravi Shekhar, Marko Pranjić, Salla Salmela, Ivar Krustok, Tarmo Paju, Carl-Gustav Linden, Leo Leppänen, Elaine Zosa, Matej Ulčar, Linda Freienthal, Silver Traat, Luis Adrián Cabrera-Diego, Matej Martinc, Nada Lavrač, Blaž Škrlj, Martin Žnidaršič, Andraž Pelicon, Boshko Koloski, Vid Podpečan, Janez Kranjc, Shane Sheehan, Emanuela Boros, Jose Moreno, Antoine Doucet, and Hannu Toivonen. 2021. EMBEDDIA tools, datasets and challenges: Resources and hackathon contributions. In *Proceedings of the EACL Hackashop on News Media Content Analysis and Automated Report Generation*. Association for Computational Linguistics.

Peng Qi, Yuhao Zhang, Yuhui Zhang, Jason Bolton, and Christopher D Manning. 2020. Stanza: A python natural language processing toolkit for many human languages. *arXiv preprint arXiv:2003.07082*.

Yaqian Shi and Lei Lei. 2020. The evolution of lgbt labelling words: Tracking 150 years of the interaction of semantics with social and cultural changes. *English Today*, 36(4):33–39.

Justin Solomon. 2018. Optimal transport on discrete domains.

Timo Spinde, Lada Rudnitckaia, and Felix Hamborg. 2021. Identification of biased terms in news articles by comparison of outlet-specific word embeddings. In *Proceedings of the 16th International Conference (iConference 2021). Springer Nature, Virtual Event China.*

Matej Ulčar and Marko Robnik-Šikonja. 2020. Finest bert and crosloengual bert: less is more in multilingual models. *arXiv preprint arXiv:2006.07890.*

Yue Zheng and Lik Sam Chan. 2020. Framing same-sex marriage in us liberal and conservative newspapers from 2004 to 2016: Changes in issue attributes, organizing themes, and story tones. *The Social Science Journal*, pages 1–13.

To Block or not to Block: Experiments with Machine Learning for News Comment Moderation

Damir Korenčić
Rudjer Boskovic Institute, Croatia
damir.korencic@irb.hr

Ipek Baris
University of Koblenz-Landau, Germany
ibaris@uni-koblenz.de

Eugenia Fernandez
euge.ft@gmail.com

Katarina Leuschel
katarina.leuschel@gmail.com

Eva Sánchez Salido
UNED, Spain
esanchez1751@alumno.uned.es

Abstract

Today, news media organizations regularly engage with readers by enabling them to comment on news articles. This creates the need for comment moderation and removal of disallowed comments – a time-consuming task often performed by human moderators. In this paper we approach the problem of automatic news comment moderation as classification of comments into *blocked* and *not blocked* categories. We construct a novel dataset of annotated English comments, experiment with cross-lingual transfer of comment labels and evaluate several machine learning models on datasets of Croatian and Estonian news comments.

1 Introduction

Comment sections are an important part of news sites, providing an opportunity for newsrooms to engage with their audience. Comment moderation aims to safeguard respectful conversation by blocking comments that are uncivil, disruptive or potentially unlawful. This is a complex task that balances legal implications and editorial guidelines. Common categories of blocked comments include: unsafe or illegal content (ex. defamation or hate speech), disruptive content (ex. trolling), advertisements, and copyrighted content (Risch and Krestel, 2018).

While newsrooms are becoming increasingly aware of the benefits provided by artificial intelligence and expect comment moderation to become more manageable, implementation of AI solutions is far from prevalent (Society of Editors, 2018; Beckett, 2019). Some newsrooms use custom automated comment moderation solutions developed in-house or third-party plugins to complement human moderation. Others rely on external companies that provide comment moderation performed by teams of contracted moderators (Society of Editors, 2018; Beckett, 2019; Woodman, 2013).

For most in-house and third-party solutions, the extent of use and details of the machine learning solutions are not publicly revealed. The stand-out third-party option is Perspective,[1] a free API developed by Google's Jigsaw, available in seven high-resourced languages (Beckett, 2019). To the best of our knowledge, there are no machine learning solutions suitable for comment moderation for under-resourced languages.

In the academic literature, the problem of comment moderation is commonly approached as a binary classification of comments into *blocked* and *not blocked* categories (Pavlopoulos et al., 2017; Risch and Krestel, 2018; Shekhar et al., 2020). In this paper, which reports the work done during the EMBEDDIA Hackashop hackathon[2] (Pollak et al., 2021), we approach the problem in the same manner and perform experiments with comment classification on datasets of Croatian and Estonian news comments (Shekhar et al., 2020).

Motivated by the lack of an English dataset of comments labelled as either blocked or not blocked, we construct such a dataset from existing datasets of news and social media comments. We then experiment with the cross-lingual transfer of English labels to Croatian and Estonian comment datasets by means of a multilingual BERT model (Pires et al., 2019; Ulcar and Robnik-Sikonja, 2020). Finally, we construct and evaluate several classification models trained on Croatian and Estonian datasets, analyze the results, and discuss the problem of automatic detection of blocked comments. We make the source code of the experiments freely available.[3]

[1] https://www.perspectiveapi.com
[2] http://embeddia.eu/hackashop2021/
[3] https://github.com/eugeniaft/embeddia-hackathon

Proceedings of the EACL Hackashop on News Media Content Analysis and Automated Report Generation, pages 127–133
April 19, 2021 © Association for Computational Linguistics

2 Related Work

Computational comment moderation includes tasks such as offensive language detection (Schmidt and Wiegand, 2017) and blocked comment detection (Risch and Krestel, 2018; Pavlopoulos et al., 2017; Napoles et al., 2017), which is the focus of our study. Most of the prior studies on comment filtering tackle the problem using text from high-resourced languages such as English (Napoles et al., 2017; Kolhatkar et al., 2019) and German (Risch and Krestel, 2018). There are only a few studies that focus on low-resourced languages (Shekhar et al., 2020; Pavlopoulos et al., 2017).

The methods for comment filtering vary from classical machine learning methods to deep learning approaches. Risch and Krestel (2018) classify comments with a logistic regression classifier using features computed from comments, news articles, and users. Deep neural networks such as RNN and CNN have also been applied (Pavlopoulos et al., 2017). Most recently, Shekhar et al. (2020) leverage Multilingual BERT (mBERT) (Devlin et al., 2019) for the moderation of news comments in Balto-Slavic languages.

3 English Dataset for Comment Moderation

There are multiple publicly available datasets in English with annotated comments that have been used in previous research about comment moderation. However, most of these datasets contain annotations of only a subset of the categories of blocked comments (Shekhar et al., 2020).

We construct a large corpus of comments containing different categories of blocked comments by unifying different datasets and defining a new label. Since comments in these datasets are not explicitly labeled as blocked, we created the *flagged* and *not flagged* labels instead. The idea is to identify comments that moderators should review and decide whether to block them or not. The *flagged* label therefore serves as an approximation of the blocking decision and classifiers that detect it automatically have the potential to save time and human effort.

3.1 Construction of the Dataset

We used five different datasets containing annotated comments from news articles, social media, and other fora. We included comments from platforms outside of news media since users are subject to a similar set of rules related to what content they can share.[4,5,6] Each dataset contains different annotations, including comments rated on a scale of toxicity, comments labelled for hateful speech and abuse, comments labeled for constructiveness and tone, etc. Our challenge was to define the labelling criteria for the binary labels *flagged* and *not flagged* and consistently apply them to the labels in the five datasets. Flagged comments are the comments most likely to require blocking based on the existing labels in the datasets, and are labeled according to the principles discussed in (Risch and Krestel, 2018) and guidelines for comment moderation in (Society of Editors, 2018) and (Woodman, 2013).

Data Source	# not flagged	# flagged	% flagged
SOCC	1,012	31	3%
YNACC	7,076	2,084	23%
DETOX	19,153	3,372	15%
Trawling	5,009	7,189	59%
HASOC	4,443	2,538	36%
Final dataset	36,693	15,214	29%

Table 1: Data source and class distribution statistics for the English dataset of flagged comments.

Our dataset consists of comments from the SOCC corpus (SFU Opinion and Comments Corpus) (Kolhatkar et al., 2019), YNACC corpus (The Yahoo News Annotated Comments Corpus) (Napoles et al., 2017), DETOX corpus (Wulczyn et al., 2017), Trawling corpus (Hitkul et al., 2020), and HASOC corpus (Hate Speech and Offensive Content Identification in Indo-European Languages) (Mandl et al., 2019). SOCC contains annotated comments from opinion articles. We used the *constructiveness* and *toxicity* labels and flagged comments whenever the toxicity level was *toxic* or *very toxic* and *not constructive*. YNACC contains expert annotated comments in online news articles. A comment was labeled flagged whenever a comment was *insulting*, *off-topic*, *controversial* or *mean* and *not constructive*. DETOX has comments from English Wikipedia talk pages. It contains annotations for *attack*, *aggression* and *toxicity*. A comment was labelled flagged whenever it was *toxic*, *aggressive* or if it contained an *attack*. We only included data from 2015. The Trawling data

[4] https://help.twitter.com/en/rules-and-policies/twitter-rules

[5] https://en.wikipedia.org/wiki/Wikipedia:Talk_page_guidelines

[6] https://www.redditinc.com/policies/content-policy

Dataset	Example	Original Label
SOCC	This has to have been written by Chinese government sponsored propagandists.	Non-constr. & Toxic
YNACC	You and at least one other person are pretty dumb, huh? Unless you have two accounts, right, moron?	Mean & Off-topic
DETOX	You should block this idiot for life!	Aggressive
Trawling	So nowadays they let models have greasy unwashed hair and man hands?	Trolling
HASOC	Too many doctors on my fucking Facebook fuck off	Hateful or Offensive

Table 2: Examples of flagged comments.

includes samples of comments from Twitter, Reddit and Wikipedia talk pages. Comments are provided with the labels *Normal*, *Profanity*, *Trolling*, *Derogatory* and *Hate Speech*. A comment was labeled as *flagged* if it belonged to any of the categories except for *Normal*. Lastly, HASOC is composed of comments from Twitter and Facebook and has annotations on whether comments are *hateful*, *offensive* or neither. We included only the English comments and labelled them as *flagged* if they were either *hateful* or *offensive*.

The resulting dataset contains 51,907 labeled comments, 29% of those being flagged comments. Table 1 gives more details on the class distribution and Table 2 contains examples of comments from each dataset that have been labelled as flagged. The dataset can be easily reconstructed by using the code we make available and applying it to the individual sub-datasets which are freely available.

3.2 Classification Experiments

We run a set of experiments to evaluate the performance of classifiers on our dataset. We split our data into train, validation, and test sets using stratified sampling to account for class imbalance. In our first experiment, we trained a Logistic regression classifier and Support vector machine classifier with linear kernel. We later fine-tuned two different multilingual BERT models: CroSloEnBERT and FinEstEnBERT(Ulcar and Robnik-Sikonja, 2020). See Section 4.2 for more details about how the models were optimized and fine-tuned.

The results of the classification experiments are in Table 3. All trained models perform better than the baseline classifier that always chooses the minority class *flagged*. The non-neural classifiers have higher recall whilst the multilingual BERT models have higher F_1 score, accuracy, and precision. The classification results support the claim that the constructed *flagged* label is well-defined and consistent and that our dataset can be further used in research related to comment moderation.

Model	F_1	Prec.	Recall	Acc.
baseline	0.453	0.293	1.000	0.293
LogReg	0.732	0.710	**0.755**	0.838
SVM	0.728	0.725	0.730	0.840
BERT-CroSloEn	0.761	**0.871**	0.675	0.876
BERT-FinEst	**0.777**	0.841	0.722	**0.878**

Table 3: Classification results on English comments labeled as flagged or not flagged. F_1, precision and recall are reported for the class of flagged comments.

4 Automatic Comment Moderation Experiments

Next, we construct and evaluate classifiers that aim to detect blocked news comments. We experiment with EMBEDDIA multilingual BERT models (Ulcar and Robnik-Sikonja, 2020) fine-tuned for classification and with standard non-neural classifiers using n-gram features.

4.1 News Comment Datasets

We use the Ekspress dataset of Estonian news comments and the 24Sata dataset of Croatian news comments (Shekhar et al., 2020). Following Shekhar et al. (2020) we focus on the comments from 2019 that have labels of higher quality. The Estonian comments are simply labelled as either blocked or not blocked, while the blocked Croatian comments are further divided into eight subcategories. We remove the subcategories 2, 4 and 7 that contain either a negligible amount of comments or non-Croatian comments. We also remove all the non-Estonian comments from the Ekspress dataset. After cleaning, 816,131 Croatian and 865,022 Estonian comments remain. Both datasets are unbalanced – only 7.77% of Croatian and 8.99% of Estonian comments are labeled as blocked.

4.2 Classification Experiments

We solve the problem of binary classification of comments into *blocked* and *not blocked* categories. We train and evaluate the comment classifiers using

Model	24Sata dataset (Croatian)				Ekspress dataset (Estonian)			
	F_1	Precision	Recall	Accuracy	F_1	Precision	Recall	Accuracy
baseline	0.144	0.078	1.000	0.078	0.165	0.090	1.000	0.090
BERT-en	0.229	0.189	0.291	0.843	0.216	0.182	0.264	0.827
BERT-en-nat	0.514	**0.960**	0.350	0.948	0.479	0.782	0.345	0.933
BERT-native	**0.535**	0.904	0.379	0.949	0.459	**0.824**	0.319	0.933
LogReg-F1	0.502	0.828	0.360	0.944	**0.532**	0.712	0.425	0.933
LogReg-recall	0.384	0.311	**0.503**	0.875	0.236	0.149	**0.565**	0.671

Table 4: Classification results for the problem of detection of blocked comments.

stratified train/development/test subsets containing 80,000/15,000/15,000 comments.

First we experiment with the two multilingual BERT models CroSloEnBERT and FinEstEnBERT (Ulcar and Robnik-Sikonja, 2020), fine-tuned for classification. We rely on the Huggingface library (Wolf et al., 2020) and use the tokenizers embedded in the BERT models, limiting the number of tokens to 128. For each dataset, we build three fine-tuned BERT models. The first model, labeled *BERT-en* and also evaluated in Section 3.2, is fine-tuned only on English comments. The second model, labeled *BERT-nat*, is fine-tuned only on the target (native) language (Croatian or Estonian). The third model is produced by fine-tuning the English model on the dataset in the target language, and labeled as *BERT-en-nat*. We train the models by setting the batch size to 16 and number of epochs to 3, and perform optimization using Adam with weight decay (Loshchilov and Hutter, 2019). We select the models that exhibit the best accuracy in the training phase.

The second classification approach is based on two standard non-neural classifiers - Logistic regression and Support vector machine with linear kernel. Both classifiers are available as part of the scikit-learn[7] framework Buitinck et al. (2013). To perform model selection we vary both the regularization strength and the method of feature construction. We find the optimal model parameters by performing a grid search on separate train and test sets containing 40,000 and 10,000 comments. Two optimization criteria are used: F_1 score and recall. The search for a model with high recall is motivated by the observation that the majority of the models tend to favor high precision. We find that the Logistic regression offers better performance across both datasets, and that the best choice of features is the binary bag-of-words-and-bigrams vector.

[7]https://scikit-learn.org

The classification results are displayed in Table 4. The performance scores are modest in terms of F_1 and show sharp precision/recall tradeoffs. All of the models outperform the baseline classifier that always chooses the minority class. Accuracy scores are deceptively high due to the prevalence of the non-blocked comments in the datasets. BERT classifiers perform better on Croatian than on Estonian comments, possibly because of differences in the original multilingual BERT models. BERT models fine-tuned only on the English dataset of flagged comments have weak but above-baseline performance, which shows that a certain amount of cross-language knowledge transfer is achieved. The weak performance could be explained both by the language difference and the fact that the English dataset represents an approximation of the blocked comments class.

Shekhar et al. (2020) classify comments from the same datasets, train the models on data containing an equal share of blocked and not blocked comments, and report recall of 0.67, precision of 0.27, and F_1 of 0.38 for the Croatian comments. This result is in line with the sharp precision/recall tradeoffs we observe. Balanced training data in (Shekhar et al., 2020) is a possible reason for higher recall scores obtained (0.70 on the Croatian and 0.58 for the Estonian dataset).

Lastly, we examine the classifiers' performance on sub-categories of blocked Croatian comments detailed in (Shekhar et al., 2020). Table 5 contains recall scores achieved by the BERT-en model trained on the English dataset, BERT-native model trained on the Croatian dataset, the Logistic regression model, and the mBERT model of Shekhar et al. (2020) that is also trained on the Croatian dataset. The performances of the Logistic regression model and the mBERT model demonstrate the benefit of optimizing for recall. The BERT-en model achieves competitive results on the "Vulgarity" and "Abuse" categories, showing that detection of these types

Model	Disallowed	Hate Speech	Deception&Trolling	Vulgarity	Abuse	All Blocked
BERT-en	0.102	0.333	0.149	0.739	0.514	0.291
BERT-native	0.432	0.510	0.299	0.435	0.324	0.379
LogReg-recall	0.515	0.647	0.388	0.783	0.473	0.503
mBERT	0.642	0.722	0.546	0.881	0.723	0.673

Table 5: Recall on the subcategories of blocked Croatian comments.

of blocked comments was successfully transferred from the English dataset. Better results on other categories could be achieved by augmenting the English dataset with additional flagged comments containing deception and misinformation, as well as the spam and copyright infringement content pertaining to the "Disallowed" category.

5 Discussion

Automatic detection of blocked comments of the Croatian and the Estonian dataset is a hard problem. This claim is supported by modest F_1 scores and sharp precision/recall tradeoffs observed both in our experiments and in the experiments of Shekhar et al. (2020). While inclusion of non-textual comment features would probably lead to better results (Risch and Krestel, 2018), we hypothesize that the main problem is the poor quality of comment labelling.

The definition of sensible text categories and consistent annotation of texts with these categories falls within the domain of content analysis (Krippendorff, 2012). Ideally, the category definitions are discussed and fine-tuned, and the measure of inter-annotator agreement (IAA) is reported. In the case of the blocked comment detection, the precise process of category definition is unknown (Pavlopoulos et al., 2017; Risch and Krestel, 2018; Shekhar et al., 2020), while the IAA is either not available (Risch and Krestel, 2018; Shekhar et al., 2020), or modest (Pavlopoulos et al., 2017). Moreover, there are indications of inconsistencies in the definition of a blocked comment class. Shekhar et al. (2020) report that the varying blocking rates are probably caused by changes in moderation policy. Pavlopoulos et al. (2017) and Risch and Krestel (2018) report that a high influx of user comments, for example during high-interest events, causes more strict comment blocking. The mentioned problems should be tackled since the consistent labelling of the comments is key to building high-quality classifiers.

The binary classification approach might be in disconnect with the true needs of the comment moderators. An engineering perspective of a machine learning system can significantly differ from the end user's perspective (Lee et al., 2017). We believe that studies including comment moderators are essential in order to define and evaluate the appropriate solution. For example, the amount of moderators' time saved might prove as a useful metric, and the best application of classifiers might not be automatic blocking but flagging and pre-filtering of comments.

Additionally, moderators operate within boundaries set by in-house rules and practices and legal regulations. An investigation of the nature and impact of such restrictions would provide perspective on the role of automatic comment moderation. For example, in a scenario where the publisher can be held accountable for the comments containing hate speech, any automatic classifier would be required to achieve very high recall.

6 Conclusion and Future Work

We plan to further develop the dataset of flagged English comments, experiment with other classification models and to improve the BERT-based language transfer models. We also plan to examine multi-task learning approaches that can lead to state-of-art results on transferring knowledge among related tasks (Zhang and Yang, 2017).

We believe that more attention should be paid to the problem of comment labelling. This could lead to better classifiers, reliable inter-annotator agreement scores that can serve as upper bounds on performance, and to a better understanding of the semantics of the composite category of blocked comments.

In our view, an essential future work direction is design and implementation of studies with comment moderators that examine real-world scenarios and user needs. We believe that such studies would be invaluable and would lead to more realistic and usable machine learning comment moderation tools.

References

Charlie Beckett. 2019. New powers, new responsibilities: A global survey of journalism and artificial intelligence. *Polis, London School of Economics and Political Science. https://blogs. lse. ac. uk/polis/2019/11/18/new-powers-new-responsibilities.*

Lars Buitinck, Gilles Louppe, Mathieu Blondel, Fabian Pedregosa, Andreas Mueller, Olivier Grisel, Vlad Niculae, Peter Prettenhofer, Alexandre Gramfort, Jaques Grobler, et al. 2013. Api design for machine learning software: experiences from the scikit-learn project. *arXiv preprint arXiv:1309.0238.*

Jacob Devlin, Ming-Wei Chang, Kenton Lee, and Kristina Toutanova. 2019. BERT: pre-training of deep bidirectional transformers for language understanding. In *NAACL-HLT (1)*, pages 4171–4186. Association for Computational Linguistics.

Hitkul, Karmanya Aggarwal, Pakhi Bamdev, Debanjan Mahata, Rajiv Ratn Shah, and Ponnurangam Kumaraguru. 2020. Trawling for trolling: A dataset. *CoRR*, abs/2008.00525.

Varada Kolhatkar, Hanhan Wu, Luca Cavasso, Emilie Francis, Kavan Shukla, and Maite Taboada. 2019. The sfu opinion and comments corpus: A corpus for the analysis of online news comments. *Corpus Pragmatics*, pages 1–36.

Klaus Krippendorff. 2012. *Content Analysis: An Introduction to Its Methodology*. SAGE Publications, Inc.

Tak Yeon Lee, Alison Smith, Kevin Seppi, Niklas Elmqvist, Jordan Boyd-Graber, and Leah Findlater. 2017. The human touch: How non-expert users perceive, interpret, and fix topic models. *International Journal of Human-Computer Studies*, 105:28–42.

Ilya Loshchilov and Frank Hutter. 2019. Decoupled weight decay regularization. In *ICLR (Poster)*. OpenReview.net.

Thomas Mandl, Sandip Modha, Prasenjit Majumder, Daksh Patel, Mohana Dave, Chintak Mandlia, and Aditya Patel. 2019. Overview of the hasoc track at fire 2019: Hate speech and offensive content identification in indo-european languages. In *Proceedings of the 11th forum for information retrieval evaluation*, pages 14–17.

Courtney Napoles, Joel R. Tetreault, Aasish Pappu, Enrica Rosato, and Brian Provenzale. 2017. Finding good conversations online: The yahoo news annotated comments corpus. In *LAW@ACL*, pages 13–23. Association for Computational Linguistics.

John Pavlopoulos, Prodromos Malakasiotis, and Ion Androutsopoulos. 2017. Deep learning for user comment moderation. In *ALW@ACL*, pages 25–35. Association for Computational Linguistics.

Telmo Pires, Eva Schlinger, and Dan Garrette. 2019. How multilingual is multilingual bert? In *ACL (1)*, pages 4996–5001. Association for Computational Linguistics.

Senja Pollak, Marko Robnik Šikonja, Matthew Purver, Michele Boggia, Ravi Shekhar, Marko Pranjić, Salla Salmela, Ivar Krustok, Tarmo Paju, Carl-Gustav Linden, Leo Leppänen, Elaine Zosa, Matej Ulčar, Linda Freienthal, Silver Traat, Luis Adrián Cabrera-Diego, Matej Martinc, Nada Lavrač, Blaž Škrlj, Martin Žnidaršič, Andraž Pelicon, Boshko Koloski, Vid Podpečan, Janez Kranjc, Shane Sheehan, Emanuela Boros, Jose Moreno, Antoine Doucet, and Hannu Toivonen. 2021. EMBEDDIA tools, datasets and challenges: Resources and hackathon contributions. In *Proceedings of the EACL Hackashop on News Media Content Analysis and Automated Report Generation*. Association for Computational Linguistics.

Julian Risch and Ralf Krestel. 2018. Delete or not delete? semi-automatic comment moderation for the newsroom. In *Proceedings of the first workshop on trolling, aggression and cyberbullying (TRAC-2018)*, pages 166–176.

Anna Schmidt and Michael Wiegand. 2017. A survey on hate speech detection using natural language processing. In *SocialNLP@EACL*, pages 1–10. Association for Computational Linguistics.

Ravi Shekhar, Marko Pranjic, Senja Pollak, Andraž Pelicon, and Matthew Purver. 2020. Automating news comment moderation with limited resources: Benchmarking in croatian and estonian. *Special Issue on Offensive Language*, page 49.

Society of Editors. 2018. Moderation guide. page 42. [Online; accessed 21-February-2021].

Matej Ulcar and Marko Robnik-Sikonja. 2020. Finest BERT and crosloengual BERT - less is more in multilingual models. In *TDS*, volume 12284 of *Lecture Notes in Computer Science*, pages 104–111. Springer.

Thomas Wolf, Lysandre Debut, Victor Sanh, Julien Chaumond, Clement Delangue, Anthony Moi, Pierric Cistac, Tim Rault, Remi Louf, Morgan Funtowicz, Joe Davison, Sam Shleifer, Patrick von Platen, Clara Ma, Yacine Jernite, Julien Plu, Canwen Xu, Teven Le Scao, Sylvain Gugger, Mariama Drame, Quentin Lhoest, and Alexander Rush. 2020. Transformers: State-of-the-art natural language processing. In *Proceedings of the 2020 Conference on Empirical Methods in Natural Language Processing: System Demonstrations*, pages 38–45, Online. Association for Computational Linguistics.

Emma Woodman. 2013. Online comment moderation: emerging best practices. a guide to promoting robust and civil online conversation. pages 45–46. the World Association of Newspapers (WAN-IFRA). [Online; accessed 21-February-2021].

Ellery Wulczyn, Nithum Thain, and Lucas Dixon. 2017. Ex machina: Personal attacks seen at scale. In *WWW*, pages 1391–1399. ACM.

Yu Zhang and Qiang Yang. 2017. A survey on multi-task learning. *CoRR*, abs/1707.08114.

Implementing Evaluation Metrics Based on Theories of Democracy in News Comment Recommendation (Hackathon Report)

Myrthe Reuver
CLTL
Dept. of Language, Literature & Communication
Vrije Universiteit Amsterdam
myrthe.reuver@vu.nl

Nicolas Mattis
Dept. of Communication Science
Faculty of Social Science
Vrije Universiteit Amsterdam
n.m.mattis@vu.nl

Abstract

Diversity in news recommendation is important for democratic debate. Current recommendation strategies, as well as evaluation metrics for recommender systems, do not explicitly focus on this aspect of news recommendation. In the 2021 Embeddia Hackathon, we implemented one novel, normative theory-based evaluation metric, "activation", and use it to compare two recommendation strategies of New York Times comments, one based on user likes and another on editor picks. We found that both comment recommendation strategies lead to recommendations consistently less activating than the available comments in the pool of data, but the editor's picks more so. This might indicate that New York Times editors' support a deliberative democratic model, in which less activation is deemed ideal for democratic debate.

1 Introduction

Recommender systems are a core component of many online environments. Such systems can be used to recommend movies or music to users where there is a large pool of potential recommendations. Their main task, as Karimi et al. (2018) put it, is "to filter incoming streams of information according to the users' preferences or to point them to additional items of interest in the context of a given object" (p. 1203). As such, they are usually designed in ways that maximise user satisfaction. Their performance is traditionally evaluated in terms of their "accuracy", which is often measured by proxies such as clicks, time spent on a page, or engagement. Simply put: the more attention a user pays to the content, the better the recommender system is deemed to be.

However, there is an increasing awareness in the recommender systems domain that "beyond-accuracy" metrics such as diversity or novelty are also important aspects of a meaningful recommender system evaluation (Raza and Ding, 2020; Kaminskas and Bridge, 2016). This is particularly true in contexts where the impact of recommendations extends beyond individual purchasing choices or movie selections, such as news recommendation. Given that exposure to diverse viewpoints is often regarded as beneficial for democratic societies (Helberger and Wojcieszak, 2018), scholars have recently highlighted the importance of exposure diversity in such systems (Helberger, 2019; Helberger et al., 2018). Not recommending diversity in news recommender systems could potentially lead to 'filter bubbles', where users only receive ideas and viewpoints they already know and/or agree with (Pariser, 2011).

Very recently, evaluation and optimization metrics by Vrijenhoek et al. (2021) have been specifically designed to align with potential goals of democratic news recommenders as suggested by Helberger (2019). As such, they move beyond the existing "beyond accuracy" evaluation metrics used in the recommender system field. These existing metrics range from "diversity", to "serendipity", "novelty", and "coverage" (Kaminskas and Bridge, 2016), but all of these implicitly aim at increasing user satisfaction rather than achieving normative goals.

In contrast, the metrics in Vrijenhoek et al. (2021) are explicitly linked to supporting democratic debate rather than user satisfaction. Specifically, these metrics are linked to models of democracy. One of these is the deliberative model of democracy, which states a functioning democracy consists of rational debate of viewpoints and ideas. Another model is the critical model, which contends a successful democracy has clashing and active debates of opposing viewpoints.

In this paper, we specifically focus on one of these metrics, "activation", and use it to evaluate

Proceedings of the EACL Hackashop on News Media Content Analysis and Automated Report Generation, pages 134–139
April 19, 2021 © Association for Computational Linguistics

two different recommendation strategies for New York Times user comments in response to news articles. In doing so, our goal is to explore the potential of, but also the challenges related to, such normative metrics, especially where it concerns Natural Language Processing (NLP) tools and strategies.

To better understand how different recommendation strategies in the NYT comment section perform in terms of this metric, we ask the following research question: *"How do different manners of recommending user comments on a news article affect the recommendation set's average activation scores?*

By comparing different comment recommendation strategies, we contribute to the ongoing discussion in three ways:

- We are the first, to our knowledge, to implement Vrijenhoek et al. (2021)'s evaluation metrics for democratic news recommenders on a dataset;
- We explicitly identify possibilities and problems related to NLP in the use of such metrics;
- We add to the literature on the deliberative value of user-comments as well as on editorial biases in comment selection.

Our goal was to "test-drive" one or more of the theory-driven evaluation metrics in Vrijenhoek et al. (2021), and see where we ran into conceptual or practical problems preventing us from answering a research question aimed at comparing different recommendation strategies on the basis of this metric.

2 Method

2.1 Dataset

Although not exactly the same as news articles in a news recommender system, user comments are particularly interesting in this context because of their deliberative implications. That is, they provide a public space where users can share, consume and engage with different ideas and viewpoints (Rowe, 2015). As such, they constitute an excellent context for the test of Vrijenhoek et al. (2021)'s activation metric.

The dataset (Kesarwani, 2018), one of the datasets linked to in the hackathon resources (Pollak et al., 2021), contains 9.450 articles with 2.176.364 comments and other related metadata from the New York Times. The articles were published from January 2017 to May 2017 and January 2018 to May 2018. The mean number of comments per article is 230, with an SD of 403.4.

The comment data set contains the text and timestamps of the individual comments, as well as unique identifiers for each comment and the article that it belongs to. In addition, for each comment it also contains the number of user likes (called "recommendations") as well as information on whether or not the comment was selected by the NYTimes editorial board. According to their website, "NYT Picks are a selection of comments that represent a range of views and are judged the most interesting or thoughtful. In some cases, NYT Picks may be selected to highlight comments from a particular region, or readers with first-hand knowledge of an issue." (Sta) In most cases, the editors select 1 comment per debate, but the spread is large, with the mean being 13 recommended comments per article (SD = 11).

2.2 Two recommendation strategies

We recommend the top 3, top 5, and top 10 comments for each news article in two ways:

- N most-liked by users
- N editorial recommendations (in order of appearance)

We also considered comparing these two recommendation strategies to maximizing intra-list diversity based on a representation with Google News word embeddings, but ran out of time to do so. This strategy is based on Lu et al. (2020), who use this strategy to implement the "editorial value" diversity.

We compare these strategies with the evaluation metric "activation" from Vrijenhoek et al. (2021). We then analyze what the different levels of Activation in different recommendation strategies say about the implicit support for the different democratic models outlined in Helberger (2019). A higher activation might indicate an implicit support of the *critical* model of democracy, where conflict needs to be emphasized in order to obtain a lively, healthy debate. A lower activation score might indicate an implicit support of the *deliberative* model of democracy, where rational and calm debate is deemed important for democratic debate.

2.3 Test and validation sets

In order to test our approaches, we used two samples of the dataset. Our validation set was February 2018. Our unseen test set was February 2017. We chose the same month so time-sensitive differences in comments or topics were avoided. February 2017 consisted of 1.115 articles, with M = 186 comments (SD = 298) per article. February 2018 had 885 articles, with M = 263 (SD = 466) comments per article.

3 Implementing the Metric

3.1 Exploring which metric to implement

Early in the hackathon, we found two of the five metrics in Vrijenhoek et al. (2021) require user data, such as previous watch or read history. The three metrics suitable to our research needs, and our data without such documentation, were "activation", "representation", and "alternative voices". However, the latter two presented too much of a challenge for the short time of a three-week, part-time hackathon.

"Representation" requires the identification of different viewpoints and perspectives in text. NLP has several manners of doing so: tasks such as claim detection, argument mining, and stance detection. For an overview of such NLP tasks and approaches useful for viewpoint diversity in news recommendation, see Reuver et al. (2021). These approaches take time to be done correctly, and we felt the short time available to us in this hackathon did not allow us to properly identify viewpoints in the comments.

"Alternative Voices" requires the identification of whether mentioned people are a member of a minority group. This metric is difficult to implement for several reasons. Conceptually, for comments it may be relevant to know whether the *commenter* has a marginalized background (rather than any mentioned named entities). However, we did not have such information in our dataset. Additionally, who is marginalized depends likely on context - which makes detection by one model difficult. There are also technical hurdles when considering this metric. It is relatively difficult to identify whether someone mentioned comes from a marginalized background based on only the text. This could possibly be solved with open data such as Wikipedia, but this allows only well-known named entities to be recognized. Furthermore, there is a bias in Wikipedia itself: especially women are less often mentioned. Another method would for instance utilize techniques such as large-scale language models to recognize names or terms related to certain marginalized groups. However, this in itself also has bias, and could lead to racist or otherwise unwelcome associations in the representation, as pointed out in Bender et al. (2021).

The "Activation" metric, in contrast, is related to the polarity in the text. Polarity detection is a common task in NLP, and one with extensive support in terms of tools and methods. For this project, we chose to specifically focus on Vrijenhoek et al. (2021)'s activation metric. The core idea behind this metric is to gauge to what extent certain content might spark action among the readers, and is related to emotion. Past research shows that both negative and positive emotions can affect the processing and effects of textual content (Brady et al., 2017; Ridout and Searles, 2011; Soroka and McAdams, 2015). As such, emotional content can produce various effects that may or may not contribute to healthy democracies. Indeed, activation is not universally appreciated in democratic theory. In the models of democracy, activation has different desired values, as outlined in Helberger (2019). For example, from a deliberative democratic perspective, it could be argued that neutral and impartial content facilitates reasoned reflection and deliberation. However, from a more critical democratic perspective one could also argue that emotional content is more valuable as it may generate additional interest and engagement.

3.2 Implementation

We implemented activation in the following manner, based on (Vrijenhoek et al., 2021)'s description of how it should be used. Each article has a certain set of comment recommendations, and also a set of all potential comments. For each comment, we calculate the "compound" polarity value. For both sets we take the mean of the absolute polarity value of each article, which we use as an approximation for Activation. We then remove the mean polarity from all possible articles from the mean of the recommendation set. This results in an output with a range [-1, 1]. According to Vrijenhoek et al. (2021), a negative value indicates the recommender shows less activating content than available in the pool of data, while a positive value means the recommendation system generally selects more activating content than generally in the data.

The use of "polarity" is related to that of "sentiment". We follow Vrijenhoek et al. (2021) and use the VADER dictionary-based approach (Hutto and Gilbert, 2014), since the "compound" value of polarity used in the operationalization of the activation metric seems to be based on this method. However, we are aware this is not the only approach of polarity analysis of text, and in fact may not have the most concept and empirical validity from the social science perspective (van Atteveldt et al., 2021), nor is considered the state of the art for sentiment analysis on user generated text in the computer science field (Zimbra et al., 2018). We discuss this in more detail in the Discussion section. As of now, we use no lemmatization or normalization on the text data. We will also discuss implications of this in the Discussion section. Our code for implementing the metrics, preprocessing the data, and eventually testing the metrics on the data can be viewed here: `https://github.com/myrthereuver/Hackathon_MediaComments/blob/main/Hackathon_comments_script.ipynb`

4 Results

Our results are visible in Table 1 and Table 2 below. Visible is that the editorial picks are considerably more negative, and thus are *less* Activated, than the recommendations based on user likes. However, both systems pick comments that are negative, and thus *lower* in activation than in the general pool of data.[1]

Recommendation	NYTimes Picks	Likes
Top 3	-0.083	-0.076
Top 5	-0.059	-0.053
Top 10	-0.041	-0.032
Mean all systems	-0.061	-0.053
all NYTimes Picks vs other comments	-0.039	X

Table 1: Results on the feb 2018 set. The left column shows the editorial picks, while the right column shows the recommendations based on user likes. Activation scores can range from [-1, 1], where a negative value denotes the recommender picks items less activating than in the general pool, while a positive value indicates the items are more activating.

[1]Note that for the Picks, we took the most recent Top N editorially picked comments. The results may differ with a random Top of recommended comments, or another manner of selecting the Top editorial picks.

Recommendation	NYTimes Picks	Likes
Top 3	-0.067	-0.078
Top 5	-0.038	-0.052
Top 10	-0.021	-0.034
Mean all systems	-0.042	-0.055
all NYTimes Picks vs other comments	-0.013	X

Table 2: Results on the feb 2017 set. The left column shows the editorial picks, while the right column shows the recommendations based on user likes. Activation scores can range from [-1, 1], where a negative value denotes the recommender picks items less activating than in the general pool, while a positive value indicates the items are more activating.

5 Discussion

5.1 "Test-driving" theory-driven metrics

We implemented Vrijenhoek et al. (2021)'s activation metric, used to assess the relation of recommendations with democratic theory. We found that even the concrete metric as described in this work requires extensive NLP (pre-)processing choices that could significantly alter the outcome of evaluation. Not only selecting which sentiment tools, but also how to tokenize and lemmatize the texts could alter the polarity scores, as does text normalization for especially spelling mistakes in comments. For instance, whether or not to normalize the word "happines" (presumably meaning "happiness") could significantly alter the polarity score of texts, especially if spelling errors are frequent - as they could be in user-generated texts such as comments.

Additionally, selecting a sentiment tool for polarity scoring is not an easy task. As noted before, recent work in social science (van Atteveldt et al., 2021) has indicated NLP sentiment tools are not as reliable and valid as one would hope, and especially dictionary-based methods do not compare to human labelling. In the computer science field, such methods are also not considered the state of the art (Zimbra et al., 2018), performing well below more complex ensemble models of several machine learning methods.

Also, we found that some of the theory-based metrics are easier to generally apply to several datasets, contexts, and research questions than others. We already pointed out that some metrics require information on individual users, such as reading history, which is often not easily available as open, shared data. Additionally, we found that implementing "Activation" generally makes sense to the comment recommendation context, while "Protected Voices" is more difficult to conceptually define, and the "Representation" metric requires more complex NLP analysis of viewpoints than available in standard tools or models.

Very important to note is that these theory-driven metrics are by no means "plug and play". Using these metrics does not translate 1:1 into a score that measures the democratic valu of content. In this context, it gives an indication if and to what extent a recommendation set lives up to democratic ideals set by different models, but drawing a meaningful line on whether content becomes valuable for a given model of democracy is difficult. These metrics also do not capture more complex concepts such as *intent* when designing recommender systems.

Moreover, these metrics are based on averages: they do not show possible spread of activation across comments as well as articles. We could assume that some articles, as well as some topics, simply attract more activating comments, while others attract a more nuanced and "deliberative" discussion. Future research may, next to implementing the other metrics, also research whether certain topics or categories of news articles and/or comments have significantly more or less activating comments when using these recommendation approaches.

5.2 Results implications for Democratic Debate in NYTimes Comments

We researched whether different recommendation strategies in the New York Times comments dataset lead to different Activation values for the recommendations as presented in Vrijenhoek et al. (2021), and in turn what this means for the democratic models related to these systems. We found editor selections are on average less activating than the most-liked comments. In 2018 this effect is clear, in the 2017 sample less so - even slightly opposite. This could mean several things from a media theory perspective. Perhaps, journalists implicitly select comments in accordance with deliberative ideals. Another explanation of these results is that more activating content is also more likely to be profane, which, as Muddiman and Stroud (2017) showed, makes their selection less likely. The idea behind the activation metric is that activating content increases engagement, maybe the fact that liked comments are more activating is due to that.

Either way, connecting our results to the idea of democratic recommendation, it appears that user selection favours a more critical notion of democracy whereas editor selection favours a comparably more deliberative notion. At the same time, our results also suggest that on the whole, both recommendation styles result in a selection of comments that is slightly less activating than the overall subset. This suggests that both recommendation strategies favour less activating content, which might indicate implicit support of a deliberative model of democracy, where rational and calm debate is preferred over activating and clashing content.

Acknowledgments

This research is funded through Open Competition Digitalization Humanities and Social Science grant nr 406.D1.19.073 awarded by the Netherlands Organization of Scientific Research (NWO). We would like to thank the hackathon organizers for organizing the event, and for excellently supporting all teams working on challenges. All remaining errors are our own.

References

New York Times Statement on Comment Moderation. https://help.nytimes.com/hc/en-us/articles/115014792387-CommentsEach, last accessed on March 1, 2021.

Wouter van Atteveldt, Mariken ACG van der Velden, and Mark Boukes. 2021. The validity of sentiment analysis: Comparing manual annotation, crowd-coding, dictionary approaches, and machine learning algorithms. *Communication Methods and Measures*, pages 1–20.

Emily M Bender, Timnit Gebru, Angelina McMillan-Major, and Shmargaret Shmitchell. 2021. On the dangers of stochastic parrots: Can language models be too big. In *Proceedings of the 2020 Conference on Fairness, Accountability, and Transparency; Association for Computing Machinery: New York, NY, USA*.

William J Brady, Julian A Wills, John T Jost, Joshua A Tucker, and Jay J Van Bavel. 2017. Emotion shapes the diffusion of moralized content in social networks. *Proceedings of the National Academy of Sciences*, 114(28):7313–7318.

Natali Helberger. 2019. On the democratic role of news recommenders. *Digital Journalism*, 7(8):993–1012.

Natali Helberger, Kari Karppinen, and Lucia D'acunto. 2018. Exposure diversity as a design principle for recommender systems. *Information, Communication & Society*, 21(2):191–207.

Natali Helberger and Magdalena Wojcieszak. 2018. Exposure diversity. In Philip Michael Napoli, editor, *Mediated Communication*, volume 7, chapter 28, pages 535–560. Walter de Gruyter GmbH & Co KG.

Clayton Hutto and Eric Gilbert. 2014. Vader: A parsimonious rule-based model for sentiment analysis of social media text. In *Proceedings of the International AAAI Conference on Web and Social Media*, volume 8.

Marius Kaminskas and Derek Bridge. 2016. Diversity, serendipity, novelty, and coverage: a survey and empirical analysis of beyond-accuracy objectives in recommender systems. *ACM Transactions on Interactive Intelligent Systems (TiiS)*, 7(1):1–42.

Mozhgan Karimi, Dietmar Jannach, and Michael Jugovac. 2018. News recommender systems–survey and roads ahead. *Information Processing & Management*, 54(6):1203–1227.

Aashita Kesarwani. 2018. New York Times Dataset. `https://www.kaggle.com/aashita/nyt-comments`, last accessed on March 1, 2021.

Feng Lu, Anca Dumitrache, and David Graus. 2020. Beyond optimizing for clicks: Incorporating editorial values in news recommendation. In *Proceedings of the 28th ACM Conference on User Modeling, Adaptation and Personalization*, pages 145–153.

Ashley Muddiman and Natalie Jomini Stroud. 2017. News values, cognitive biases, and partisan incivility in comment sections. *Journal of communication*, 67(4):586–609.

Eli Pariser. 2011. *The filter bubble: What the Internet is hiding from you*. Penguin UK.

Senja Pollak, Marko Robnik Šikonja, Matthew Purver, Michele Boggia, Ravi Shekhar, Marko Pranjić, Salla Salmela, Ivar Krustok, Tarmo Paju, Carl-Gustav Linden, Leo Leppänen, Elaine Zosa, Matej Ulčar, Linda Freienthal, Silver Traat, Luis Adrián Cabrera-Diego, Matej Martinc, Nada Lavrač, Blaž Škrlj, Martin Žnidaršič, Andraž Pelicon, Boshko Koloski, Vid Podpečan, Janez Kranjc, Shane Sheehan, Emanuela Boros, Jose Moreno, Antoine Doucet, and Hannu Toivonen. 2021. EMBEDDIA tools, datasets and challenges: Resources and hackathon contributions. In *Proceedings of the EACL Hackashop on News Media Content Analysis and Automated Report Generation*. Association for Computational Linguistics.

Shaina Raza and Chen Ding. 2020. A survey on news recommender system–dealing with timeliness, dynamic user interest and content quality, and effects of recommendation on news readers. *arXiv preprint arXiv:2009.04964*.

Myrthe Reuver, Antske Fokkens, and Suzan Verberne. 2021. No nlp task should be an island: Multi-disciplinarity for diversity in news recommender systems. In *Proceedings of the EACL Hackashop on News Media Content Analysis and Automated Report Generation*. Association for Computational Linguistics.

Travis N Ridout and Kathleen Searles. 2011. It's my campaign i'll cry if i want to: How and when campaigns use emotional appeals. *Political Psychology*, 32(3):439–458.

Ian Rowe. 2015. Deliberation 2.0: Comparing the deliberative quality of online news user comments across platforms. *Journal of broadcasting & electronic media*, 59(4):539–555.

Stuart Soroka and Stephen McAdams. 2015. News, politics, and negativity. *Political Communication*, 32(1):1–22.

Sanne Vrijenhoek, Mesut Kaya, Nadia Metoui, Judith Möller, Daan Odijk, and Natali Helberger. 2021. Recommenders with a mission: assessing diversity in news recommendations. In *SIGIR Conference on Human Information Interaction and Retrieval (CHIIR) Proceedings*.

David Zimbra, Ahmed Abbasi, Daniel Zeng, and Hsinchun Chen. 2018. The state-of-the-art in twitter sentiment analysis: A review and benchmark evaluation. *ACM Transactions on Management Information Systems (TMIS)*, 9(2):1–29.

Association for Computational Linguistics
209 N. Eighth Street
Stroudsburg, Pennsylvania 18360

ISBN 978-1-7138-2960-7

CURRAN ASSOCIATES INC.
proceedings.com